15/07/24

The Craces: Royal Decorators
1768–1899

HONI SOIT QUI MAL Y PENSE

DIEU ET MON DROIT

Grace and Son

House Painters & Decorators

TO THE QUEEN

14, Wigmore Street,

Cavendish Square.

The Craces: Royal Decorators 1768–1899

Edited by Megan Aldrich

John Murray
The Royal Pavilion, Art Gallery and Museums, Brighton

Published to accompany the exhibition *The Craces: Royal Decorators 1768–1899*
at The Royal Pavilion, Art Gallery & Museums, 9 October–30 December 1990
Guest Curator: Megan Aldrich.

© The Royal Pavilion, Art Gallery and Museums, Brighton, 1990

British Library Cataloguing in Publication Data
The Craces: Royal decorators 1768–1899.
  1. Great Britain. Royal residences. Interior design. Crace (Family), history.
  I. Aldrich, Megan
747.22

ISBN 0 7195 4854 3 (hardback)
     0 948723 13 0 (paperback)

Frontispiece: The Trade Card of Crace and Son, *c.*1837

Printed by BAS Printers Limited,
Over Wallop, Hampshire

Contents

Preface by His Grace the Duke of Devonshire

I am lucky to be writing this Preface in a room designed and decorated by John Gregory Crace in the 1840s, surrounded by furniture he had made for the room to his own design. My ancestor, the 6th Duke, employed J. G. Crace here at Chatsworth after seeing his showrooms in Wigmore Street. I was also lucky to acquire last year a painting of the ceiling he designed for this room. I am, therefore, in the fortunate and unusual position of sitting under the original and looking at its reproduction.

Appropriately, Crace also decorated the 6th Duke's house in Brighton, a place with which the name Crace is forever linked by the firm's work at the Royal Pavilion. It was, happily enough, the 6th Duke who opened the Pavilion to the public in 1851 after its presentation to the town of Brighton.

This book is the first published attempt to survey in depth the remarkable achievements of the Crace decorating business from its origins in the elegance of the eighteenth century to its last days in the grandiose 1890s. It is an extraordinary tale and I am sure will lead to a renewed understanding and appreciation of the interiors of the period and their importance.

Devonshire

Introduction

The Crace firm was undoubtedly the single most important firm of decorators working in Britain in the nineteenth century by virtue, at the very least, of the sheer number of its commissions and their importance. In this book the history of the firm is divided into two main periods: the Georgians (Edward, John and Frederick) who each worked for royal patrons and were on easy terms with the leading architects and decorators of the day, but whose business remained relatively small and limited in scope; and the Victorians (John Gregory and John Dibblee) under whom the firm greatly expanded – J. G. Crace was recognised as the foremost decorator in Britain of his day – until J. D. Crace eventually wound up the business in 1899 in order to devote himself to writing and lecturing. Both sections commence with a survey of the work of the Craces by Megan Aldrich, based upon her 1987 doctoral dissertation on the Crace firm, followed by shorter essays on specific aspects of the period in question by experts in these areas.

The realisation of the exhibition and this book has been a lengthy process and we are indebted to a large number of people for their assistance. To Megan Aldrich go our warmest thanks and praise for everything she has done to bring this project to fruition, combining a fine appreciation of the materials with a tremendous dedication to the details of the Crace story. I would also like to thank the six essayists in this book: Gordon Lang, Jessica Rutherford, Michael Snodin, Clive Wainwright, Alexandra Wedgwood and Stephen Wildman.

I would like to thank the members of the honorary committee for their support and encouragement: His Grace the Duke of Devonshire who, as well as being a major lender, has kindly written the Preface to this book, Sir Geoffrey de Bellaigue and Lord Briggs.

The responsibility for the organisation of the exhibition rested in the capable hands of John Filkin until he left the Department in January 1990; Sarah Carthew and Shelley Tobin have brought it to fruition with their usual enthusiasm and professionalism. The exhibition would not have taken place without the willingness of individuals and institutions to lend items in their possession. It should be acknowledged that many of the lenders have also contributed substantially in terms of information and assistance. The exhibition catalogue has been produced with the financial support of Sotheby's.

I would also like to express my gratitude to the following for their help: James Aldrich, Stephen Astley, David Beevers, Neil Bingham, Stephen Calloway, Julia Clements, Frances Collard, Peter Day, Elaine Evans Dee, John Dinkel, Frank Galvin, Ian Grant, Hans de Groot, Ian Gow, John Hardy, Kate Harris, Margaret Henderson Floyd, Gerhard Hojer, Roger Hudson, Simon Jervis, John Kenworthy-Browne, Susan Lambert, Kathryn Lochnan, Hans Karl Lücke, Katherine McTaggart, Michael McCarthy, John Morley, Judy Neiswander, Catherine Niles, Charles Nugent, Linda Parry, Douglas Richardson, Hugh Roberts, Hugh Samson, Peter Thornton.

Special thanks are also due to the late Mrs Eileen Crace and Sir John and Lady Johnston.

It is a commonplace to say it these days, but a project like this would never have progressed beyond the hypothetical stage without external funding. It is entirely thanks to the supreme generosity of the Coral Samuel Charitable Trust that it has been possible to make the idea into a reality.

Richard Marks
Director
Royal Pavilion, Art Gallery & Museums, Brighton.

Crace Family Tree

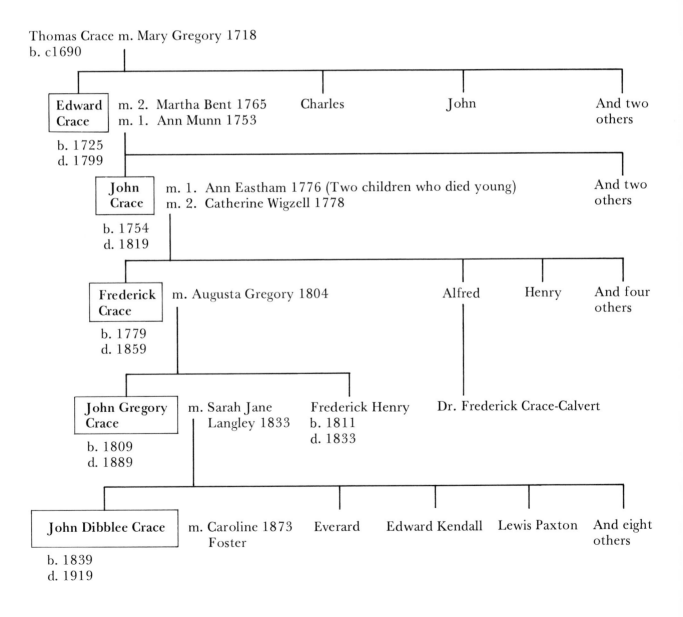

Thomas Crace m. Mary Gregory 1718
b. c1690

Edward Crace   m. 2. Martha Bent 1765   Charles   John   And two
b. 1725   m. 1. Ann Munn 1753   others
d. 1799

John Crace   m. 1. Ann Eastham 1776 (Two children who died young)   And two
b. 1754   m. 2. Catherine Wigzell 1778   others
d. 1819

Frederick Crace   m. Augusta Gregory 1804   Alfred   Henry   And four
b. 1779   others
d. 1859

John Gregory Crace   m. Sarah Jane   Frederick Henry   Dr. Frederick Crace-Calvert
b. 1809   Langley 1833   b. 1811
d. 1889   d. 1833

John Dibblee Crace   m. Caroline 1873   Everard   Edward Kendall   Lewis Paxton   And eight
b. 1839   Foster   others
d. 1919

Contributors

DR MEGAN ALDRICH. Tutor, Sotheby's Educational Studies, London. She specialises in furniture and interiors of the nineteenth century and has published articles on a variety of subjects in architectural and furniture history, including three articles on the work of the Craces at Abney Hall, Longleat House and Windsor Castle.

GORDON LANG. Senior Tutor, Sotheby's Educational Studies, London. A specialist in Chinese porcelain and decorative art and the Honorary Keeper of Porcelain at Burghley House, he is an expert in this field for Sotheby's and has published a number of articles on ceramics, the China trade, and Oriental influence on the West.

JESSICA RUTHERFORD. Assistant Director and Principal Keeper of the Royal Pavilion, Brighton. In addition to a number of articles on the Royal Pavilion and the nineteenth and twentieth centuries, she has published catalogues of the late nineteenth- and twentieth-century decorative art collections of the Brighton Museum (1983 and 1986).

MICHAEL SNODIN. Head of Designs Collection, Department of Prints, Drawings and Paintings, Victoria and Albert Museum, London. He has published numerous articles on design and decorative art, especially of the eighteenth century. He was organiser and editor of the catalogue of the V & A's exhibition *Rococo Art and Design in Hogarth's England* (1984), and he is organising a new permanent gallery of European ornament opening in 1991.

DR CLIVE WAINWRIGHT. Assistant Keeper, Department of Furniture and Woodwork, Victoria and Albert Museum, London. He has published many articles on nineteenth-century design, edited a reprint edition of Benjamin Ferrey's *Recol-*

lections of Pugin (1978), and was a principal contributor to the recent exhibition and catalogue on George Bullock (1988). His most recent book is *The Romantic Interior: The British Collector at Home, 1750–1850* (1989).

ALEXANDRA WEDGWOOD. Architectural Archivist at the House of Lords Record Office, London. She is a leading authority on the work of A. W. N. Pugin and has published the definitive catalogues of Pugin's drawings in the collections of the Royal Institute of British Architects (1977) and the Victoria and Albert Museum (1985).

STEPHEN WILDMAN. Deputy Keeper (Fine Art), Birmingham Museum and Art Gallery, in charge of the Prints and Drawings collection. His publications cover many aspects of British nineteenth-century art and design, including watercolours (*David Cox*, 1983), the Pre-Raphaelites and their circle (*Morris & Company in Cambridge*, 1980) and the etching revival (*Sir Henry Rushbury*, 1989), as well as International Exhibitions.

Part One

I

The Georgian Craces, *c.*1768–1830

by Megan Aldrich

The Crace Firm of Decorators

THE CRACE 'FIRM' was founded in the year 1768 by Edward Crace. It then continued in unbroken succession, being headed by four of his direct descendants, until 1899, when it was dissolved by his great-great-grandson, John Dibblee Crace. The daybooks and accounts of the firm – if indeed, they survive – have yet to be discovered. The single exception to this lack of documentation is to be found in a bound volume entitled, 'Partnership', covering the period of 1872 to 1888. It was begun when J. D. Crace formally entered into partnership with his father, and it will be discussed within the context of J. D. Crace's career.[1] Some information on the day-to-day workings of the firm has come to light from bills, Crace family memoirs, and contemporary comments in newspapers and journals. This information is discussed, where pertinent, within these pages.

It is clear that during its 131 years of operation the Crace firm corresponded to the idea of the 'upholder', or upholsterer, in the eighteenth-century meaning of the word. Therefore, a considerable amount of the work of the Crace firm consisted of supplying and installing wallpapers, textiles, and upholstery for fashionable interiors, as well as arranging furniture and decorative objects and re-hanging collections of paintings. This work corresponds most closely with that of the twentieth-century 'interior decorator'.

However, the role of the Craces did not stop here, for it is also clear from the hundreds of their signed drawings which survive in various public collections that they were designer-decorators.[2] Each of the five heads of the Crace firm played an active role in designing the decoration of interiors and furnishings, including the design and execution of mural and ceiling painting in the full range of artistic styles current during the firm's history. Of particular interest to the historian of interiors is the fact that their work was informed by continual study of the leading decorative schemes of the day. Beginning with Frederick Crace they often travelled to major European centres, recording in sketches and notes the sources of their inspiration. It is therefore the Craces as designers which will form the focus of this book, supplemented by information on the working practice of the firm where known.

The first section of this book examines the careers of the so-called 'Georgian Craces', Edward, John and Frederick Crace.[3] Edward worked closely with King George III as did John and Frederick for his son George, Prince of Wales. Indeed, the careers of these three Crace decorators are principally identified with royal patronage and with the circle of artists and craftsmen surrounding the court.

In comparison with the two later Crace decorators, John Gregory Crace and John Dibblee Crace, the 'Victorian Craces', the number of commissions secured by the Georgian Craces was relatively few. The artistic styles practised by each were the predominant styles of the day – that is, Rococo until the mid 1760s, followed by Neo-classicism until the early nineteenth century, with Orientalism, or the Chinese style, being used concurrently in the first two decades of the nineteenth century.

Despite the existence of a large body of material concerning the family,[4] relatively little is known about the careers of the Craces in the first half of the eighteenth century. Thomas Crace set up business as a coach-maker in Rochester Row, London, in about 1718. In the same year he married Mary Gregory, the daughter of the Surveyor to Westminster Abbey. This was a useful connection for the Crace family, who married into the influential Gregory family no less than three times in the eighteenth and early nineteenth centuries.[5] Thomas Crace trained his three sons, Edward (b.1725), Charles (b.1727) and John (b.1728) in different branches of the coach-making trade. All three sons lived and worked in Long Acre in London. John remains a shadowy figure, as little is known about his career. However, Charles and Edward Crace specialised in the design and decoration of coaches, and surviving drawings by Edward testify to his skill. Charles published six plates of Rococo designs for coaches.[6]

Edward Crace, 1725–1799

It is the career of Edward, the eldest son of Thomas Crace, which is of greatest interest amongst those of the early Craces, since it was he who founded the decorating firm (which lasted until 1899, when it was dissolved by his great-great-grandson). Perhaps owing to his superior abilities, in 1741, at the age of 15, Edward Crace was apprenticed not to a coach-maker but to an artist, William Atkinson, a member of the Painter Stainers Company.[7] In 1753 he married the daughter of another artist, James Munn of Greenwich. A small book of drawings by Crace for coach decorations of about 1760 demonstrates the competence and facility with which he designed in the then fashionable Rococo style. This album is examined elsewhere by Michael Snodin (see p.34). Edward Crace's small book of coach panel designs gives little idea of the direction he was next to follow in his career, for in 1768, after the death of his second wife, Crace set up business as a decorative house painter to the nobility and gentry.[8] The contacts he had developed in the coach-decorating business must have been useful in attracting a clientele, but nothing is known of the private houses he decorated. The interior of the Pantheon in London remains the sole, spectacular example of Edward Crace's work as a decorative painter.

In 1770 Crace was engaged to decorate the Pantheon on Oxford Road (now Oxford Street) in London.[9] This interior certainly ranks as the most important commission of his career. An obscure newcomer named James Wyatt, later famous as the architect of Fonthill Abbey, designed the London Pantheon. It can be considered as among the first large-scale, non-domestic buildings in the Neo-classical style in England. The Pantheon opened its doors in 1772 as a place of amusement and social gatherings particularly during the winter months, when outdoor meeting places such as Ranelagh or Vauxhall Gardens were impractical. Horace Walpole, who recorded the reaction of the public when the building was first opened, cited a cost of £60,000 for the Pantheon. This figure seems to have been inflated, but it was the lavishness of the furnishing and decoration which amazed him and his contemporaries. Walpole wrote to a friend: 'If we laugh at the French, they stare at us. Our enormous luxury and expense astonish them. I carried their Ambassador and a Comte de Levi to see the Pantheon, which is almost finished. Imagine Baalbek in all its glory. It amazed me.'[10] In referring to the Temple of Baalbek, Walpole links Wyatt's Pantheon to contemporary Neo-classical country house interiors, inspired by the publication of Robert Wood's and James Dawkins' *Ruins of Baalbek* of 1757.

A painting by Zoffany and Hodges of *c.*1772 gives an idea of the appearance of the interior scheme for the Pantheon [Plate 1].[11] The interior was dominated by a vast dome supported on pendentives painted with scrolling, foliate arabesques which enclosed cameos with classical figures, all executed in cream on a stone-coloured ground. Trotter's *London* of 1839 described the walls and ceiling of the Pantheon as 'delicately and tastefully embellished in panels, with scroll ornaments, into which are introduced foreign birds . . . exquisitely painted on a light ground by Crace'.[12] The decorations by Crace for the Pantheon came barely ten years after the radical Painted Room at Spencer House, London, designed by James Stuart and considered to be the first Neo-classical interior in existence. Crace's decoration of the Pantheon, which Walpole likened to

'Raphael's loggias in the Vatican',[13] must surely be the first painted Neo-classical interior in a public building in Europe. It is therefore an important milestone in Western art.

In addition to his painted arabesques for the walls and central dome of the Pantheon, a payment of £63 was made to Edward Crace 'for painting and gilding glass frames, table frames, seats and chairs'.[14] The furniture has long been dispersed, but this type of work would have been consistent with Crace's experience as a coach decorator and the practice of gilding remained a consistent aspect of the firm's work throughout its history. To execute the interior of the Pantheon in London he must have had assistants to carry out the painting and gilding. One name has come to light. His great-grandson, John Gregory Crace, stated that, 'In his last years he was greatly assisted by his confidential friend, Mr. Kingham, who had been his apprentice'.[15]

The great public success of the Pantheon promoted Wyatt as an architect and furthered Edward Crace's reputation as an authority on the arts. King George III had visited the Pantheon and was sufficiently impressed by it to send his librarian, Mr Dalton, to engage Edward Crace for the cataloguing and care of the paintings in the Royal Collection.[16] This curatorial work occupied most of Crace's time from the mid 1770s until his death in 1799, given that the Royal Collection was dispersed between Queen's House (now Buckingham Palace), St James's Palace, Kew, Hampton Court, and Windsor Castle.

Frederick Crace later described accompanying his grandfather to the room called 'Crace's Room' in Queen's House, where Edward Crace arrived at ten o'clock each morning. The king himself would occasionally look in to watch the progress in cleaning and re-varnishing the collection.[17] By 1778 the catalogue of the Royal paintings in Kensington Palace had been published and an undated manuscript for Queen's House survives.[18] Each catalogue is a straightforward list of paintings by room, with artists noted, including descriptions of the decorative and mural paintings by artists such as William Kent in each residence. Edward Crace must have been cataloguing the royal pictures at Hampton Court in 1782, for in this year his residence was listed as Hampton Wick in a legal action brought against him by Miss Alcock for breach of promise.[19] During the later 1780s he lived at Windsor, 'For he was always anxious to attend upon the King – and remained there for some time as the Pictures were in a very bad State.'[20] Edward Crace retired to London in the 1790s and was succeeded in business by his son John. He died in 1799.

1:1   John Hoppner, Portrait of John Crace, c.1800.

John Crace, 1754–1819

In personality Edward Crace was reserved and quiet, but his son John was every bit as handsome, gregarious, and outgoing as his portrait by the fashionable painter John Hoppner suggests [Fig.1:1].[21] A breach occurred between them for a time in 1776 when John Crace eloped with Ann Eastham, the niece and heiress of Henry Gregory.[22] According to family tradition, John Crace began his house decorating business in 1776 with £100 that a friend had lent him.[23] His wife's large fortune undoubtedly assisted him in immediately establishing himself as a decorator in London independently of his father.

Crace began his career at the age of 16 by assisting his father in coach decoration, but it was not until 1785, at the relatively late age of 30, that he was admitted to the Freedom of the Painter Stainers Company by patrimony.[24] In 1778, after Ann Eastham had died in childbirth, John Crace settled at 55 Great Queen Street, London, with his second wife, Catherine Wizzell. His trade card, dating to about 1785, shows a classical female figure seated amongst billowing drapery and displaying a tablet with the words 'Crace, Painter and Gilder', followed by the Great Queen Street address [Fig.1:2].[25]

1:2   Trade card of John Crace, c.1785

An insight into the work carried out by John Crace is provided by the survival of a handful of his bills for decorating between 1780 and 1804.[26] For example, in a bill of 1780 to his relation and patron, Mr. Lulham, John Crace lists painting four houses in Barbican Court, London, which included painting sashes, skirting boards, and window frames, as well as giving the yardage for areas painted 'twice in oil' and those painted 'three times'.[27] The houses apparently were rental properties owned by Lulham. In 1780 Crace was trading as 'John Crace & Co.', indicating that he must have had a certain number of regular employees.

Between 1801 and 1804 John Crace worked in conjunction with John Robins, like himself a member of the circle of the architect John Soane. Robins supplied furniture for Soane at the Bank of England, Pitzhanger Manor, and 12 Lincoln's Inn Fields.[28] He and Crace worked together on a number of occasions, and John Crace and his three sons were employed to decorate Robins' own house at 18 Park Lane, London. An example of the range of decorating work carried out by John Crace & Co. is illustrated by a bill for a house in Hammersmith owned by Mr. Scott. In 1802 Crace supplied bedsteads, blankets, mattresses and textiles, as well as, '39 Yards of Yard wide Morone Chints', 'Cutting out and making up Field Bed furniture as before', 'cutting out and making up a four post Bed Furniture with full Valens and Drapery head Cloth, the Curtains only lined with Dark Green Dy'd Callico', 'a turkey Patern Brussells Carpet with a neat Border', and other items of upholstery and soft furnishings.[29]

There has been some confusion about the career of John Crace owing to the fact that he had a less prosperous cousin of the same name. This John Crace lived at 158 Drury Lane in London and was employed by 'John Crace & Co.'. For example, John Crace of Drury Lane worked at Althorp House in 1790 and 1792 cleaning and revarnishing some of the pictures in the house, as well as regilding their frames.[30] It is not clear how many regular employees John Crace had, but his sons Frederick, Henry and Alfred, and his cousin John, numbered among them. Crace seems to have been on close terms of friendship with a number of men from Soane's office such as, 'Mr. Chawner, Mr. Leverton Jun., Mr. Kendal, Mr. Laing, and many other young men from Mr. Soans . . . they spent many happy years and enjoyed themselves very much'. In addition, 'his Wife took a very active part in his business until her decease', which was in 1809.[31]

Frederick Crace described his father John as 'a house and decorative Painter' who was 'considered very Eminent in his profession being patronized by King George 3rd and 4th.'[32] John Crace held the appointments of Painter to the Board of Works and Painter to the Royal Hospital at Greenwich for a number of years. Like the majority of his commissions, these two appointments involved the supervision by Crace of his workmen, who were responsible for cleaning, restoration, and the repainting and gilding of interiors. He must have fulfilled the

1 :3   J. M. Gandy, The Breakfast Room at 12 Lincoln's Inn Fields, 1798.

same supervisory role in work he undertook at the Bank of England for Sir Robert Taylor and Sir John Soane, at the Drury Lane and Covent Garden Theatres for Henry Holland, and at a number of country houses for Soane and Holland, most notably at Althorp and Woburn. There are, however, some commissions in John Crace's career where he acted as his own designer of decorative mural and ceiling painting. These will be worth considering briefly, beginning with two ceilings Crace designed and executed for Sir John Soane, including that of the famous house at 12 Lincoln's Inn Fields close to Crace's own.

Shortly after Soane remodelled the house at Lincoln's Inn Fields for his own use in 1792, he employed John Crace to design and paint a boldly trellised ceiling with flowering vines to ornament the unusual star-shaped vault of the Breakfast

Room [Fig.1:3].[33] Contemporary watercolours by J. M. Gandy in the Soane Museum illustrate this ceiling and a similar trellised ceiling of c.1802 by Crace for the Back Parlour at Soane's country house, Pitzhanger Manor, in Ealing [Plate 2]. The ceiling at Pitzhanger differs slightly from that at Lincoln's Inn Fields, for here Crace decorated the crossing of the star vault with four classical cameo heads set in laurel wreaths with scrolling ribbons. It has recently been re-painted, and the Breakfast Room ceiling in Lincoln's Inn Fields has been uncovered beneath no less than sixteen layers of paint.[34] In both cases the trellis ceilings by John Crace give a fresh and open appearance to two interiors which are not large and which could have easily appeared confined owing to the number of bookcases which were originally housed in them. In the watercolours by Gandy both rooms look onto gardens which complement the greenery of these trellised ceilings.

A small group of designs demonstrates the interest of John Crace and his son Frederick in trellis ceilings.[35] This seems to have been one of the ways in which they were directly inspired by Carlton House, the splendid London town house of the Prince of Wales. According to Frederick Crace, his father John may be credited with improving the contemporary English style of architectural decoration by means of the techniques he learned from 'foreign artists' employed at Carlton House. Frederick Crace criticised English Neo-classical decorative schemes of the later eighteenth century, which featured 'Ornamental plaister work on the ceiling and Wall with a small pannel of an Historical subjects [sic] painted . . . and the plaister Ornament picked out [in] different shades of Colour.' This sounds like a description of the later work of Robert Adam, which the Craces evidently felt was lacking in vitality. Frederick Crace stated proudly that his father had re-introduced 'Imitation of Marbling and Graining of Wood Work etc.' into English decoration during the 1790s.[36] It is precisely this interest in graining, marbling, and other illusionistic techniques of painting, along with an interest in the use of bold colour, which characterises the work of John Crace, influenced as he was by the decorative techniques he observed while working at Carlton House in London. He had begun work here late in the 1780s.

It would be difficult to over-estimate the importance of Carlton House to contemporaries. The house was given in 1783 to the Prince of Wales, who refurbished it as a sumptuous town house expressing his own artistic tastes. Horace Walpole, who had been amazed by the Pantheon, said the apartments at Carlton House ranged from 'elegant' to 'noble and rich' to 'inexpressible . . . greatness and splendour'.[37] John Britton's and A. C. Pugin's publication of 1828 on London buildings praised fulsomely the Prince's architect, Henry Holland, and his team of decorators.[38]

It was particularly the first phase of decoration of the 1780s which influenced the Craces. A team of French decorative painters at Carlton House worked under the supervision of Jean Jacques Boileau and his principal assistant, Louis André Delabrière. This team was brought to England by the upholsterer Sheringham of Great Marlborough Street, London.[39] Many of the state rooms decorated by the French artists featured illusionistic sky ceilings, the use of rich colour and gilding, and striking marbling and graining. John Crace, who painted imitation porphyry columns in the front parlour at Pitzhanger c.1802, may have been inspired by the enormous imitation porphyry columns in the Circular Room of Carlton House, which were painted by the artist Bartoli in about 1790. Britton and Pugin described this room as being 'most remarkable for architectural beauty and picturesque form'.[40] In addition to these enormous marbled columns, the ceiling of the Circular Room was decorated with billowing clouds against a blue sky. Sky ceilings were soon to appear in designs by John and Frederick Crace for the Royal Pavilion at Brighton.

The exact work that John Crace carried out at Carlton House is unclear, but by 1793 he had billed the Crown for over £1500 for his work as a 'painter' there.[41] Therefore he and his men must have executed a substantial amount of work, much of which may have involved carrying out the sophisticated painted decoration in the state rooms with Boileau and his team. In addition, it was Carlton House that served as the testing ground for Frederick Crace, the talented son of John Crace.

John and Frederick Crace

Frederick Crace was born in 1779 and apprenticed at the age of fourteen to Richard Holland, a builder who was the cousin of Henry Holland.[42] In an autobiographical account, Frederick Crace recalled that he had first tried his skill at decorating in 1793 with his father at 148 Piccadilly, the home of a Mr. Tollemache. In the same year he went to Woburn Abbey, where his father was working as part of the Holland team 'to learn painting and gilding'; Frederick then returned to London in 1794 'to superintend the Work at Carlton House – where I was first noticed by the Prince of Wales and Mrs Fitzherbert being at work upon gilding the Iron Railing of the Staircase'.[43] In the same account, Frederick Crace stated that he learned graining and marbling 'which was then being introduced into noblemen's houses', at Carlton House and that he was busy using these skills in commissions for his father.

John and Frederick Crace seem to have finished their work at Carlton House in about 1795, when they began work on a series of country houses for Henry Holland and undertook several commissions for Sir John Soane.[44] Shortly after

1:4   Design for Neo-classical Hall, attributed to Frederick Crace, perhaps at the Royal Pavilion Brighton, *c*.1800.

1800 the Craces began work on the first series of chinoiserie interiors at the Royal Pavilion in Brighton for the Prince of Wales. A very small number of their drawings for Neo-classical designs may represent work for the earliest phase of the Pavilion[45] [Fig.1:4], but the overwhelming majority of surviving drawings by John and Frederick Crace for Brighton are in the Chinese style.

John Crace's own interest in things Chinese was profound. According to family tradition, as a young man he was on a visit with his father Edward to

1:5   A view of the Prince of Wales' Chinese Drawing Room at Carlton House, reproduced from Thomas Sheraton, *The Cabinet-maker and Upholsterers Drawing Book*, 1793.

Queen's House (later Buckingham Palace) in about 1775 when he darted forward to save a Chinese vase which Queen Charlotte had accidentally upset.[46] The Queen, a well-known connoisseur of Chinese decorative art, was pleased enough to reward John Crace with an enamel pin.[47] Whether or not he had been inspired by this early experience, he owned a considerable collection of 'Chinese curiosities' at his death in 1819. The catalogue of the sale of his library in the same year by Sotheby's documents an outstanding personal collection of books on the art, topography, and the inhabitants of oriental countries.[48] Crace owned fourteen books on China alone, besides books on Japan, Oceania, and Asia generally. His books on China included Duhalde's *History of China* of 1741, Kircheri's *China Illustrata* of 1667, and the Earl Macartney's *Embassy to China* of 1797. John Crace's library included many other books on British antiquities, heraldry, plays, biographies, and works by Horace Walpole, among others.

In terms of John Crace's early designs in the Chinese style for Brighton Pavilion, there was perhaps a closer source of inspiration than the contents of his fine library. Significantly, at Carlton House John and Frederick Crace could see the Chinese style used for decorating and furnishing. The Prince of Wales shared Queen Charlotte's interest in Oriental art, and by January of 1789 Henry

Holland was at work on designs for the 'Sallon Chinois', or Chinese Drawing Room, at Carlton House, made famous when a view of the room was published by Thomas Sheraton in 1793[49] [Fig.1:5]. It is apparent that certain elements of Holland's elegant scheme for the Chinese Drawing Room were used by the Craces in their subsequent work for the Royal Pavilion. For example, the suspended temple bells and Chinese figures beneath the cornice of the room, the painted chinoiserie wall panels framed in *trompe-l'oeil* bamboo, and the painted trellis patterns to ornament the dado of the room, are all features which appear later in the interiors at Brighton. Likewise, the trellis work dado indicated in Sheraton's view of the Chinese Drawing Room parallels the bold interior decoration designed by John Crace for the Chinese Dairy at Woburn – and may even indicate Crace's design contribution to the Drawing Room.

Henry Holland was also the architect of the Chinese Dairy at Woburn Abbey, begun in 1787. However, John Crace decorated the interior of this little garden structure. He was paid over £81 in 1789 for unspecified painting at Woburn and this must include the Chinese Dairy.[50] The bold, abstract, almost primitive nature of the trellis patterns and the arabesques used in the interior of the Dairy are entirely consistent with the designs in the Chinese style produced by John Crace shortly afterwards for the Royal Pavilion, Brighton, as will be discussed. Indeed, it is tempting to view this garden structure by Holland and Crace, along with the Chinese Drawing Room at Carlton House, as the first step in the development of chinoiserie at the Royal Pavilion.

The interior of the Chinese Dairy at Woburn has been painted with bold trellis patterns in black, gold and red shaped into panels which cover the flat surfaces of the walls and ceiling [Fig.1:6]. The lantern of the roof and the coves of the wall niches have been ornamented with rather ponderously drawn arabesques that are identical in character to the arabesques which appear in a drawing by John Crace of about 1801 for the initial phase of chinoiserie decoration at Brighton Pavilion[51] [Fig.1:7]. This drawing, which has been identified as a design for the Glass Passage in the Royal Pavilion, Brighton,[52] shares with the decoration of the Woburn Dairy the use of boldly outlined forms and an overall patterned effect produced by the use of abstract ornamentation. The Woburn Dairy interior and the design for the Glass Passage display the use of strong colour and vigorous, if occasionally crude, draughtsmanship that characterise the hand of John Crace, as opposed to that of his son Frederick.

The firm attribution of drawings and designs to John Crace remains somewhat problematic, since there is only one signed drawing by him in existence. It is not a design for decoration but rather a drawing of a very large pear which grew in Crace's garden in Hammersmith in 1794.[53] This drawing exhibits the vigorous draughtsmanship and bold outlining of forms seen in the other draw-

1:6 Mural decoration and furniture by John Crace for the interior of the Chinese
Dairy at Woburn Abbey, *c.*1789.

1:7 John Crace, design for the decoration of a canopied passage, probably the Glass Passage at the Royal Pavilion, Brighton, *c*.1801–4.

1:8   John Crace, design for the Entrance Hall at the Royal Pavilion, c.1801–04.

ings attributed here to John Crace. A further relationship between the signed
drawing of a pear and the drawing for the Glass Passage at Brighton is evidenced
by the scrolling letter 'C' with which Crace signed his name. It is surely uninten-
tional that this 'C' so closely resembles the curlicue pattern used to decorate
the floor of the design for the Glass Passage. Another design belonging to the
group by John Crace in the Cooper-Hewitt Museum has his handwriting, with
its distinctive curlicues, on the reverse side.[54] Shortly after the Cooper-Hewitt
Museum acquired the group of drawings by the Craces they were published by
Maurice Bloch. The drawings assigned to 'Anonymous Designer II' by Bloch
can, for the most part, be assigned to the elder Crace. Bloch has characterised
this designer's work as 'less interested in precise draughtsmanship and fine detail,
but somewhat more concerned with the achievement of unusual impressions of
texture and colour, generally using marbleized surfaces, and trellis-work patterns
in gay abandon.'[55] This is a reasonable description of the drawing style of John
Crace. Fig.1:8 is an example of another Cooper-Hewitt drawing, again for the
Royal Pavilion, probably by John Crace.
    Although nearly all the original Crace bills for work at the Royal Pavilion

have been lost, a typescript survives at Brighton to document their work.[56] This covers the period 1802 to 1822 and gives a detailed account of the wide range of decorating activities John and Frederick Crace undertook on behalf of the Prince of Wales. Aside from the vast amount of painted decoration and gilding they executed, a sizeable quantity of Chinese porcelain and decorative objects such as painted glass appears in the Crace bills, especially during the years 1802 to 1804. The Craces were evidently supplying these objects to furnish the Pavilion at Brighton.[57] The possible relationship of these objects to Chinoiserie designs by Frederick Crace is discussed in the essay by Gordon Lang (see p.42). By examining this aspect of the Craces' activity – namely, that they worked as agents acquiring Chinese objects for the Prince – the intriguing idea is raised that these objects served as first-hand sources for decorative motifs which appear in the Crace designs for the interiors at Brighton.

Much furniture for the Pavilion came from Elward, Marsh & Tatham of London early in the nineteenth century.[58] However, from the typescript of Crace bills it is apparent that they acquired a large amount of furniture for the Pavilion. For example, in 1802 the Crace firm billed the Prince £14 for 'One very Fine Japan India Cabinet', over £8 for 'Two Bamboo Tables with Japan tops', £30 for 'One Fine Japan Screen', £38 for '8 Arm Bamboo Chairs and one Sopha', and nearly £41 for '18 Bamboo Chairs'.[59] The reference to 'Japan' indicates a decorative finish either of real lacquer, or a Western imitation of it, usually done in black and gold and called 'japanning'.

In 1803 furniture continued to appear in the Crace accounts. The Prince was billed for a variety of bamboo furniture, including stands, tables, sofas, stools, and chairs. Also amongst the items billed were five 'Japan' cabinets and three 'Japan' screens. One cabinet cost as much as £15.[60] In 1804 an unspecified Crace employee japanned a stand for a cabinet in black and gilt, perhaps one of those referred to above,[61] while more bamboo stands for porcelain, and another 'Japan' screen, appear in the accounts.[62] In addition to the limited importation of Oriental furniture, the Craces decorated Western furniture. For example, in 1802 the Craces billed £29 for 'Furniture etc. (not in E. G. Saunders account)'. This furniture included '2 Dressing tables 3 [times in] oil and flatted white and striped blue', various seat furniture, and '48 Chairs 3 oil Green and striped black', with four armchairs *en suite*.[63]

In 1968 an unusual rosewood table of about 1800 with chinoiserie decoration appeared on the London art market [Fig.1:9].[64] The form of the table itself is that of a 'Pembroke table', a common type during the Regency, which could have been made by a number of different cabinet-making firms. However, the simple silhouette of this table has been complicated by the addition of Chinese-style brackets at either end and at its base, along with decorative end panels

1:9   Rosewood table with Chinoiserie decoration, *c*.1801–04.

in bamboo pattern with small coloured spheres and painted fretwork designs resembling the abstract trellis work patterns found in the Chinese Dairy at Woburn and in John Crace's designs for Brighton Pavilion, particularly that for the Glass Passage.[65] Although there is no evidence to suggest that the Crace firm was engaged in making furniture at this date, the rosewood table could have been designed and painted by them. The decoration on this table is primitive enough to have been designed by John Crace.

Professional services provided by John and Frederick Crace were an important part of their business with the Prince of Wales. John Crace billed £78 for expenses in 1803 and 1804, which included travel to collect furniture and porcelain. He billed a total of £179 for the period of 1802–04 for 'attending the Prince at Brighton and arranging the furniture, china etc.', which occupied 358 days over these three years. John and Frederick Crace were paid £10 for 'attending at the Balls the whole night by order of His Royal Highness', and the two men also charged £7 for overseeing the removal of 'old furniture' from Carlton House.[66]

Another duty performed by Crace Senior was negotiating at the Customs House for the importation of furniture, porcelain, and decorative objects.[67] Work by the Crace firm at Brighton ceased from the end of 1804, until 1815, when the late phase of chinoiserie decoration was begun under the supervision of Frederick Crace.

In 1805 John Crace finished his work at Pitzhanger Manor, and not long afterwards he retired with an unmarried daughter to the elegant comfort of his house in Knightsbridge, surrounded by his fine library and his collection of Oriental porcelain. His three sons, Frederick, Alfred and Henry, worked as 'John Crace & Sons' at 34 Curzon Street from 1806 to 1812, moving to 55 Great Queen Street in 1812. As will be discussed, they worked at this address until 1826, when the partnership was dissolved and Frederick Crace took over the sole manning of the firm. In some respects Frederick Crace can be viewed as the most artistically talented of the early Crace decorators, having a broad range of activities and interests.

Frederick Crace, 1779–1859

Frederick Crace's early designs for interiors are close in style to those by his father John. One of these early designs, for the Entrance Hall of the Pavilion of about 1801,[68] shares with the drawings of John Crace characteristics such as the use of sky and cloud painting, trellis work, and bold outlining to delineate forms [Fig. 1:10]. However, the execution of the drawing displays a certain lightness of touch and an element of nervous linearity which distinguishes it from the cruder work of the senior Crace. This distinction is perhaps a fine one, but further evidence for the authorship of this design is contained in its inscription. The top of the drawing bears the inscription, 'Brighton Pavilion – Decoration for one side of the Hall', while in the lower margin are the words, 'For Mr Crace'. From the dozen or so documents in the hand of Frederick Crace that are amongst the Mostyn-Crace papers in the Victoria and Albert Museum, it can be established that these inscriptions were written by Frederick Crace himself. 'Mr Crace' would, of course, refer to John Crace, who is consistently referred to as 'Mr Crace' in the typescript accounts at Brighton, and Frederick Crace is cited as 'Mr F. Crace'. The inscription on the reverse in the same hand reads: '(illegible) to Mr. Crace's designs (for the State?) B(edroom?) will be followed by the rest of the drawings immediately'; thereby suggesting that Frederick Crace was involved to a considerable degree in designing for his father at the Pavilion c.1801–04.

1:10   Frederick Crace, design for the Entrance Hall of the Royal Pavilion, *c.*1801–04.

Over the course of the next thirty years Frederick Crace was to become a
proficient draughtsman and an accomplished watercolourist. Another design of
about 1801 attests to his ability as a designer. This is an alcove with tented ceiling
in calico which can be established as the design for the Prince of Wales's bedchamber [Fig.1:11].[69] A description of the Prince's bedchamber appeared in the
London Chronicle of 1802:

> The Prince's bed-chamber is divided into three compartments: the centre
> encloses, by sliding partitions, the bed intended to be fitted up as a tent, with
> looking glasses and reflectors, exhibiting to His Royal Highness the Promen-
> ade on the Steine very distinctly, while he reclines on his pillow. On one side
> is an ante-room, and on the other a breakfast room for the accommodation
> of the Prince.[70]

Later in the same article, the 'inimitable skill' of 'Mr Crace, jun.' is referred to,
leaving no doubt as to the designer of the calico-tented bedchamber. For a date
of 1801–02, the design is advanced in style, looking to interiors of the late 1790s
in France where rooms were boldly draped to suggest the military tents of
Napoleon's campaigns.

1:11   Frederick Crace, design for an alcove with a tented ceiling, *c*.1801.

1:12   Japanned cabinet attributed to Frederick Crace, *c*.1815–20.

An interest in the use of drapery is apparent in several designs for the Pavilion by John and Frederick Crace.[71] The supply and use of textiles was to become an important aspect of the business of the Crace firm during the nineteenth century. Gilding was another important activity of the firm from its inception and Frederick Crace seems also to have been proficient in this skill. Several bills for gilding executed by him at the Pavilion in 1818 are among the Mostyn-Crace papers in the Victoria and Albert Museum.[72] Furthermore, in at least one instance he seems to have turned his talents towards the lavish decoration of a suite of furniture in the Chinese style.

In the collection of the Victoria and Albert Museum is an imitation black and gold lacquer, or japanned, cabinet that has been attributed to Frederick Crace [Fig.1:12].[73] The cabinet was designed as part of a suite of furniture which was in the collection of Sir Stamford Raffles, at the time of his death in 1826.[74] No connection between Frederick Crace and Raffles has been established. However, several points of similarity between the decoration on the cabinet and a design by Crace for the Music Room at the Pavilion of c.1817 are apparent [Plate 3].[75] The dragons which ornament both side and base of the cabinet have the same whimsical faces and scrolling bodies as do those seen above the red and gold imitation lacquer panels in the Music Room design. Typical of Frederick Crace's work is the use of a small-scale trellis or diaper background against which the larger motifs of the design are placed.[76] The trellis patterning is found in the centre front portion of the Victoria and Albert Museum japanned cabinet. The curlicue wave pattern on the front of the cabinet also appears in designs by Frederick Crace for Chinese ornament.[77]

The designs by Frederick Crace for the Music Room at Brighton, begun in 1817, form an instructive contrast to his early designs for the Pavilion, illustrating how he had developed as a draughtsman and as a designer over the intervening thirteen years. The Music Room designs indicate how much he had absorbed from working at Carlton House as a young man. By using slender colonnettes, temple bells suspended from the cornice, imitation lacquer panels on the walls, and a chimneypiece with caryatid figures surmounted by a large, rectangular looking glass, Frederick Crace placed his designs for the Brighton Music Room squarely within the elegant, French-inspired tradition of Henry Holland's Chinese Drawing Room at Carlton House.

The Corridor and the Music Room of the Pavilion are the two interiors remaining in the Royal Pavilion today which best express the decorative intentions of Frederick Crace. Designs for the Corridor, begun c.1815, feature lively masks set in cartouches of strapwork ornament which are thoroughly French in terms of their inspiration, owing as much to the designer Jean Bérain as to contemporary sources for Chinese design. In addition to mural decoration, Crace designed

1:13   Frederick Crace, rejected scheme for the Music Room at the Royal Pavilion,
c.1817.

stained glass for the laylights of the Corridor ceiling. His designs have been published by John Morley.[78]

In the Cooper-Hewitt Museum are rejected schemes for the Brighton Music
Room.[79] These feature a blue diaper ground with large pink panels filled with
fantastic dragons, ho-ho birds, and Chinamen [Fig.1:13]. The scheme which was
eventually adopted featured a dazzling colour scheme of a blue mural ground
with an overlay of gold trellising, scarlet and gold temple tops with bells over
each doorcase, canopied areas with enormous, *trompe-l'oeil* bundles of bamboo,
and a giant dome decorated with silver dragon's scales. In addition to the carpet,
which has recently been rewoven, and the decorative, carved dragons in the
room, Crace designed a small forest of stained glass lanterns and possibly the
suite of furniture for the Music Room that was later removed to Buckingham
Palace. This suite of twelve side chairs and four armchairs was made by the firm
of Bailey and Saunders, but the issue of their design has never been resolved.[80]

The wall and door panels of the room have been treated with a rich scarlet
ground painted in gold to represent the landscape scenes found in oriental
lacquer. Thus the Music Room features panels and doors which have been
'japanned' like some of the furniture supplied for the Pavilion in about 1802
by the Crace firm. These japanned panels were painted by a Mr. Lambelet,[81]
who seems to have been one of the thirty-four men working in the Music Room
under Frederick Crace between 1817 and 1820. In 1838 the Music Room of the
Pavilion received lavish praise from the distinguished nineteenth-century architectural historian, Edward Brayley.

1:14   Frederick Crace, unexecuted design for the exterior of the Fishing Temple at Virginia Water, *c.*1827.

No verbal description, however elaborate, can convey to the mind or imagination of the reader an appropriate idea of the magnificence of this apartment . . . Yet luxuriously resplendent and costly as the adornments are, they are so intimately blended with the refinements of an elegant taste, that everything appears in keeping and in harmony . . . The professional skill of Mr. Frederick Crace, and his assistants, has been especially exhibited in the ornamental work and painted decorations, which display great invention and elegance.[82]

Frederick Crace's Music Room at Brighton represents the masterpiece of his career and fully expresses his talent and penchant for detail.

As seen today, the interiors of the Brighton Pavilion represent the final phase of chinoiserie, from about 1815 to 1822, reflecting the work of Frederick Crace and, increasingly in the 1820s, that of Robert Jones. For example, Jones seems to have designed the decoration of the Saloon and parts of the Banqueting Hall.[83] There is some evidence to suggest that the King may have tired of some of Frederick Crace's schemes and planned to replace these with schemes by Jones in the 1820s. Frederick Crace's later work at the Pavilion has been thoroughly researched and published[84] and will not be discussed at length here; his sketchbooks in the Mostyn-Crace Bequest simply confirm his known rôle in the decoration of the Pavilion, as well as the sense of fantasy, whimsy, and technical skill that he brought to the execution of these well-known designs.

After completing his work at the Pavilion in the 1820s, Frederick Crace began work for George IV at Windsor Castle. His final exercise in the Chinese style was the Fishing Temple at Virginia Water, Surrey, near Windsor. Crace was paid £2150 in 1827 for decorating the interior, while the architect of the temple, Jeffry Wyatville, received substantially less (£400) for his contribution.[85] Two drawings by Frederick Crace, now in the Cooper-Hewitt Museum[86] [Fig.1:14], reveal that he attempted to design the exterior of the building. His design is more ornamental than that by the King and Wyatville, in keeping with his designs for Brighton. The *Observer* of 1827 reported (somewhat belatedly) that 'The King is going to erect a temple upon the verge of Virginia Water from a pure and chaste design made by himself. The decorative part is given to Mr Crace.'[87] This quotation assigns the design of the exterior of the building to the King. Wyatville's relatively small payment may be explained by the fact that he acted in the capacity of a consultant to carry out the wishes of the King. Crace's interior, now vanished, was described as 'brightly coloured trellis work and gilded dragons'[88] and was most likely consistent with his work at Brighton. He was, however, sufficiently proud of the Fishing Temple to pose for a portrait by his son, Frederick Henry Crace, holding the plans for it, in the manner of an eighteenth-century architect. This little portrait, executed in pencil in about 1830, is in a private collection [Fig.1:15].

Without question, the major work undertaken by Frederick Crace during the 1820s was the painting and gilding of the private apartments at Windsor Castle for George IV during its refurbishment by Wyatville, which took place between 1824 and 1834. No bills to document this work by Frederick Crace have been discovered. Information on his contribution is limited and comes chiefly from contemporary notices in the press, probably collected by Frederick Crace himself.[89] For example, in the *Morning Herald* of 1827, it was reported that, on June 29th, George IV inspected the progress made by Mr Crace in painting and gilding the ceiling at Windsor Castle.[90] In the obituary of Frederick Crace which appeared in the *Leader* of 1859, it was stated that Crace had been 'engaged in the principal decorative work at Windsor Castle'.[91] In his account of the career of Sir Jeffry Wyatville, Derek Linstrum has stated 'The painting and gilding of the ceilings [of the private apartments at Windsor] was executed by Frederick Crace, who could have been partly responsible for the design of the wall and ceiling panels'.[92] While there is little evidence to suggest what Frederick Crace might have designed for the interiors at Windsor, it is difficult to believe that, with his wealth of experience designing for the Pavilion at Brighton and the interior of the Fish-

1:15   F. H. Crace, Portrait of Frederick Crace, *c.*1830.

ing Temple, he would have acted merely in the capacity of painter and gilder.

The feature of Wyatville's remodelling of Windsor which attracted the greatest attention amongst contemporaries was the remarkable Long Corridor he created in order to link the private apartments with the state rooms. In 1829 a visitor to Windsor, Lady Georgina Ellis, described the Long Corridor thus:

> The first coup d'oeil of the long gallery or corridor is the most strikingly beautiful thing you can conceive . . . splendidly furnished and lighted, filled with pictures and admirably arranged, and with busts and bronzes which made it as interesting as it is magnificent. There is perhaps too much gilding, but this heightens the fairy-like appearance, and excepting this, all the ornaments and decorations are in the best possible taste.[93]

The architecture of the corridor is rather severe, which sets off the works of art displayed in it to good advantage.[94] It features a series of broad, pointed arches in light-coloured stone which have been decorated with blind Gothic tracery. The spandrels of the arches, as well as the bosses of the Perpendicular ceiling, have been richly gilded and seem to represent the contribution of Frederick Crace and his firm.

It is interesting to consider Frederick Crace's work at Windsor in the light of an unfinished album which belonged to his son, John Gregory Crace.[95] In this album are contained nearly 100 individual studies for designs pertaining to the decoration of Windsor in the 1820s [Fig.1:16]. A number of these studies have been inscribed in the hand of John Gregory or Frederick Crace, in order to identify which interior at Windsor they represent. For example, folio 1 contains four studies of leaf-scroll ornament for capitals of pilasters in the Ballroom and Library of Windsor, dated 1829. The dates given for these studies range from 1827, for details of the Audience Chamber and Ladies' Dressing Room, to 1831 for studies of the Ballroom and Library. In a few examples, designs and studies have been inscribed in the hand of Frederick Crace.[96] It is tempting to conclude that the album may represent studies by John Gregory Crace of his father's decoration at Windsor Castle in the 1820s, since some of these studies resemble closely designs in one of Frederick Crace's sketchbooks, now in the Victoria and Albert Museum, London.[97]

In addition to the revived Rococo, or 'Louis Revival', interiors at Windsor Castle, reflected in the leaf-scrolls and capitals in J. G. Crace's album, Windsor in the 1820s was well-known for its Gothic interiors. Frederick Crace was clearly developing an interest in the Gothic style in the 1820s, as evidenced by the sketchbook mentioned above. Several studies of Windsor Castle are included here, along with a drawing of the west façade of King's College Chapel, Cambridge dated 1829. Further studies include the west porch of Durham Cathedral and a detail of its famous medieval lion door-knocker. The feathery quality of the drawing of the porch and the somewhat whimsical character of the face of the lion knocker link these later drawings in the Gothic style to earlier studies for decoration in the Chinese style at the Royal Pavilion.

In the same Frederick Crace sketchbook there is an incomplete drawing of an architectural feature in the Perpendicular Gothic style. This element seems to be either a fire surround or an arched doorcase, and ornamental details such as the quatrefoils inscribed in roundels and the trefoil frieze across the top of the sketch bear a close resemblance to the same features seen in the drawings from the so-called 'Wyatville Project'. This was a large group of highly finished designs for Gothic interiors at Windsor.[98] A number of these designs have been convincingly attributed to the young A. W. N. Pugin.[99] It is intriguing to speculate whether Frederick Crace was actually recording some designs by Pugin for Windsor in his sketchbooks, and whether the two men met at Windsor. Certainly, Frederick Crace could not have foreseen that, in less than twenty years, his son would be working in collaboration with Pugin.

By 1826 payments of over £600 for painting and gilding at Windsor Castle had been made to the firm of 'John Crace & Sons', a relatively small sum when compared with the payments received for work at the Royal Pavilion. The three brothers, Frederick, Alfred and Henry Crace, had been in partnership under the leadership of Frederick Crace since their father's retirement in about 1806. Due to financial difficulties experienced by Alfred and Henry Crace, who had drawn substantially more than their share of the firm's profits, the partnership was dissolved in 1826.[100] Frederick carried on the business assisted by his two sons, John Gregory and Frederick Henry Crace. The latter was working with his father at Windsor in 1827.[101]

The decade of the 1830s was something of a transitional phase in the career of Frederick Crace. He was in his fifties and reaching the time in his life when he might look towards retirement from the day-to-day work of the firm. Some decorating work did, of course, continue. King George IV had died in 1830, and his brother William IV completed works which had been under way, including that at Windsor.[102] Frederick Crace received further commissions from the Board of Works after his work at Windsor, for in July of 1834 he was awarded a contract for gilding the rooms of the west range of Buckingham Palace.[103] Increasingly during the 1830s, however, a number of family and administrative commitments seem to have diverted his attention away from the business of decorating.

In 1818 Frederick Crace had been elected Commissioner of Sewers in London. This post, which perhaps reflected his long-standing interest in the topography of the city, may have given impetus to his collecting the vast quantity of prints

1:16   J. G. Crace, Studies of ornamental details at Windsor Castle, c.1827–30.

and drawings which now comprises the 'Crace Collection' in the British Museum.[104] Included in the sale of the library of John Crace in 1819 was a collection of topographical views of London, and some objects from his father's collection may have been reserved by Frederick Crace to form the nucleus of his own, which ultimately numbered 5000 prints and drawings. The views ranged in date from the sixteenth to the nineteenth centuries, and some watercolours were commissioned from Thomas Shepherd to fill gaps in the collection.[105]

In addition to the Sewer Commission and the Crace Collection, Frederick Crace seems to have taken over the administration of the estate of his wealthy relation by marriage, John Gregory, who owned a considerable amount of property. Frederick managed the Gregory estate during the later 1820s and 1830s on behalf of the heirs, of whom he and his wife were two.[106] A number of sheets of calculations of income, bills for work at the various Gregory properties, and memoranda left by Frederick Crace on this subject indicate that managing the estate was virtually a full-time task even without additional commitments.[107] In 1815, the Gregory estate was worth about £40,000, which was a considerable amount of money.

Therefore it does not seem surprising that, as early as 1826 at the age of seventeen, John Gregory Crace should have begun to work for his father. With the advent of J. G. Crace into the decorating business, the Crace firm entered the second phase of its history. Never again was the work of the firm to be so closely connected with the royal circle. The work of the so-called 'Victorian Craces' is characterised by its astonishing range and diversity and by the eclecticism of its inspiration. This, however, will be discussed in the second long essay.

2

Charles and Edward Crace and Rococo Coach Painting

by Michael Snodin

EIGHTEENTH-CENTURY coach making employed a very wide range of skilled trades working with a great many different materials. In London the trade was dominated by a group of makers and associated craftsmen centred on Long Acre, Covent Garden,[1] including Thomas Crace's three sons, Edward, Charles and John. While the information on trade cards makes it clear that a number of coach painters were independent operators, many more may have been employed directly in the workshops of the larger coachmakers. Indeed, an advertisement for Charles, probably dating from 1756, some eight years after completing his apprenticeship, suggests that after a number of years designing for the trade (perhaps as a sub-contractor) he was setting up as an independent designer of coaches both for the trade and for private clients.[2] While Charles Crace designed complete coaches as well as, perhaps, being a coach painter, Edward Crace, trained by a Painter Stainer, designed and executed the decoration alone.

Among the independent operators, coach painting was often part of a range of decorative painting on offer. Typically such painters were also engaged in painting signs, hatchments, window blinds, floorcloths and lettering. The common feature of most of this work was the depiction of coats of arms and some coach painters were also herald painters working on a small scale on vellum. Also frequently undertaken was general house painting and picture framing and cleaning.[3] A number of coach painters made the transition to easel painting;[4] after 1768 Edward Crace made the more natural move to house decoration and looking after pictures.

Charles and Edward Crace were part of an accomplished group of designers and draughtsmen which became increasingly prominent amongst craftsmen working in the West End from the 1730s, coinciding with the beginnings of the developed Rococo style. By the 1750s training in draughtsmanship and the design education of craftsmen was being carried out in a number of local drawing schools as well as being encouraged by annual prizes awarded by the Society of Arts.[5] The drawing masters were often themselves craftsmen or from a craft background, like Charles Crace. Perhaps the most accomplished of these Rococo craft designers of the 1750s and 60s was the furniture maker John Linnell, whose graphic and ornamental style is close to that of the Crace designs.

The study of English Rococo coach painting is greatly hampered by the disappearance of all but a handful of the coaches. The surviving design records are therefore of particular importance, none more so than the Crace design book and its associated drawings in New York.[6] The Crace designs represent a number of different stages in the design process, ranging from rough sketches in which ideas are worked out to carefully finished drawings in body colour which probably served as the last stage before the full-size cartoon for transfer to the coach panel. Most of the drawings show intermediate stages between these points, and many have been folded, perhaps for sending to customers for approval.

In terms of design the leading characteristic of the Crace drawings is their use of a consistent vocabulary of elaborate Rococo scrollwork. They can be divided into three main groups. The first, and smallest, consists of complete schemes for the decoration of carriage sides (below the windows), in which unified compositions are created which ignore the break caused by the door, shown as a pair of ruled lines [Fig.2:1]. The lack of surviving coaches decorated in this manner makes it difficult to determine how the painted decoration was intended to relate to the carved door and body framing members which are usually present on all other coaches of this date. In general the painted scrollwork is conceived as being on the plane of the panel or carving. One extremely elaborate design for a town chariot (or *carrosse coupé*) shows several layers of receding scrollwork [Fig.2:2], its handling of space echoing the illusionistic landscape paintings covering whole carriage sides which were popular on the Continent.

The second design category in the Crace drawings covers designs for single panels, almost certainly for doors, which are generally filled with scrollwork compositions incorporating in the centre oval cartouches for armorials. This series of variations on a theme runs from pencil drawings through designs in pencil and watercolour to larger drawings coloured with metallic paint [Plate 4]. The formal variations are slight except for one design which has broken away from convention into a series of elegant loops [Fig.2:3]. Also in this panel group is a charming sketch for a horizontal panel of uncertain use which shows a dog attacking a swan, between which is the armorial cartouche [Fig.2:4]. The third category of Crace drawings consists of free-standing illusionistic scrollwork structures often incorporating trees and flower garlands, the upper parts of which are solid or open cartouches for coats of arms. These designs, which play vari-

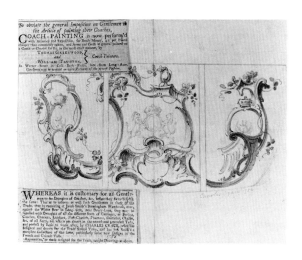

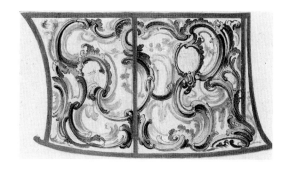

2:1 Edward Crace(?), design for painting a Berlin coach, c.1755–60.

2:2 Edward Crace(?), design for the decoration of a *carrosse coupé*, c.1755–60.

2:3 Edward Crace(?), design for a painted coach panel, c.1755–60.

2:4 Edward Crace(?), design for a painted coach panel, c.1755–60.

2:5 Edward Crace(?), design for a painted coach panel, *c.*1755–60.

2:6 Edward Crace(?), design for a painted coach panel, *c.*1755–60.

2:7 Pierre Edmé Babel, plate from *Différents Compartiments d'Ornements*, *c.*1740–50.

2:8 Edward Crace(?), design for coach decoration, *c.*1755–60.

ations on three basic types, often markedly asymmetrical, are among the most striking designs in the Crace drawings [Fig.2:5].

It is useful to compare the Crace drawings with those in a design book at the Avery Library attributed (almost certainly correctly) to the painter G. B. Cipriani, 'one of the great backroom figures of the neo-classic style in England'.[7] Although Cipriani started painting ceilings soon after his arrival in England in 1756, he is known to have executed the figurative compositions on the Royal State Coach (1760–61) and probably on the Lord Mayor's coach (1757). The Avery book, however, is evidence that he was involved in non-figurative coach painting as well as other work characteristic of the decorative painter. While the drawings contain a copy after a Boucher cartouche (as well as figures after Bloemaert),[8] most of the ornamental designs in the book are for decorative surrounds to armorials. Very different in style to the Crace drawings, they are later Rococo adaptations of the airy grotesque devices of Watteau. Close comparisons can be drawn with published prints after the designs of J. F. Cuvilliés, which very probably influenced them.[9] While there is some evidence to suggest that Cipriani was not the only coach painter employing this style, connections can also be made with the very different manner of the Crace drawings. A single panel repeats, albeit in the Cuvilliés style, the compositional schema of the Crace door panels, while a design for mantling repeats a formula found on two other Crace drawings. In addition, two other pencil drawings come very close to the Crace fantasy structures.

The Crace designs are amongst the most vigorous and accomplished exercises in French *Genre Pittoresque* in English Rococo. Particularly close to French *morceaux de fantaisie* are the imaginary structures, with their pierced forms and indications of landscape [Fig.2:6], closely comparable to such French print suites as P. E. Babel's *Différents Compartiments d'Ornements* of 1740–50 [Fig.2:7].[10] Particularly French in feeling is a pair of pencil designs for structures incorporating fountains, putti, and remarkably fat scrollwork [Fig.2:8].

In their solid forms and smooth graphic handling these drawings are markedly different from the spiky designs of the dominant school of London carver-drawing masters represented by Matthias Lock and Thomas Johnson. They can, however, be compared both in form and graphic handling with the drawings of another Rococo furniture maker and designer, John Linnell. Not only do the drawings share the same type of easy handling (so different from the fussy style of the carvers) but formal comparisons can also be made, notably in the use of smooth cartouches and elongated and overlapping scrollwork [Fig.2:9]. Little is known of Linnell's training in draughtsmanship, except that he attended the St. Martin's Lane Academy, the stylistic influence of which is unclear. Perhaps more significant in this context is Linnell's connection with the coachmaking

2:9   John Linnel, design for a bed, *c*.1755.

trade. Together with his coachmaker uncle he published in 1760 a design for the Royal State Coach. Such compositions as the title page for his *New Book of Ornaments useful for Silver Smiths etc.*, of the same year, with its sculpturesque asymmetrical vases on a fat scrolling base, also show that he had fully absorbed the rich Rococo-Baroque style characteristic of state coaches in this period.[11] Apparently out on a limb in the context of English Rococo, painted coach decoration of the Crace type immediately makes sense as part of a trade in which the highest achievement was a massively carved product, wholly continental in style, such as the Lord Mayor's coach, described by Mark Girouard as the 'Apotheosis of the Rococo'.[12] Indeed the elaborately scrolled schemes for complete coach sides on bodies of plain profile may have been largely intended as a substitute for the far more expensive fashionable French body, with its complex curved profiles.

The disappearance of all the carriages painted in the Crace manner might suggest that the style was unique to that family. That this was not the case is indicated by the few other visual records of coach painting in the period. Interesting comparisons can be made between the graphic style of an armorial in the Crace book and the designs for armorials in a design book at the Yale Center for British Art.[13] The latter are executed in pen and ink with a confidence and brio which make one doubt the inscribed dates in the 1750s; given the manner in which such drawing is generally covered by strong heraldic colours the hesitation is excusable.

Equally full of dash is a set of cartouche decorations for coach panels recently identified in the Victoria and Albert Museum.[14] Extraordinarily fresh and bright in colouring, the drawings not only display a graphic handling similar to both the Linnell and Crace drawings but they also share a number of key motifs. The most important is an oval cartouche (for armorials) supported by a long tail-like moulding [Fig. 2:10]. This cartouche motif is also found (together with fat scrolls)

:10   Anonymous, design for a painted coach decoration, *c.*1790.

2:11   J. Hall after Edward Abbott, title page of *A Set of New Designs for Coach and Chariot Builders,* 1763.

2:12   F. Patton after Charles Crace, design for a coach, 1750.

on the title page of *A set of New Designs for Coach and Chariot Bodies* by Edward
Abbott of 1763[15] together with the tendril ornament which is also characteristic
of the designs discussed so far [Fig.2:11].

Interestingly, none of the designs in the Abbott set displays complete panels
of scrollwork as in the Crace designs; coach bodies of delicately varying
curvilinear outline are decorated in two cases with complete scenes across the
whole body[16] while the other designs show relatively small coats of arms supported in some cases by Crace-type scrollwork. This set tends to support a few
other pieces of evidence which suggest that most English coaches of the Rococo
period were restricted in their painted decoration to more or less elaborate
armorials, as was to be the case later in the century.[17]

While there can be no doubt that the Crace drawings are by a member, or
members, of the family, attempts to distinguish among them the hands of Charles
or Edward Crace are faced with considerable difficulties, not the least of which
is the wide variety of media and varying purpose of the designs. The spine of
the volume gives it to Edward Crace, and it contains a loose drawing of a motif
inscribed 'Edward Crace 1760'. A drawing in New York for the painting of
a coach side, which is an alternative to one in the volume, is inscribed 'Charles
Crace 1754'.[18] While it would be tempting to suppose that Charles, the coach
designer, was responsible for the coach while Edward tackled the motif, no

reliance can be placed on the inscriptions, which are almost certainly not auto-graph. Confidence is not increased by the widely divergent dates on drawings so similar in treatment and design. In fact certain features, notably the use of vases of a simplified late Rococo type and fantastic flowers of a kind probably associated with Jean Pillement,[19] strongly indicate that the designs date from about 1755–60. Indeed the entirely undecorated carriages in Charles Crace's pattern book of 1750[20] [Fig.2:12] suggest that we should give entirely to Edward, Painter Stainer and future interior decorator, the elaborate painted designs discussed here.

Whoever was their author, the Crace designs were part of a distinct mid-eighteenth-century school of London coach painting, now largely lost, whose skills ranged from simple armorials to schemes for whole carriages, executed in a smoothly curvilinear style closely allied to that of John Linnell but ultimately indebted to French models.[21] Even without further evidence it is clear that the Crace designs must represent some of the most adventurous purely ornamental coach painting of the period.

3

The Royal Pavilion Brighton: The Chinoiserie Designs by Frederick Crace

by Gordon Lang

THE FALL OF Constantinople to the Ottoman Turks in 1453 discouraged western Christian trade in the eastern Mediterranean. The difficulty in obtaining supplies of silks, spices and other exotica from the Far East through the normal channels via Arab and Persian middlemen resulted in the exploration of alternative routes. Within fifty years the Portuguese had rounded the Cape of Good Hope and crossed the Indian Ocean to India where they began to establish their trading empire. By 1514 their tentacles extended into Chinese waters, and shortly afterwards they began shipping Chinese commodities, including silks and porcelain, directly to the west. The development of trade created a greater demand for Chinese goods and designs so that by the middle of the seventeenth century northern Europe was in the grip of 'chinamania'. If it proved impossible to obtain real Chinese lacquer, porcelain or silk then the Portuguese, Dutch, French or English parodied them. Although there were accurate copies of Chinese artefacts such as those manufactured at Delft in Holland, most European produced goods were simply fanciful pastiches. Thus we have the first phase of 'Chinoiserie'. A second period of orientalism occurred during the Rococo period in the middle of the eighteenth century as the designs of Watteau, Boucher, Pillement, Chippendale and Matthias Lock confirm. The continued import of Chinese decorative items kept this fascination with the Orient alive, even if at times interest waned, as it did, for example, during the Neo-classical period at the end of the eighteenth century. It was at this time that the Prince Regent, flying in the face of stylistic convention, commissioned work on his fantastic pavilion at Brighton. Thus the Prince was at least partly responsible for another, if not the final phase of Chinoiserie, perhaps most clearly represented by the hybrid oriental designs on English ceramics and wallpapers of the early years of the nineteenth century.

The oriental designs of the Royal Pavilion range from the truly bizarre confec-

3:1   Frederick Crace, design of Chinoiserie scrolls, shapes and flowers, *c.*1815.

tions of Robert Jones to the often more prosaic treatments by Frederick Crace. The former appears to have been a highly imaginative designer whose depictions are, with the possible exception of his figure subjects, almost entirely divorced from recognisable traditional Chinese design. In this sense Jones's designs are true Chinoiserie: fanciful western interpretations of Cathay. On the other hand, much of the work of Frederick Crace shows a very close, almost slavish adherence to original Chinese sources, using motifs from eighteenth century 'famille-rose' exportware porcelain, Canton enamel or even Mandarin robes. Crace generally borrowed ancillary motifs such as border panels, rarely employing a complete design. Although most of the designs of Frederick Crace for the Pavilion were executed around 1802–03 or 1815, his Chinese source material is usually somewhat earlier, mostly dating from the reign of the emperor Qianlong (1736–95).

Canton enamel, with its well-defined and crisply painted patterns, seems to have had a greater appeal to his draughtsmanship than the more loosely treated porcelains. There are many examples to illustrate this preference. Catalogue entry no.220 in John Morley's *The Making of the Royal Pavilion, Brighton*, a design of Chinoiserie scrolls, 'is a convoluted symphony of cloud scrolls, florettes and *ruyi* heads' [Fig.3:1]. Painted in the soft pastel colours of the early 'famille-rose' palette, the design is an accurate rendition of a popular pattern of the Qianlong period. This is one of the most complicated repeating designs that Crace copied, the designer following precisely every twist and turn of the original, and thereby emphasising his reliance on Chinese decorative sources. No.197 in Morley's book [Fig.3:2] is a study of Canton enamel decoration, as indeed are many other Crace designs. To sinologists this is a familiar configuration, that of bats (often five in number) flying above a lotus medallion.[1] Many Chinese motifs are symbolic and the present arrangement can signify happiness and fertility. It is usually found on the centre of a dish or bowl especially in the Qing dynasty (1644–1912).

The group of rectangular panels of scrollwork (no.85 in Morley) are conventional filler decoration, invariably occupying a continuous band between the central zone and the outer border on dishes or trays. It is interesting to note Morley's understandable misinterpretation of the largest of these panels. He refers to 'the abstract treatment of the serpents that form the scrolling pattern at the base of (85), a device that is seen quite often in this period and afterwards.' This device is a descendant of the so-called vine scroll introduced into China during the Tang dynasty (618–906 AD) which was revived and became very popular on Japanese porcelain towards the end of the seventeenth century. In Japan this scroll was termed 'karakusa' or 'octopus scroll', probably because of the small lateral projections which resemble the suckers on this creature. From Japan the scroll was re-introduced into China, where it was altered slightly, making it look a bit like a centipede, although it is purely vegetal.

Another subject, of which Crace did several versions, either in outline or in watercolour, was the phoenix or ho-ho bird. Nos.122, 123, 124 and 125 – each described by Morley as a 'design for an exotic bird' – are very accurate copies of Chinese designs of this bird of good omen, for although it is a mythical and composite creature it has, like the dragon, certain changeless features, even if its plumage varies in colour [Plate 5]. To the Chinese the phoenix has the form of a swan with a scaly body, a serpentine head, the tail of a fish, the mouth of a chicken and the throat of a *yen* bird, and his back has dragon's markings.[2] The phoenix, emblematic of the Empress, often accompanies the dragon (the Emperor), and when seen together they symbolise a happy and peaceful reign. Another study (no.192), described as a 'design for a moth/bird' which shows the phoenix in the slightly unusual head-on attitude, is a meticulous copy of a Canton enamel original. For some of his other designs Crace looked to eighteenth-century Chinese porcelain; no.222 'chinoiserie design in tones of blue' is based on a blue and white porcelain jar painted with stylised lotus scrolls between *ruyi* heads on the upper border and adjoining lappets on the lower edge [Fig.3:3].

The *ruyi* motif was a popular motif in the Chinese decorative arts,[3] particularly during the Ming and Qing dynasties. It resembles an inverted double-ogee or Islamic arch, and is a stylised version of the head of the sacred fungus (*lingzhi*),

3:2   Frederick Crace, design of bats and lotus medallion, *c.*1815.

3:3   An eighteenth-century Chinese blue-and-white jar in the Ming style with a frieze
of stylised *ruyi*-heads.

a plant believed to possess the ingredients to make an elixir of immortality. The
lower frieze is a development of the lotus petal panel introduced as a decorative
element probably during the Tang dynasty where it was usually modelled in
high relief. In its painted form the petal appears *ab initio* on blue and white
porcelain, an innovation of the Yuan dynasty (1278–1368 AD). Another design
for 'chinoiserie repeat pattern in green, pink, yellow and blue' (no.224) is taken
from a 'famille-rose' porcelain vessel. Crace seemed more at ease with flat or
linear prototypes such as those cited here, and he was less successful with complicated three dimensional objects. His design for a 'Chinese dog' (no.121), borrowed from a porcelain joss-stick holder complete with slab socle and tubular
holder, is a delightful parody.[4]

3:4   Frederick Crace, design for a Chinese boy and flowers, *c.*1815.

The design for 'a Chinese boy and flowers' is a very early theme, first appearing in China during the Tang dynasty [Fig.3:4]. The child's attire and anklets suggest that the subject was probably Indian in origin. Similar designs were carved on *Dingyao*,[5] an early porcelain made in the north of China and of which Crace would have had no knowledge. It is more likely that he based his design on seventeenth or early eighteenth-century porcelain when this particular theme enjoyed a revival in popularity.

For some larger designs Crace has referred to Chinese silk robes as a source of inspiration. Fig.3:5, which replicates closely the design on a conventional Manchu robe[6] [Fig.3:6], shows a four-clawed dragon careering directly towards the viewer above rocks and foaming waves.[7] Both cloud and sky are populated

3:5   Frederick Crace, design based on traditional Chinese dragon robes, *c*.1815.

3:6 A traditional Chinese dragon robe, Qing Dynasty (1644–1912).

3:7 Frederick Crace, design with crane, c.1815.

with precious objects, which the designer has imperfectly understood. The dragon, in spite of his ferocious appearance, is a benign spirit of the waters and symbolises the eastern quadrant in his role as one of the creatures of the four directions. This scaly, serpentine creature is an entirely mythical beast yet is always shown precisely delineated in one of his nine forms. The present configuration and frontal attitude is typical of dragon robe embellishment. In Fig. 3:7, the familiar bat, here probably symbolising the Five Happinesses of human existence (longevity, wealth, virtue, tranquillity and a good end to one's life), emerges as an antennaed butterfly. Bobbing along the waves are conch shells, looking more like gaily-painted Easter eggs than Buddhist emblems of good fortune. Other objects include the musical stone and the pair of scrolls or books, all typically displaced as on the original vestment. Although many robes are embellished with a seemingly random selection of Buddhist, Daoist or precious objects, there is often an overall theme or an indication of rank, such as the double *shou* or happiness character found on marriage robes.[8]

Whilst Crace quite obviously made religious copies of Chinese sources it would be unfair to suggest that he was incapable of originality or of adapting designs. Certainly many of his interpretations of Chinese themes, especially for the skylights, are embellished with grotesques or other renaissance motifs, or are given a fuller and more natural European feel.

In conclusion, it is impossible to say why Crace was often so literal in his decoration. Was he following the wishes of the Prince of Wales, or simply copying porcelain, enamel or textiles in the royal collection or from his own stock? The lists of such materials in the Crace bills for the Pavilion are, sadly, too vague to answer that question. Perhaps the solution lies buried somewhere in the present Royal Collection.

Part Two

4

The Victorian Craces, *c.*1830–1899

by Megan Aldrich

J. G. Crace and the 'Old French Style'

IN 1826, WHEN he was seventeen years old, John Gregory Crace began to work for his father Frederick. A few bills exist to document this early work.[1] One bill has been made out by J. G. Crace to Frederick and Henry Crace, the latter being Frederick's brother and partner until 1826, for 'posting' and 'glazing'. Another two bills, which must have come later in the year, have been made out to Frederick Crace alone for posting the firm's accounts and glazing. The early work of J. G. Crace therefore involved relatively routine office and work-shop duties.

The year 1826 was a significant one in the history of the firm, since the partner-ship of 'John Crace & Sons', established during the work at Brighton Pavilion, was dissolved due to discord over financial matters between Frederick and his two brothers, Henry and Alfred Crace. The latter two seem to have brought little credit to the firm. Henry Crace became embroiled in an incident of industrial espionage whereby he pirated a process of painting in imitation of damask from the prominent Edinburgh decorator D. R. Hay. Crace apparently had the full co-operation of Hay's staff in the matter.[2] Alfred Crace seems to have been chronic-ally in debt. He fled first to France and then, in 1830, to Canada, where he assumed the surname Crace-Calvert and died in 1849. J. G. Crace was sent to Rouen in 1830 to settle his uncle's debts.[3]

Between the tumultuous events of 1826 and the year 1830, when J. G. Crace entered into formal partnership with his father, young Crace made several visits to the Continent. In 1827 he had first travelled to Paris in the company of his father Frederick, who was a great admirer of French decoration. In 1829 he embarked on a more extensive study tour of northern Europe. The meticulous notes and descriptions made by J. G. Crace about the buildings he studied have been recorded in his 'Diary of a Journey to Paris and the Rhine'.[4] This study tour served as an important source of ideas for Crace in the practice of his profession, and the time he spent in France sparked a lifelong admiration of French decorative art.

For the duration of his very long career, J. G. Crace remained an unapologetic eclecticist, for he enthusiastically admired the art of all centuries. He expressed great appreciation of Gothic and Renaissance structures. When making his way towards Paris in 1829, he remarked that the great Gothic cathedral at Amiens was 'one of the richest Gothic Edifices I have ever seen'. The Renaissance chateau at Chantilly was pronounced 'very elegant', and the early Gothic cathedral of St. Denis 'agreeably surprised me . . . [being] very light and elegant'.[5]

In particular, buildings which he described as having 'lightness' and 'elegance', especially those of the seventeenth and eighteenth centuries, attracted J. G. Crace's attention, reflecting the preoccupation of his early career with the 'Old French style' which is now associated with the Rococo Revival of c.1825 to 1845. In about 1830 this term denoted French art from the late seventeenth to late eighteenth centuries, comprising the Baroque, Rococo and Neo-classical styles of decoration prevalent during the reigns of Louis XIV, Louis XV, and Louis XVI. In the English mind these styles were often confused with one another, and the term 'Old French style' was occasionally applied to English Rococo designers such as Matthias Lock and Thomas Johnson.[6] It is the vagueness of the term 'Old French style' which is appropriate in describing the rich mixture of Baroque, Rococo and Neo-classical motifs used by J. G. Crace in his earliest designs of the 1830s.

Crace was equally enthusiastic about the decorated interiors of contemporary buildings in Paris, which he examined in great detail during his visit of 1829. On 29 June he made notes in his diary concerning Les Invalides: 'the Richness of the Interior of the Chapel quite surprised me.' This included the lavish use of gilt and the ornamental painting of the ceiling and its spandrels. On the same day J. G. Crace visited the new building of the Bourse by Brongniart, an architect trained before the Revolution. Crace remarked that the Bourse had, 'a very fine Ceiling which I could never have discovered to be so, had I not looked for some that my Father told me were *excellent*.'[7] It is interesting to note the professional influence of Frederick Crace on his son's ideas of decorative practice. Less enthusiasm was evident in J. G. Crace's notes on Soufflot's famous domed church of Ste-Geneviève, later christened the Panthéon, in Paris. This building must have brought to mind the contemporary Pantheon in London, decorated by his great-grandfather. On 30 June he noted in his diary that it was 'very light and beautiful' in the 'general effect of the interior', yet he thought that 'great fault could be found with the Details' of the ornaments used in the scheme.[8] He did not elaborate further.

It was not Soufflot's Panthéon but the Opéra Comique in Paris which Crace praised most highly. On 6 July he noted in his diary that the interior decoration of the Opéra Comique was 'the neatest I have yet seen in Paris: top tier, light painted ornament on white ground, the next tier, a Cameo Pattern, the next imitation of Tapestry thrown over each Box, which looked very rich, and the next a painted scroll ornament in white and gold.'[9] The description of this decoration, with its scrolls, cameos, and imitation textile effects, mentions what were to become the standard features of J. G. Crace's designs for interiors in the 'Old French style' in the 1830s and early 1840s.

In particular, Crace's comments suggest that it was the decoration of the Opéra Comique in Paris which directly inspired his own interiors for two theatres designed by the architect Samuel Beazley in 1836. These must rank as J. G. Crace's earliest independent decorating commissions. They were the Theatre Royal in Leicester and St. James's Theatre in London. Both are now demolished, but designs by J. G. Crace for their interiors have recently come to light.[10] Although the interior of St. James's has been described as 'Louis Quatorze style',[11] in fact the drawings by Crace illustrate a decorative scheme which takes its cue from the French Rococo decoration typical of the reign of Louis XV. The balconies of the theatre were painted with scrolling cartouches, vines, trellis work, and asymmetric leaf scrolls. Term figures were used to support the upper, domed ceiling, and the whole was painted in pastel colours and gilt on the white ground. The designs by Crace for the interior of the Theatre Royal in Leicester are in a Neo-classical style, with symmetrical swags, arabesques, and geometric cartouches with cameo figures. This type of decoration was prevalent during the reign of Louis XVI, indicating Crace's use of the full range of French eighteenth-century styles of decoration which he saw during his travels.

There is evidence in J. G. Crace's travel diary of 1829 that he was entrusted to carry out business for his father's firm during this visit to Paris. On 7 July he noted there was 'business all day – saw Mr Delille . . . Different Paper Factories and Print Shops.'[12] The supply of wallpaper was to become a consistent aspect of the business of the Crace firm in the nineteenth century. Textiles had formed a major portion of the firm's work since John Crace's work at the Royal Pavilion, and Crace toured the Gobelins tapestry works and the Royal carpet factory during his 1829 visit to Paris.[13] In this year Frederick Crace would have been in the middle of decorating work at Windsor Castle for King George IV, a great connoisseur of French decorative art. Perhaps the business with Mr. Delille was for this very important commission.

On 15 July J. G. Crace left Paris and arrived at Rheims, which he described as a 'fine old town'. He noted that the cathedral had 'the Richest stained Glass I have seen', but 'unfortunately the Roof is spoilt by being painted blue on which are yellow Fleurs de Lis'. This criticism seems a curious one in view of the fact that Crace was to design polychromatic ceilings in the medieval and Renaissance styles later in his career. It may have been the contrast of blue and yellow to which he objected, but the use of contrasting, primary colours became characteristic of his work in the later 1840s. On 19 July Crace and his companion, Mr. Buchan, entered Bavaria, where he was pleased with the many 'fine Ruins of the Castles'. He particularly cited the castle at Heidelberg, which 'surpassed in grandeur and beauty what we had expected' to such an extent 'as to render us incapable of utterance for a minute or two'.[14] Crace then described the nearby Fountain of the Wolf's Glen as 'a gloomy, desolate, romantic place'. On another page of his diary, Crace had referred to the 'Picturesqueness' of a view.[15] From his use of terms such as 'gloomy', 'romantic', and 'Picturesque', it is apparent that J. G. Crace's sense of aesthetics was not confined to the elegance of Parisian interiors of the eighteenth century. He also appreciated the concerns of the early nineteenth century with those more powerful, evocative aspects of design associated with the Romantic Movement.

In describing the architecture of the ruined chateau at Heidelberg, Crace noted that a later addition to the medieval building was 'built in 1600 in the richest French style, thus in the same ruins you have the vastness and grandeur of the Ancient and the Richness of the more Modern Building.'[16] Crace began experimenting with combining the 'grandeur' of the Gothic style with the 'richness' of the Renaissance style in interiors he created with his father at Taymouth Castle, Scotland, early in the 1840s. In 1829, however, he was still chiefly concerned with studying decorative schemes in France of more recent date. Of a church in Mayence, he noted 'the Interior was pretty, in the old French style, the Ceiling is very beautifully painted in Fresco, the Colouring of the Ornaments blending in with the figures . . . with very good effect.'[17]

From Mayence Crace and Buchan travelled by packet boat down the Rhine. They admired many of the castles and arrived in Cologne on 28 July, when Crace noted in his diary that the cathedral was 'of beautiful execution'. From Cologne to Calais their route lay through Belgium, where Crace found much to appreciate. He praised 'the Belgian carved oak pulpits' and the tower of the Hôtel de Ville in Brussels, which he thought 'very light and elegant', as well as the ceiling of the council chamber, which Crace described as 'very well painted'.[18] On 10 August Crace attended a service in the 'superb' cathedral of Antwerp. He remarked, 'I always think the swelling of the organ in a large Gothic Building causes it to be viewed with much stronger feelings and more effect.' His future colleague Pugin would have sympathised with this observation. Crace also saw the famous painting of *The Deposition* by Rubens in Antwerp Cathedral. 'The Descent from the Cross certainly affected me more than any picture I ever saw.'

In the same entry, Crace cited the fresh, brilliant colouring and the naturalism of Rubens's painting as a model for other artists.

Although J. G. Crace returned to France a number of times and to Germany and the Netherlands on future occasions, his journey of 1829 and the notes he made in his travel diary give an indication of the kinds of sources he was to use throughout his career. Overall, the models upon which he based his work were to be found in French decoration of the eighteenth century. Frederick Crace would have served as a strong influence upon his son in this, having spent his early years training among the French decorative artists who worked at Carlton House.

In his travel diaries, J. G. Crace recorded the most detailed information about interiors in France and, specifically, Paris. The impact of colour upon architecture, the overall effect of an interior, and the use of decorative ornament to set off figurative mural or ceiling painting were major concerns of Crace when he travelled and studied abroad, and these concerns formed the basis of his career in the decoration of interiors. His inspiration must be characterised as 'French' in a broad sense, however, for he borrowed ideas from a variety of cultures and periods. It is rather his concern for the details of a decorative scheme, his care in making the various elements of an interior harmonise, and his rational, logical approach to the organisation of a room which indicate that ultimately the interiors created by Crace derive from eighteenth-century French sources.

One designer who influenced J. G. Crace was Gilles Marie Oppenord, the Parisian-born son of a Flemish father who was a cabinet-maker for Louis XIV.[19] Oppenord received an education in architecture and travelled through Italy before returning to Paris and publishing a series of plates for designs early in the eighteenth century. He is now regarded as a designer of interiors who spanned the transition between the older Baroque and the new, lighter style of Rococo decoration shortly after the death of Louis XIV. In at least one instance, J. G. Crace copied designs by Oppenord. From the work of Oppenord and Jean Bérain, another French court designer who straddled the Baroque and Rococo styles, Crace observed the use of naturalistic foliate designs in combination with abstract ornament such as strapwork and cartouches. Early drawings by J. G. Crace in the 'Old French style', displaying these features, are now in the collections of the Victoria and Albert Museum and the Metropolitan Museum in New York.

The Renewal of the Firm

The 1830s were a crucial period in the history of the Crace decorating firm. In 1830 John Gregory Crace had come of age to inherit a substantial sum of money from his mother's estate, thereby enabling him to become a full partner in business with his father. 'On May 26 1830 I became 21 years old and the property inherited from my dear mother was made over to me . . . and . . . about £3,200 cash. The latter I at once put into the business and I became partner with my father—at this time we kept no Clerk—I had to manage the books and to make out all accounts. I rose always at 5.30 and opened the shop gates myself. I called the men's names—and arranged them on their several works. We had no general foreman.'[20] He remarked that his father was completely pre-occupied with work for the Crown, most notably at Windsor Castle, and that the number of private commissions had greatly fallen off.[21] This was clearly a worry to him. Among the Mostyn-Crace papers is a draft of a memorandum written on paper watermarked '1831' entitled, 'Supposing my Father determines on remaining at Brighton'. In this memorandum J. G. Crace discusses various options concerning the future of the firm, including whether he should dissolve the partnership with his father, whether he should attempt to legally restrain him with respect to the firm's activities, or whether they should revert to the same situation as 'before I was of age' (when Frederick Crace was the head of the firm and J. G. Crace simply an employee, with his inheritance not invested in the firm). Crace expressed concern that, owing to 'our present extensive premises', the business should remain based 'in Town' and not at Brighton, where Frederick Crace was living.[22]

J. G. Crace's relationship with his father seems to have been complicated by the latter's strong attachment to his younger son, Frederick Henry Crace, who worked with him at Windsor from an early age.[23] Frederick Henry Crace was a talented draughtsman who won a silver medal at the Royal Academy, where he studied drawing in about 1830. He lived with his father at Brighton until his premature death in 1833 after a long illness. This sad event evidently helped to close the gap between Frederick Crace and his eldest son, for the house in Brighton was sold shortly afterwards and Frederick Crace began to spend more time at the London premises of his business, now 'Frederick Crace and Son', located at 14 Wigmore Street since 1827.

Aside from the fact that J. G. Crace displayed a natural aptitude for business, there was genuine pressure on him to ensure things were running smoothly. In January of 1833 he married Suzanne Langley, the daughter of the Superintendent of Works at the Royal Naval Hospital at Greenwich, where Crace had been supervising painting during the early 1830s.[24] After their marriage Mr. and

Mrs. J. G. Crace lived in the firm's premises in Wigmore Street off Cavendish Square. J. G. Crace later stated that the ground floor was always reserved for business, and it was extended twice, the first instance being in 1836. Until 1845, the year of his retirement, Frederick Crace kept two rooms on the third floor of the house.[25]

With father and son established at Wigmore Street, the younger Crace was able to increase the number of the firm's private decorating commissions, as he had wished. Shortly after having finished the decoration of the two theatres for Beazley in 1836, Crace was determined to create a showroom at the firm's premises in order to demonstrate its capabilities and to attract new custom. In search of inspiration, he set out once again for Paris in 1837. On this trip he examined in detail the decoration of the interiors of the principal private and public buildings.[26] Crace concluded that England lagged behind France in the excellence of its decorative art, and during this visit he engaged a few French artists who agreed to come to England and work for the Crace firm when a commission required them.[27] In 1837, upon his return from Paris, Crace arranged a showroom at Wigmore Street which was, as his son later recalled, 'a picturesque room richly decorated in the Early French Renaissance manner which remained unaltered . . . until . . . 1899.'[28] In this showroom Crace gave receptions for clients and people in the art world. He even designed a French Renaissance-style invitation card for his open houses [Fig.4:1].[29]

A watercolour by Thomas Shepherd, commissioned by Frederick Crace, documents the exterior of the now-demolished Crace premises at Wigmore Street. In the front window of the Shepherd watercolour, the Renaissance-style decoration of the window screens is visible [Fig.4:2].[30] Dating to the same time, about 1837, is a trade card inscribed 'Crace and Son/House Painters and Decorators to the Queen/14 Wigmore Street, Cavendish Square' (Frontispiece).[31] This white card has been decorated in gilt with strapwork in the manner of Fontainebleau. Thus J. G. Crace's 'Old French style' now extended as far back as the sixteenth century!

The open house evenings at Wigmore Street were a great success and saw a renewal of the firm's scope and decorating activities. Almost immediately the Crace firm was engaged to work at Arlington Court in Devon for J. D. Chichester. John Cornforth has suggested that the Crace firm may have supplied the unusual Rococo-revival wallpaper now in the Morning Room of the house[32] [Plate 6]. The paper is almost certainly French,[33] and it is interesting to consider whether it might have come from a shop in Paris, which J. G. Crace had visited in 1829. A letter from J. G. Crace to J. D. Chichester, dated 3 November, 1839, discusses some of the work the Craces executed at Arlington Court. In it, Crace says he 'trusts that the Pilasters by this time arrived'.[34] This seems to refer to

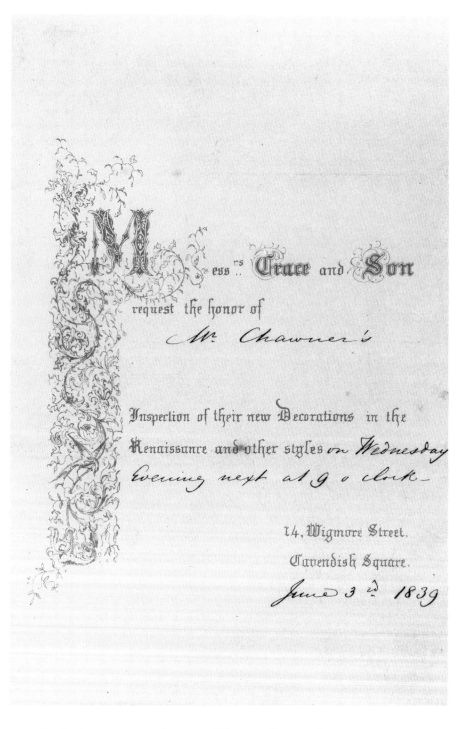

4:1   Invitation to an open house at Wigmore Street, 1839.

4:2   Thomas Shepherd, the Crace premises at 14 Wigmore Street, *c.*1837.

the pilasters in the Boudoir, which display arabesque decoration similar to the
ornament of Crace's invitation cards of 1837. Although it is not mentioned in
the Chichester papers, the Crace firm could have supplied the red, Louis XVI-
style silk damask with which the Boudoir walls were hung.

The 6th Duke of Devonshire

In 1838 at one of his open houses, J. G. Crace met his most important early
patron, the 6th Duke of Devonshire. This knowledgeable and cultured aristocrat
must have been exactly the type of patron Crace sought, and the two men shared
a mutual regard for one another which lasted the rest of their lives. According
to J. G. Crace it was the Duke who suggested that he add 'upholstery and cabinet
work' to his business.[35] By 1840 the Crace firm was working at Devonshire
House, the residence of the Duke in London, and at Chatsworth, the Duke's
palatial seat in Derbyshire. The importance of these two commissions must have
immediately enhanced the Crace firm's reputation.

In about 1840 J. G. Crace was designing a ceiling for the Saloon of Devonshire House, London (now demolished). Several drawings by Crace which appear to be alternate treatments for this ceiling are in the Victoria and Albert Museum.[36] It is not clear whether a first Crace design for the Devonshire House Saloon was executed, for in 1840 a fire swept the house and destroyed much of the interior decoration, including some of the early eighteenth-century schemes by William Kent. The design for the Saloon ceiling which was executed after the fire is in the Victoria and Albert Museum[37] [Plate 7]. It has been signed 'John G. Crace' and inscribed by J. D. Crace as 'executed in 1844'. The architectural framework of Crace's design was taken straight from Kent's interior scheme. Crace complemented the Palladian architectural style of the room sufficiently well to have his ceiling design mistaken for that of Kent's by a writer in 1908.[38]

This ceiling design displays a greater degree of sophistication than some of the alternate schemes by Crace. While retaining the pastel palette of colours used in the early drawings for Devonshire House, Crace's executed design of 1844 is more complex and displays a greater unity of its elements than do the earlier designs, which are generally composed of separate panels of ornament. In the centre panel of the Saloon ceiling where the Star of the Garter is displayed, Crace has used vine scrolls which embody the robust curves found in contemporary French 'Restauration' decoration. A sketch of a similar vine scroll drawn by J. G. Crace c.1831 in France is in a notebook in the V & A.[39] In some ways, it can be said that Crace's design for the Saloon ceiling at Devonshire House anticipates the so-called 'Second Empire' style in France of the mid-nineteenth century, a style exemplified by Garnier's Opera House in Paris which looks back to French Baroque design. The richness of colours and textures, the contrast of dark and light, and the illusionistic painting of features such as the cast-shadow indicated in Crace's design, are all decorative practices he adopted from the Baroque. To decorate the corners of his Saloon design, Crace has used a gilt diaper pattern against a blue ground to form a ground for the putti which support heavy swags. This practice of using a small-scale, repeated pattern as a ground for larger designs was to become a typical feature of the work of J. G. and J. D. Crace.

According to the household accounts at Chatsworth, Crace & Son worked at Devonshire House from 1840 to 1845, for which they were paid a total of £2581.[40] The breakdown is as follows: for unspecified decorating at Devonshire House between 1840 and 1845, the firm was paid £1883, which probably includes payments for the ceiling designs discussed above. For upholstery supplied to Devonshire House in 1840, the firm was paid £698. Another £2500 was paid to the firm for upholstery at Devonshire House between 1846 and 1848.[41] Even more important, however, was the work executed at Chatsworth. The

Chatsworth Household Accounts, which are primarily extracts from the itemised bills submitted by the Crace firm, show that the firm was paid an enormous sum, £9329, for unspecified decorating carried out in 1840 at Chatsworth.[42] In addition, between 1841 and 1843, the firm was paid £3902 for decorating and upholstery for Chatsworth, in 1846 the Craces received £588 for work carried out between 1840 and 1845, with a final payment of £737 in 1848.[43] Of this latter sum, £303 went towards carpets supplied to Chatsworth in 1846, £354 went for upholstery supplied in 1848, and £80 was paid for 'sundry items' in 1841.

A substantial portion of the £9329 paid to the Craces for work at Chatsworth in 1840 must have represented payment for the splendid private library that J. G. Crace designed for the 6th Duke. The Lower Library of Chatsworth ranks as Crace's first masterpiece. This room had been a rather featureless breakfast room with white walls in 1840,[44] when a group of artists brought over from Paris by Crace transformed the room with painted decoration that, as the Duchess of Devonshire has observed, closely resembles the decoration of the Café Véfour in the Palais-Royale in Paris.[45] J. G. Crace may have seen this decoration when he visited Paris in 1837 and engaged French artists to work for him.

A handsome coloured design for the ceiling of the Chatsworth Lower Library, signed by J. G. Crace, is now in the collection of the Duke of Devonshire [Plate 8]. The pastel colours used and the luscious foliate scrolls of the design firmly link the Chatsworth ceiling to two other Crace commissions of the 1840s, namely the state rooms of Taymouth Castle and Knebworth House, which will be discussed shortly. Here at Chatsworth Crace has used a flat, painted ceiling divided into panels which are carefully defined by illusionistically painted mouldings. The clever painting of the ceiling suggests, at first glance, that it has been modelled in relief like the ceilings of Baroque state apartments in the seventeenth century. The ceiling at Chatsworth also displays the cameo heads and light-coloured ornament on a cream ground which the young J. G. Crace had admired in the decoration of the Opéra Comique in Paris during his visit of 1829.

The Lower Library has been fitted with bookcases of varying shape which succeed in making the room appear square. Besides these Crace designed a suite of maplewood furniture inlaid with rosewood and upholstered with deep maroon leather [Plate 9]. The delicate inlay designs feature strapwork and vine scrolls which closely resemble the ornament designed by Jean Bérain and used for metal marquetry by A. C. Boulle, the renowned French court cabinet-maker of the early eighteenth century. Crace knew of and admired the work of Boulle.[46] Additionally, the X-frame stool designed by Crace for the Lower Library might have been used at the court of Louis XIV, although the X-frame chair is an earlier furniture type. However, the dark inlay against a light ground and the slow, ponderous curves of the outlines of Crace's furniture are in keeping with contemporary French furniture of the Restauration era. The Lower Library at Chatsworth illustrates J. G. Crace's eclectic use of French design from a variety of historic styles, and represents his richest and most satisfying essay in the Old French style.

The novelty of the decoration used by Crace for the Lower Library at Chatsworth is evinced by the comments made by the 6th Duke. In his Handbook of 1844 he remarked, 'I had wished to have one room in the new style of decoration.'[47] J. G. Crace and his son were not primarily innovators who set the taste of their day. Instead, they should be viewed as highly competent, knowledgeable, and discriminating decorative artists whose work reflected current styles. The mural and ceiling decoration, the textiles and papers, the upholstery and the furniture supplied by the Crace firm throughout the nineteenth century were of excellent quality. More importantly, as a contemporary remarked, 'Probably, until the last few years, the Messrs. Crace have been the only heads of a large decorative business who have habitually designed and directed their own work.'[48] By doing so, the Craces ensured the originality and distinctiveness of the interiors they created.

'Gothic Arabesque'

While J. G. Crace was still working for the Duke of Devonshire at Chatsworth, Devonshire House, Chiswick, and 1 Lewes Crescent in Brighton,[49] he began two more important commissions. These were the re-decoration of the state rooms at Taymouth Castle, Perthshire and Knebworth House, Hertfordshire in a rich, polychromatic style intended to evoke the sixteenth century. When viewed together, the Lower Library at Chatsworth and the State Drawing Rooms at Taymouth and Knebworth represent the three early masterpieces of J. G. Crace's career, before his association with Pugin began.

Frederick Crace and Son were engaged in about 1841 to decorate the state rooms at Taymouth Castle, Perthshire, for the 2nd Marquis of Breadalbane. Late in the 1830s Lord Breadalbane had hired James Gillespie Graham to alter and improve parts of the castle.[50] It is not clear why Lord Breadalbane should have chosen the Craces, but he may have attended one of the open houses at Wigmore Street. However, the Crace firm was not employed at Breadalbane House, the London residence of Lord Breadalbane, until 1854. It has been noted that, 'the impetus to undertake such improvements [to Taymouth] must surely have been provided by Lord Breadalbane's intention to entertain the young Queen Victoria' when she and Prince Albert visited Scotland in September of 1842.[51] In her journal, the Queen described the rooms of Taymouth as 'newly and exquisitely furnished . . . the Drawingroom, especially, is splendid'.[52] The work of the Crace firm at Brighton Pavilion, Windsor Castle, and Buckingham Palace was most likely known to the Queen and Prince Albert. Frederick and John Gregory Crace's involvement at Taymouth for the visit of the Royal couple may have brought about further Royal commissions in the 1850s.

The Large, or State, Drawing Room at Taymouth has its painted ceiling intact [Plate 10]. The drawing for this ceiling, now in the V & A, has been signed 'F. & J. Crace' and dated to 1841 [Plate 11].[53] Evidently it was the result of a collaboration between Frederick Crace and his elder son. In the bills of 1842, this ceiling is described as having 'richly illuminated Ornament introducing armorial shields and Heraldic figures the Cove with figures intermixed with Coloured Ornament, Griffins, etc. The Border an elaborate pattern in blue & gold ground.'[54]

Even more revealing is the description of the ceiling of the Small Drawing Room, which formed a kind of ante-room to the Large Drawing Room, where the ornament was characterised as 'Gothic Arabesque' in the Crace bills. This extremely interesting descriptive term implies that the Craces were deliberately fusing the classically-inspired arabesque ornament that had played a large part in the decoration of both men up to now, with ornament of a medieval character. In the Taymouth ceilings, the medieval elements include the use of armorial shields, the knights on horseback, and the papier-mâché pendants which suggest Late Gothic pendant vaulting, such as the well-known ceiling in the Chapel of Henry VII in Westminster Abbey.

The delicate, interlaced borders are also found in the design for the Refreshment Room of Swindon Railway Station, signed 'F. & J. Crace' and dated 1841 [Fig.4:3]. It is contemporary to the work at Taymouth.[55]

The use of 'Gothic Arabesque' decoration was perhaps appropriate to a building which exhibited a variety of interpretations and revivals of medieval architecture.[56] In fact, the dividing up of the wall surface of the Large Drawing Room into vertical panels, now covered in silk damask which has faded from its original emerald green, is an idea which developed in France in the seventeenth century. Frederick and John Gregory Crace consistently used this French wall treatment of vertical panelling which many English designers abandoned during the Gothic Revival.

The splendid pelmets designed by the Craces for the Large Drawing Room at Taymouth are still intact [Fig.4:4]. In the bills of 1842 these are described as, 'a suite of Gothic Vallances for the 5 windows in Drawing room of rich silk Brocade bordered with Velvet and trimmed with silk fringe and tassels and

4:3   Frederick and J. G. Crace, design for ceiling of Swindon Railway Station, 1841.

4:4   Frederick and J. G. Crace, design for mural and window decoration of the State Drawing Room at Taymouth Castle, 1841.

swags of silk Drapery Cord suspended from ditto'.[57] Each of these pelmets cost the Marquis of Breadalbane £23, which meant that the drapery supplied by Crace was costly. As at Devonshire House and Chatsworth, the upholstery and drapery supplied by the Crace firm constituted the single most expensive item on their bill. It is interesting to compare the appliqué designs used by the Craces for the drapery at Taymouth to French drapery of the seventeenth century.[58] J. G. Crace had gained much of his knowledge of textiles from seeing historic buildings and the work of commercial firms in Paris.

In addition to the Large and Small Drawing Rooms of Taymouth, the Crace firm decorated the Library, Gallery, Grand Hall, Tapestry Rooms, and several bedrooms and dressing rooms in preparation for the visit of the Queen and Prince Albert. Details concerning the furniture, household items, and even the reproduction armour supplied by the Craces to the Marquis of Breadalbane are described in the bills of 1842 in the Scottish Record Office. Frederick Crace & Son also decorated 'Boats for Her Majesty's Excursion' and billed the Marquis £15 for 'Mr. J. Crace's attendance at Taymouth during Her Majesty's Visit'.

The luxury and expense of such grand-scale preparation for a visit of the Queen brings to mind the notoriously expensive entertainments prepared by courtiers of Queen Elizabeth I during her 'progresses' through the country in the sixteenth century. The state rooms at Taymouth stand as the most satisfying example of the collaboration of Frederick and John Gregory Crace and should be viewed not as the antecedent to their work in the Gothic style at the Houses of Parliament, but rather as the final manifestation of work by the firm in the tradition of Carlton House and the Royal Pavilion, Brighton, where classical French ideas of decoration were adapted to suit the needs of an individual commission.

Polychromatic Decoration and the Influence of Munich

Shortly after completing the work at Taymouth, in 1843 J. G. Crace travelled abroad to Munich. The interiors he saw there profoundly influenced his ideas on interior decoration. The letters he sent to his parents during the autumn of 1843 from Munich are now among the Mostyn-Crace papers in the Victoria and Albert Museum, London.[59] They chronicle Crace's route from Coblenz through Switzerland to Venice, and then back to Munich. In his letter of 7 October to his father, Crace wrote that he had arrived in Munich and had so many things to see that he lacked the time to write a full account of them. Rather it is through his two lectures on the art and architecture of Munich that we are able to understand what captured the imagination of J. G. Crace to such an extent in the Bavarian capital. The first of these lectures, 'Some Account of the Frescoes in Germany and the North of Italy', was read to the Institute of British Architects on 6 November 1843, shortly after his return. Crace stated, 'My principal object in Travelling was first, to learn the processes employed in Fresco and Encaustic Painting, – Secondly, to form an opinion as to the effects produced – and thirdly, to judge how far those effects would surpass Painting in Oil, in appearance and in durability.'[60] He also remarked that he had chiefly been interested in modern fresco painting, which was undergoing a revival in Bavaria.

It is illuminating to consider how Crace's interest in fresco painting had come about, as he must have been aware of the visit to London in 1841 of the artist Cornelius, a fresco painter working in Munich for Ludwig I. Also in 1841 there took place the deliberations of the British Parliament's Select Committee, which was considering, 'the promotion of the fine arts of this Country in connexion with the rebuilding of the Houses of Parliament.'[61] The Select Committee was especially interested in fresco painting. Prince Albert was equally interested, and commissioned a series of frescoes by the German artist Grüner to decorate his pavilion in the gardens of Buckingham Palace in 1843, the year in which Crace travelled to Munich.[62] The other possible influence upon J. G. Crace at this time was his new acquaintance, A. W. N. Pugin, to whom he had recently been introduced at Alton Towers, Staffordshire, by Lord Shrewsbury. Certainly Pugin's reaction to the nineteenth-century decorative painting in Munich was as negative as Crace's was positive.[63]

4:5   J. G. Crace, ceiling of the Staircase, Royal Library, Munich, 1843.

While Crace commented briefly upon the fresco painting of Northern Italy, praising its separation of figurative from purely ornamental elements, his comments chiefly concerned the fresco painting he had seen at Munich. He cited the Ludwigskirche (now the University church), the Allerheiligen Kapelle, St. Boniface, the Glyptothek, and the Pinakothek as the most noteworthy buildings for study, alongside the Halls of the Niebelungenlieder in the Munich Residenz.[64] All these interiors date to the first third of the nineteenth century and were created as part of Ludwig I's programme for refurbishing and expanding the city.

Between 1843 and 1851 J. G. Crace was at work completing a series of finished studio drawings based on sketches he had made in 1843 of the buildings in Munich [Fig.4:5]. This series of drawings is now in the collection of the Royal Institute of British Architects in London.[65] The drawings were used by Crace to accompany his lecture to the RIBA on 10 February, 1851, entitled 'On the Decoration of Some of the Buildings at Munich'.[66] This lecture can be viewed as Crace's manifesto for the next twenty years of his career. In his introductory paragraph to the lecture, Crace stated he was going to discuss the use of colour and ornament in some important buildings in Munich, which had, 'risen into importance almost entirely through the genius of its artists, fostered and encouraged by a prince, enthusiastic in his love for art. It is a glorious instance of what may be accomplished by the enterprise, perseverance, fine taste, and good judgement of an individual.'[67] Such a statement may reveal Crace's vision of Pugin and himself as artistic geniuses, with Prince Albert acting as the encouraging prince, in order to enhance the quality of decorative art in nineteenth-century Britain.

His lecture on the buildings of Munich consisted of a careful, clear description of the decoration used in each of the examples he considered. J. G. Crace gave his own opinion of the merits of several of the decorative schemes, particularly with respect to the Glyptothek, designed by the architect Leo von Klenze to house the famous collection of ancient art in Munich. Crace approved of the 'vivid colouring of the walls', quoting von Klenze as saying, 'deep colours should be used on the walls, to make these antique statues appear to advantage.'[68]

In adopting the attitudes of von Klenze and his colleagues, J. G. Crace began to depart from his earlier sources of inspiration – namely, French interiors of the late seventeenth and eighteenth centuries. Throughout his later career, he was to demonstrate an awareness of how strongly coloured interiors could enhance the objects contained in them. Indeed, Crace has been credited by contemporaries with, 'having been the first English decorator to revive the use of harmonious colour as distinguished from mere tints in the decoration of our houses.'[69] In shifting his emphasis from pastel colours and gilding to deep colouring with stencilling, and responding to collections of objects contained within an interior, Crace can be said to exemplify the preoccupations of Victorian decorators, as opposed to their eighteenth-century predecessors.[70]

According to Crace, strong colouring did not necessarily mean the use of primary colours. Describing the Ludwigskirche in Munich by the architect von Gärtner, completed c.1830, he remarked in his lecture, 'the decoration of this church is different from any I have seen, on account of the neutral quality of the colouring employed.' After describing the ochre and red hues of the large fresco by Cornelius in the church, Crace continued 'it seems to me that the decoration of the church was calculated with reference to this fresco.'[71] He was particularly struck by the juxtaposition of 'dull lilac' and 'neutral fawn' with 'interlacings of blue and red' [Plate 12]. In later works such as the decoration of large exhibition halls in 1857 in Manchester and in 1862 in London, J. G. Crace was to use abstract borders of unusual colour contrasts, just as he had described them in his lecture on the buildings of Munich to the Royal Institute of British Architects.

Crace was intrigued with the way that Bavarian artists used colour to emphasize the architectural composition of a building and to set off figurative paintings on the wall surfaces. The purely decorative polychromy he had seen in Munich was to inspire him in his work in the Gothic style, most notably when he worked at the new Palace of Westminster in the 1840s and 50s. Despite his admiration for the interiors of the Glyptothek and Ludwigskirche, it was the Königsbau, or new wing, of the royal palace in Munich, known as the Residenz, which most impressed him. The Königsbau, which was begun in 1826 for Ludwig I, was again the work of Leo von Klenze.

In the Königsbau, Crace focused on the sequence of rooms painted in fresco by Julius Schnorr von Carolsfeld, with two principal assistants. These illustrate the medieval saga of the defeat of the Niebelung dynasty and were painted between 1827 and 1867.[72] Crace, of course, was more interested in the decorative paintings of these interiors. He noted the way narrow borders of white and contrasting colours were used to add liveliness to the effect of the room, thereby emphasizing its architectural features. For example, in the Hall of Treachery the lunettes of the room had been brought into prominence by means of grey bands bordered on either side by narrow bands of white. As with the ornament of the Ludwigskirche, Crace was struck by the use of a small-scale band of abstract ornament to give a 'neutral' effect. He and his father had, in fact, used this technique of decorating for some time with respect to classical ornament. The powerful use of colour with strong contrasts rather than the actual ornament used in the buildings in Munich fascinated J. G. Crace, and he returned to England with a changed eye to begin decorating at Knebworth House.

In December of 1843 Sir Edward Bulwer Lytton, an antiquary and a highly successful novelist, inherited Knebworth House in Hertfordshire. The earliest parts of the house dated to the end of the fifteenth century, but it had undergone a series of alterations by 1840.[73] Almost immediately Bulwer Lytton engaged J. G. Crace to undertake a major re-decorating of the house. He must have known Crace through his friend and fellow MP, Charles Tennyson d'Eyncourt, for Crace had decorated the latter's seat, Bayons Manor in Lincolnshire, in 1841.[74]

The decoration of Knebworth House incorporated heraldic shields, and before commencing work Crace had to wait until the consultant genealogist, Mr. Courthope, had thoroughly researched Bulwer Lytton's family tree.[75] The majority of the rooms decorated by Crace in 1844, including the library, drawing room, and a bedroom, were later altered. However, a collection of late nineteenth-century photographs at Knebworth House records these interiors. (Although an impressive oak staircase in the Elizabethan style was made by J. G. Crace, it was designed by the architect H. E. Kendall, junior.) The spectacular survival from the 1844 decorations is the State Drawing Room, located on the first floor of the house, and its two ante-rooms.

The ceiling of the first ante-room, which was used by Bulwer Lytton as a study, represents the early Gothic decoration by Crace [Plate 13]. The colours of this ceiling are ochre yellow, red, and blue, with small amounts of white ornament, a scheme which comes straight from the interiors Crace had admired in Munich, most notably in the Ludwigskirche and the Halls of the Niebelungs. A stylised daisy forms an ornamental pattern on the blue borders. The ceiling marks a turning point in J. G. Crace's decorative art. Gone is the refinement and pastel colouring of his 'Old French style', to be replaced by stronger, almost jarring, coloration and more primitive, vigorous draughtsmanship.

The second ante-room to the State Drawing Room at Knebworth features a ceiling in the 'Gothic Arabesque' style very similar to the ceilings designed for Taymouth Castle by Frederick and John Gregory Crace in 1841. This ceiling must represent the contribution of Frederick Crace towards the end of his career. (In 1844 he would have been 65 years old.) The work of J. G. Crace in the 'new' medieval style is illustrated by the ceiling in the next room.

The State Drawing Room at Knebworth also displays unmistakable similarities to the decoration of the State Rooms at Taymouth [Plate 14]. The lacy, almost Arabic-looking cartouches used to ornament each compartment of the painted, heraldic ceiling and the small-scale diaper pattern ornamenting the grounds of the cartouches, also appear in the Large Drawing Room at Taymouth. However, at Knebworth the Drawing Room ceiling and frieze are virtually abstract in decoration. Heraldic devices are featured and the inhabited vine scrolls used at Taymouth have been confined to the second ante-room. In addition to the abstraction of this scheme, which J. G. Crace described as 'very Gothic',[76] the adoption of red, blue and green as the principal colours of the interior represents a radical departure from the pastel colouring used at Taymouth in the Craces' 'Gothic arabesque' style. Crace had much admired the contrast of red with blue in interiors in Munich, such as the staircase of the Royal Library.[77] The use of diagonal bands with mottoes along the frieze of the room may represent an early example of Pugin's influence, since the two men had met by 1843.[78]

In addition to decorative painting, the Crace firm supplied curtains, stained glass, and some furniture at Knebworth. The velvet pelmets designed by J. G. Crace for the State Drawing Room and two ante-rooms are sumptuous and remain *in situ*, although the colours of the velvets have altered over time. The Crace firm supplied stained glass worth £150 to Knebworth. Included in this was a full-length figure of Henry VII for the Gothic window of the State Drawing Room, whom the diligent Mr. Courthope had linked to the ancestors of Bulwer Lytton. J. G. Crace designed the splendid Gothic overmantel mirror in the Knebworth State Drawing Room which features carved medieval figures placed under canopied niches. A coloured sketch by Crace for this mirror is in the Drawings Collection of the Royal Institute of British Architects.[79]

A pair of Gothic side tables in the State Drawing Room must have been the work of the Crace firm but they are not mentioned in the bills of 1844[80] [Plate 15]. These extraordinary carved tables with marble tops closely resemble the grilles for the hot water pipes in the second ante-room, which do appear in the Crace bills. The narrow vine scroll band under the marble tops of the tables is identical to that used as a cornice around the room. The most peculiar aspect of the design of these tables is the use of bold primary colours and green for the ground of the diamond lozenges which cover their legs.

It is worth noting that this decoration is close in character to that on a suite of carved and gilded armchairs which bear a Windsor Castle inventory mark and date to the 1820s.[81] The connection between Knebworth in the 1840s and Windsor Castle in the 1820s is, of course, Frederick Crace who may have designed the Windsor chairs and assisted his son in designing the tables in the State Drawing Room at Knebworth.

In his interiors for Knebworth House, J. G. Crace began to digest the new ideas of using bold, primary colours and abstract patterning which had so impressed him at Munich. With the judicious use of small amounts of red, blue and green for a drawing room decorated with heraldic themes, Crace created a quietly opulent interior in the medieval style which managed to evoke a Romantic image of Knebworth's sixteenth-century past, just as its new owner had intended. By 1844, when the decoration at Knebworth was completed, Crace had become involved in a business partnership with a man who was to influence his career for the next eight years and perhaps, indirectly, for the rest of his life.

A. W. N. Pugin and the Gothic Style

In 1894 John Dibblee Crace paid tribute to the influence that the theories of Pugin had upon his own work and that of his father, J. G. Crace, during the second half of the nineteenth century.[82] Indeed, despite the large numbers of designs by Pugin which were used by the Crace firm in the 1840s, 50s and later, it is probably in the area of theory that Pugin's influence upon the two Victorian Crace decorators was greatest. In particular, Pugin's stress on the appropriateness of ornament and on the uniting of form with function as set forth in his various writings[83] was enthusiastically, if on occasion inappropriately, seconded by J. G. Crace. There can be no doubt that, despite his earlier interest in the Gothic style, as evidenced at Taymouth, Crace's Gothic became more accurately observed and more archaeological in character as a direct result of the influence of Pugin.

In terms of numbers, commissions executed in the Gothic style represent a minority of the work of J. G. Crace. However, these included some important country houses and what was arguably the single most important public structure of the nineteenth century, the Palace of Westminster. Between 1844 and 1851 Crace's commissions in the Gothic style were undertaken with Pugin, the latter acting as principal designer. The nature of their collaboration is discussed in the essay by Alexandra Wedgwood.[84] A chronology of their major joint work can be established on the basis of Pugin's letters to Crace, now in the Royal Institute of British Architects Library.[85] Crace's letters to Pugin have not survived.

Pugin's letters begin in January 1844 and indicate that, by this date, he and Crace had commenced work together at Alton Towers in Staffordshire, where they had met when working separately. The house, now ruined and the site of an amusement park, was begun about 1810 in the Gothic style by the architect James Wyatt.[86] By 1837 Pugin was working there as an architect, and by late in 1842 J. G. Crace was decorating at the house. By the spring of 1844, Crace was supplying furnishings at Alton Towers such as printed papers, and by the summer of 1844 he was supplying textiles and furniture, all to Pugin's designs.[87] Unfortunately, these were dispersed in sales held in 1857 and 1924.

Later in 1844 Crace began to supply Gothic furnishings for The Grange, Pugin's house, and his private church in Ramsgate, Kent. This continued until 1851, and the letters indicate that work at The Grange was extensive, comprising the Drawing Room, Dining Room, Library, Nursery, East, West and South Bedrooms, the Dressing Room, Passage, and Closets. While the great majority of the designs for the house must have come from Pugin himself, he did not object to the occasional use of the luxurious, Continental textiles with which Crace was familiar and which he used frequently in other country house commissions.[88]

Pugin seems to have considered the decoration of The Grange as a 'showroom' for the kind of house decoration in the Gothic style which he thought he and Crace could offer to clients. A letter of 1844 from Pugin to Crace, reveals that Pugin was expecting 'some persons to come to me very shortly' and he wanted Crace to send him 'his things' in order to be able to show them to his visitors. He continued, 'I would not press you if there was not necessity. But it is of *consequence to me*. I may say *great consequence* and perhaps to you. in the long run. for if this sort of thing takes we may do wonders.'[89] Clearly Pugin hoped for a flourishing practice in Gothic house decoration to grow out of the furnishings that he designed and Crace supplied for The Grange. In some respects, he was not mistaken about this, for a cluster of country house commissions followed in the 1840s. However, Crace was a businessman and at times seems to have used his partner's designs in a far more commercial way than the latter had intended. In a letter of 1846 Pugin took Crace to task for selling wallpapers Pugin had designed for his own house to, 'a gentleman in Newcastle'. Pugin wrote,

> nothing can annoy me more than to see a paper which is quite a family thing handed about as a *mere pattern* in the possibility of finding its way into a tap room. I never felt so inclined to repaper my rooms in my house . . . I should never for a moment have thought of having my own motto & crest made a marketable commodity & stuck up anywhere.[90]

Nonetheless, despite occasional hiccups, the collaboration continued into the later 1840s. Without question, the most important product of their collaboration was the decoration of the new Palace of Westminster, rebuilt after the disastrous fire of 1834. Frederick Crace & Son were awarded the contract for painting and gilding at Westminster in 1846, although Pugin's letters to Crace suggest that the Crace firm was involved with the decoration of the House of Lords as early as 1845.[91] This work has been extensively researched and documented.[92] Undoubtedly the principal interior at Westminster was that of the House of Lords[93] which Phoebe Stanton has claimed gave rise to a group of country houses in 'the House of Parliament style'.[94] Among this group are Chirk, Eastnor and Lismore Castles, Bolton Abbey, and Leighton and Abney Halls.

In the spring of 1846 Crace and Pugin were decorating Chirk Castle in Wales, a thirteenth-century structure which had been repeatedly altered during its history. In 1855, three years after Pugin's death, an amusing incident occurred regarding the Pugin-Crace interiors there. On 18 August 1855, a letter from the Shrewsbury Archaeological Institute was published in *The Builder* criticising the decoration of the Saloon at Chirk, which members of the Institute had recently visited. These criticisms, and J. G. Crace's reply to them, appeared in the 22 September issue of *The Builder*.[95]

It was the strong colouring used by Pugin and Crace in the Chirk Saloon which provoked 'horror' on the part of the Shrewsbury Archaeological Institute, since the walls of the room had been decorated with bright green and gold, and the ceiling was coloured in a strong blue. Crace stated that a 'deep warm green flock, on brown leather ground, relieved with gold' was the scheme chosen for the wallpaper of the Saloon, because it was felt that this scheme would harmonise with 'a series of valuable portraits having to be arranged on the walls'. Accommodating old paintings with yellowed varnish was a continual professional problem that Crace faced in his decorating schemes. Crace defended the choice of blue for the ceiling of the room saying that they had wished to find a colour which would harmonise with existing painted decoration on the ceiling panels, and that the contrast of the blue had been relieved by means of 'vellum and gilt' ornament. He concluded that, 'Any two colours may be brought together by a proper modulation of tone, and interposition of suitable contrast between them.'[96]

This final statement sums up J. G. Crace's approach to the use of colour in interior decoration. It is this principle of 'modulation' and 'interposition of suitable contrast' which typifies his mature work in commissions such as the building for the International Exhibition of 1862. In the defence of the juxtaposition of green with blue, Crace cited the work of his German contemporary Ludwig Grüner, who had published a book on polychromatic decoration in 1844.[97]

It is clear from Crace's defence of the Saloon at Chirk that he was responsible for choosing the colours of the scheme. He stated that Pugin 'directed the architectural restorations at this fine old building', and 'I carried out the various decorations of the interior, subject to the approval and directions of Mr. Pugin.'[98] It is difficult to judge the merits of the colouring of the Saloon since the controversial blue and green scheme disappeared earlier in this century. However, the article in *The Builder* demonstrates the strength of J. G. Crace's interest in the use of colour by the mid-1840s.

Pugin and Crace were decorating the House of Lords at the same time that the work at Chirk was being done – that is, from about 1846 to 1848. It was not surprising that Frederick Crace & Son were awarded a contract by the Office of Works in 1846 for decoration at the Palace of Westminster. Frederick Crace would have been familiar to the Office of Works from his time at Windsor Castle and Buckingham Palace in the 1820s and 30s; in the eighteenth century the Crace firm had been employed by the Board of Works at Greenwich Hospital.

It is interesting to consider the sheets of trial designs for the ceiling of the House of Lords which were produced by J. G. Crace in 1846 [Fig.4:6].[99] These seem to have been attempts to work out Pugin's ideas in finished drawings.[100] Crace's ornament is generally more loosely drawn, more naturalistic, and less tightly organised than designs by Pugin of the same date.[101] Some panels of Crace's trial designs have been coloured with the deep pastel palette he used at Knebworth and Taymouth. The ideas received by Crace in Munich in 1843 are evident in them too. These include the use of clearly defined areas of white and gold against a solid ground – most commonly, as in this instance, deep blue – and the use of outlines and large areas of flat colour.

It is important to bear in mind that John Gregory Crace was an eclectic designer who never worked exclusively in any one style. The influence of Pugin's Gothic style upon Crace was great, but in 1846, the year in which the trial designs for the House of Lords were done, Crace travelled to various chateaux in the Loire Valley in order to study French Renaissance decoration. In 1847 he lectured

4:6   J. G. Crace, trial designs for the ceiling of the House of Lords, 1846.

on their restoration to the Royal Institute of British Architects.[102] Crace was effusive in his praise for the decorative artists of sixteenth-century France, and he particularly admired the stencilled decoration of the beams of certain of the state rooms. In addition, he cited the 'elegant arabesques' used at Blois, which Pugin had not admired, and stated his pleasure in sketching such a 'rich fund of *renaissance* art'.[103] Even more surprising than Crace's admiration for French Renaissance art is the fact that, when deeply involved in work with Pugin, Crace undertook a commission in the 'old French style'.

At Gilling Castle in Yorkshire he 'came from London to decorate the gallery . . . and did it beautifully, not having as yet developed his heavy, gloomy style of interior decoration.'[104] This was late in 1845, as recorded by Barbara Charlton. The Gallery at Gilling was illustrated by *Country Life* in 1908[105] [Fig.4:7], and it is clear that Mrs. Charlton much preferred the light, pastel Parisian style of decoration here to the work in the Gothic style he had already begun with Pugin. Crace decorated the walls of the eighteenth-century Gallery by means of light, scrolling arabesques which correspond to the vertical architectural panels of the room. The ornament has been carefully arranged around each of the eighteenth-century paintings which hang on the walls.

Another commission which represents a variation on the French Neo-classical theme was Ince Blundell in Lancashire. Crace decorated the Dining Room, Drawing Room and Picture Gallery between 1847 and 1850. Pevsner has described Crace's decorations here as, 'pretty, very light Raphaelesque stuff'.[106] Particularly striking was the design for the Picture Gallery, which featured patterns of stylised ivy leaves with anthemia and vine scrolls [Fig.4:8]. Drawings by Crace for the Picture Gallery at Ince Blundell are now in the Victoria and Albert Museum.[107] The latter two motifs had been used by Crace when designing the ceiling of the Saloon of Devonshire House, London, in 1844, but a telling change in his style of draughtsmanship is illustrated by these two examples. The Devonshire House design retains the three-dimensionality and pastel colours of Crace's earlier style, while the ornament used in the later design for Ince Blundell has the flattened, abstract quality and strong colouring which Crace seems to have adopted after his trip to Munich. This abstraction and use of strong colour were doubtless reinforced by his association with Pugin.

Eastnor Castle represents an important late example of the collaborative work of Pugin and Crace, begun in 1849. Crace departed to some extent from Pugin's original designs when executing decoration and furniture.[108] By this time, Pugin's ideas were sufficiently known to Crace to enable him to interpret a design, when appropriate. Pugin was not always pleased with the results of these variations on his themes, as evinced by a letter to Crace after he had visited Eastnor. The castle had been built in 1812 by Sir Robert Smirke for the 1st Earl Somers, and

4:7   The Gallery at Gilling Castle, decorated by J. G. Crace in 1845.

4:8   The Picture Gallery at Ince Blundell, decorated by J. G. Crace, *c*.1847.

between 1849 and 1850 Pugin and Crace were modernising the Gothic style of its interiors, most notably in a sumptuous Gothic Drawing Room which featured pendant vaults in plaster by Francis Bernasconi. In 1850 Pugin wrote to Crace, 'I think the chimney piece quite ruined by the way the gilding is done . . . I assure you I never saw a fine job so completely ruined and cut to Fritters.'[109] This splendid chimneypiece remains at Eastnor Castle, with its faulty gilding intact, as do Bernasconi's plaster vaults and Crace's lacy Gothic painted ceiling.

A drawing by J. G. Crace showing the scheme for the furnishing of the Drawing Room is in the Metropolitan Museum in New York. It illustrates the pendant vaults of the ceiling, as well as an upholstered settee and oak buffet. In addition, a number of designs by Pugin for furniture are in the Victoria and Albert Museum.[110] These designs were made up by the Crace firm and much of this furniture remains in the house. Of particular interest is a small marquetry work table which Pugin designed in 1850, remarking to Crace that it had cost him too much trouble. 'It will not bear the proper price to make any decent return for the time.'[111] The design of the Eastnor work table is perhaps surprisingly elaborate, featuring carved imbricated legs, interlacing pendant drawer handles, and scrolling vines executed in coloured marquetry. The use of rich coloured marquetry was repeated in an octagonal table and a library table for Eastnor and directly inspired the furniture made by Crace for Abney Hall in 1853.[112]

Lismore Castle in County Waterford was the final commission that J. G. Crace executed for his great friend and patron, the 6th Duke of Devonshire, who died in 1858. By 1849 Crace had begun work on the Duke's seventeenth-century Irish castle, altered during the Regency.[113] In the spring of 1850 he wrote to Pugin to request designs for heraldic motifs for ceilings and wallpapers.[114] Of particular note today is the Banqueting Hall, formerly a ruined chapel, with its splendid stencilled roof timbers and brass chandelier and sconces made by Hardman's of Birmingham to Pugin's design. Crace supplied a number of Gothic chimney-pieces and items of furniture based upon the designs of Pugin. In one instance, a sideboard for the Dining Room, Crace adapted the motifs and ideas of Pugin according to his own design. The squat legs of the piece, ornamented with large rosettes, and the lusciously carved grape vines which meander along the back panel, closely resemble furniture Crace was to create for his Gothic commissions of the 1850s and 1860s.

The decorative work at Lismore Castle continued into the 1850s, after Pugin's premature death in 1852. Sir Joseph Paxton, the 6th Duke's head gardener who had designed the Crystal Palace (the 1851 Exhibition building in London), was supervising structural repairs to Lismore from 1853 to 1858. Crace was at Lismore to record some of this work, as evidenced by a collection of his photographs of the exterior of the castle contained in his photograph album in the Victoria and Albert Museum.[115]

Eclecticism circa 1850

The furniture and decorations Crace exhibited in the Great Exhibition of 1851 in London helped to increase his renown as a house decorator. He also served as a juror for furniture and 'works of decoration' in the exhibition.[116] Although his name is most often associated with Pugin's Medieval Court, he exhibited a painted arabesque in conjunction with Jackson & Sons of Rathbone Place, who made the border of composition ornament [Fig.4:9].[117] While it recalls the early designs of J. G. Crace in the Old French style of the 1830s and 1840s, the arabesque panel of 1851 displays the deeper colour and controlled use of ornamental detail which characterises his work in commissions such as Ince Blundell.

4:9   J. G. Crace, design for ornament exhibited at the
1851 exhibition in London.

Nonetheless, Crace received the greatest acclaim at the 1851 Exhibition for
his exhibits in Pugin's Medieval Court [Fig.4:10]. The *Art Journal* catalogue of
the exhibition reported that,

> The furniture of the Medieval Court forms one of the most striking portions
> of the Exhibition, and has attracted a large amount of attention. The design
> and superintendence of these articles are by Mr. PUGIN, . . . ably seconded by
> Mr CRACE, who has executed his designs. The two specimens on this page
> are their joint productions. The PRIE-DIEU is very elegant, and is enriched with
> painting and gilding. The CABINET is of oak, richly carved, and is decorated
> with characteristic brass-work of exceedingly bold design.[118]

4:10 The Medieval Court at the Great Exhibition of 1851. Reproduced from the *Art Journal Catalogue of the Great Exhibition.*

The prie-dieu referred to above was made for Charles Scott Murray, a Pugin client, for his house at Danesfield, Buckinghamshire.[119] The oak cabinet, described by the *Art Journal* as 'one of the most important pieces of furniture in the Medieval Court', was purchased after the exhibition for the national collection.[120]

Also displayed in the Medieval Court were 'stuffs for hangings . . . a great variety of elaborate and most effective old patterns, executed by Mr. Crace, some in tapestry, others in silk and woollen stuffs, which, by their design, perfectly recall those gorgeous bandekins so often mentioned in the pages of the old historian.'[121] A collection of sample textiles which the Craces would supply for clients is now in a private collection. This contains a wide variety of fabrics, from silk damasks to calicos, and some of these textiles appear to be French rather than English. There is no evidence that the Crace firm made wallpapers or textiles at its premises in London. These seem to have been produced by commercial manufacturers and supplied by the Craces when appropriate.

At about the same time that the Great Exhibition was under way, Crace designed a striking ceiling in the Greek style for the residence of Raikes Curry M.P., facing Hyde Park. This ceiling featured precisely drawn, geometrically arranged classical ornament in a bold black, white and terracotta colour scheme [Fig.4:11].[122] The design can be viewed as something of a departure for J. G. Crace, in which he experimented with bolder alternatives to the refinement and the softer quality of his work in general, whether it was in the Gothic, Renaissance, or Old French styles. Indeed, the use of earth tones and outlining, combined with the geometry of the design, are more typical of the work his son was to execute in the 1870s.

The Pompeian style had been established since the mid-eighteenth century as an option for European designers, and Crace had especially admired several rooms in this style at the Munich Residenz.[123] Since the later eighteenth century, English designers had sought to create archaeologically correct, antique interiors such as Robert Adam's startling Dressing Room in the 'Etruscan' style at Osterley. Adam had in fact based this black, white and terracotta scheme upon Greek red-figured vase paintings, which also seem to have provided Crace's inspiration for the room for Raikes Curry. Crace did have a more recent example than Adam to follow, for in 1848 Ludwig Grüner had decorated the Grand Staircase at Buckingham Palace in a severe Greek style for a ball held by the Queen and Prince Albert.[124]

The ceiling for the London house of Raikes Curry indicates Crace's willingness to experiment with new styles. His appreciation of Pugin's Gothic was sincere, but it was not exclusive. During the 1850s he increasingly adopted aspects of the Gothic style he learned from Pugin and combined them with other elements from his decorative vocabulary to create interiors which reflected his own ideas.

J. G. Crace's Gothic

The outstanding example of the eclectic Gothic style Crace developed after Pugin's death is Abney Hall in Cheadle, near Manchester. Between 1852 and 1857 J. G. Crace worked for James Watts, a successful merchant who eventually

4:11   J. G. Crace, ceiling design in the Greek style for Raikes Curry M.P., *c.*1850.

became Mayor of Manchester. Watts had been delighted with the Medieval Court in the Great Exhibition, and had originally intended Pugin and Crace to decorate the 1840s Gothic brick villa which he had recently purchased.[125]

Despite his increasing ill health, Pugin did supply some designs for Abney early in 1852, before his death later that year.[126] However, scarcely any of these were used. Instead, for the first time since Knebworth in 1845, Crace acted as his own designer in the Gothic style. Moreover, the commission from James Watts represents something of a departure for Crace in terms of patronage. Up to this point, nearly all his commissions had been for the nobility and gentry, or for public buildings. As the residence of a *nouveau riche* industrialist, Abney Hall indicates the shift of patronage in Britain during the middle of the nineteenth century.[127]

Only one of the interiors at Abney Hall has survived with its 1850s decoration intact. This is the spectacular Drawing Room, decorated by Crace in 1852–53 [Fig.4:12]. Early in 1852 Pugin had sent designs for this room to Crace, and the way in which Crace adapted these designs is instructive. Pugin initially advised a stencilled, beamed ceiling in the room, but Crace's design features pendant vaults and pointed spandrels.[128] The pendant vaults were executed in *carton pierre*, a substance similar to papier mâché. These were probably made by Jackson's of Rathbone Place, London, with whom Crace had exhibited at the 1851 Exhibition. Pugin's spandrels with coats of arms were not used. Instead, Crace designed a flat ceiling with square panels into which the pendants were set, joined to the wall by means of a small, 'Gothic' cornice. The ceiling was coloured in blue and gilt, with red and white accents.

Crace did not follow Pugin's suggestion of wood linenfold panelling up to the height of the chimneypiece, which would have been true to late medieval interiors, for the walls of the Drawing Room. Instead, Crace created dado panelling of recessed quatrefoils picked out in gilt against a stone-coloured ground [Plate 16]. He divided the walls into vertical sections, a feature of grand French interiors of the seventeenth and eighteenth centuries. The walls were hung with emerald green silk damask with stylised pineapples, a luxurious fabric made to a Pugin design for wallpaper of 1852.[129] With J. G. Crace's love of rich effects it is not surprising that he translated this design into silk. Pugin's designs were used for the frieze of the room featuring shields with the arms of the London guilds, and for the vertical bands of coloured ornament which divide the walls into panels.[130]

The fireplace Pugin suggested for the Abney Drawing Room featured a Perpendicular Gothic arch and spandrels decorated with shields. Crace designed a more luxuriant chimneypiece of white marble with a deep pointed arch and spandrels decorated with entwining grape vines. A giant overmantel mirror was a

4:12   The Drawing Room, Abney Hall, in 1912.

Crace trademark previously used at Knebworth and Taymouth. The doorcases and the dado panelling were designed with the same carved and stencilled tracery designs in gilt. The handsome brass chandelier by John Hardman of Birmingham, after a design by Pugin, remains in the house today. However, most of the furnishings were removed in 1958 when the house was sold. A group of photographs dating to 1912 illustrate how the interiors of Abney Hall appeared before they were dismantled [Fig.4:13].[131]

Crace supplied a large quantity of furniture for Abney Hall. This may explain why, by 1854, the firm had acquired the premises at 4 Little Welbeck Street, directly behind the Wigmore Street building, for furniture workshops.[132] A suite of padded seat furniture upholstered in silk in Pugin's pineapple design, and fringed, is clearly visible in the photograph illustrating the Drawing Room.

4:13   The Dining Room, Abney Hall, in 1912.

Furniture of very similar design was made by Crace for Pippbrook House in Dorking, Surrey. The architect George Gilbert Scott added three Gothic rooms to the house in about 1855 for the owner, W. H. Forman. Crace's furniture seems to have been made for these new rooms.[133]

Of higher artistic quality is a suite of carved furniture with coloured marquetry vine scrolls designed by Pugin and made by Crace for the Drawing Room at Abney. The suite consists of a large octagonal table and side cabinet, two small tables and a large table similar to that made for Eastnor[134]; however, the Abney tables have been 'customised' by the inclusion of small honeybees in the marquetry, taken from the Watts coat-of-arms [Fig.4:14]. Most of these pieces are now owned by the Stockport Borough Council and displayed at Bramall Hall, Cheshire, and the large octagonal table is now in the Victoria and Albert Museum,

London.[135] This suite of furniture is visible in the photograph of 1912; the octagonal table is of particular interest [Plate 17]. It was once thought that James Watts had actually purchased the octagonal table shown in the Medieval Court of the 1851 Exhibition, but this has since been discovered in a private collection. Shipping labels on other furniture supplied by Crace to Abney show a date of April 1853,[136] which seems to be a reasonable date for all the furniture supplied by Crace for the ground floor rooms of the house.

The octagonal table from the Drawing Room at Abney has superb quality carving on its square oak base which has been reinforced by four ogee arches carved with vine scrolls. The table top displays splendid coloured marquetry vine scrolls and a central lozenge. Similar designs had been sent by Pugin to Crace for marquetry furniture at Eastnor.[137] However, the sumptuous walnut veneer divided into four symmetrical parts on the table's top has puzzled students of Pugin's design. This type of veneering dates to the later seventeenth century and seems to indicate the preference of Crace and his client Watts for more luxurious effects than those favoured by Pugin.

Crace also supplied a great deal of furniture for the rest of the house: handsome oak bookcases for the library (now at Bramall Hall), a large oak octagonal table which was far less elaborate than the marquetry one (now at Lyme Park in nearby Disley), and several upholstered X-frame chairs and stools similar in shape to those supplied for the Lower Library at Chatsworth in about 1840. However,

4:14   J. G. Crace after A. W. N. Pugin, a small writing table for the State Drawing Room, Abney Hall, c.1853.

the Abney examples were carved in oak with medieval motifs. For the Dining Room, a large oak table with an ogee arched base was supplied, along with Puginesque chairs and an enormous carved sideboard which is still in the house [Fig.4:15]. This piece displays the same squat legs and richly carved vines seen on the smaller piece at Lismore, and it represents another of J. G. Crace's adaptations of Pugin's designs.[138]

The work at Abney continued until 1857. A design by Crace for the ceiling of the downstairs corridor in Abney is Islamic in character and may, perhaps, be dated to the spring of 1855, after his return from a period of rest in the south of Spain following a breakdown caused by overwork. He had spent late March of that year travelling in Moorish Spain with his camera. Crace had taken up photography in 1852 and was a founder member of the Photographic Society in London.[139] He was among the first to photograph the Alhambra in Granada.

In letters written to his son from Spain,[140] he cited the delicate interlace designs and the subtle but rich colouring of Islamic architectural ornament. Both these qualities are present in his corridor ceiling design, now in the Royal Institute of British Architects Library [Plate 18]. This design features a scalloped lozenge in the centre of a panel surrounded by a trefoil frieze. The colours are strong pastels – rose pink, medium blue, and gold. The ceiling, as executed, was quite different, with a much simplified Gothic design of stylised leaves and flowers executed in stencilling. It is illustrated in the group of photographs of Abney Hall dating to 1912.[141] Perhaps this design was felt to be more in keeping with the Gothic character of the house. During his absence in 1855, J. G. Crace also wrote to his son with instructions for a set of 'light Elizabethan chairs' and some needlework chairs for Mr. Watts.[142]

From an historical point of view, possibly the most interesting room at Abney Hall is the Prince Consort's Bedroom, prepared by J. G. Crace for the visit of Prince Albert when he came in May of 1857 to open the Manchester Art Treasures Exhibition. The *Illustrated London News* showed Prince Albert setting out from Abney *en route* to the exhibition [Fig.4:16].[143] His Gothic bedroom by Crace was one of the interiors photographed in 1912 [Fig.4:17]. Crace chose a wallpaper designed by Pugin for the Palace of Westminster to decorate a bedroom for the husband of the Queen.[144] A fragment of the original paper in a colourway of chocolate brown and blue on a cream ground was recovered by Mrs Mostyn in 1958.[145] The bold colouring of the wallpaper would have been balanced by Crace's grained oak woodwork and by the relatively simple carved oak furniture he supplied.

The focal point of the room was the splendid half-tester bed which resembled that supplied for the Speaker's residence in the Palace of Westminster in 1859.[146] Throughout the 1850s, J. G. Crace was active in the Palace of Westminster

4:15　J. G. Crace after A. W. N. Pugin, carved oak sideboard for Dining Room, Abney Hall, *c*.1853.

4:16   The Departure of Prince Albert from Abney Hall, 1857, from *The Illustrated London News*.

supplying furnishings which were based upon the large collection of designs by Pugin that he had acquired during their association.[147] In the Prince's bedroom at Abney, the bed and writing table in the room were close to these designs. However, the Gothic cheval mirror and daybed illustrate Crace's willingness to clothe entirely un-medieval types of furniture in Gothic dress. He supplied a similar mirror and daybed for Pippbrook House at almost exactly the same date.[148]

The decade of the 1850s saw the realisation of J. G. Crace's plans which he had drawn up in the 1830s for expanding the business of 'Frederick Crace & Son'. The success of his campaign may, indeed, have resulted in his breakdown in 1854. In addition to the ongoing work at Abney Hall and the Palace of Westminster, an important commission for a suite of state rooms at Windsor Castle brought his eldest son, J. D. Crace, into the firm in an active role.[149] In 1854 J. G. Crace also designed the Queen's Apartments in the south wing of the re-erected Crystal Palace in Sydenham in an Elizabethan style with a triumphal arch opening onto Sir Joseph Paxton's famous Italianate gardens.[150]

J. G. Crace was confirmed as one of the most fashionable London decorators

4:17   The Prince Consort's Bedroom at Abney Hall in 1912.

when his former patron the Marquis of Breadalbane, for whom he had decorated
Taymouth to receive the Queen and Prince Consort, engaged him to decorate
a temporary structure as a 'dancing saloon' at Breadalbane House in London.
This was for a ball held in 1854 in honour of the Queen and Prince Albert.[151]
The builder George Myers, a member of the Pugin-Westminster circle, constructed a large extension to Breadalbane House with a giant hammerbeam roof decorated in a spectrum of pastel-coloured stencilled designs and heraldic shields
by J. G. Crace.[152] This commission for the ball at Breadalbane House may have
given rise to one in 1863, when Crace decorated the Guildhall in London for
a ball held in June to honour the Prince and Princess of Wales. As shown in
the *Illustrated London News*, he executed Gothic stencilled beams for a ceiling
similar to that for the Marquis of Breadalbane.[153]

It was doubtless a combination of the weighty reputation Crace acquired at
the Palace of Westminster and his association with Pugin which led the Governor
of Australia, John Stephen Hampton, to seek his assistance in furnishing Government House in Perth, Western Australia in 1862. This was being built of brick
and stone in a vaguely Jacobean style from 1861 to 1863.[154] Crace supplied

4:18   J. G. Crace, Gothic chairs designed and made
for Government House, Perth, 1862.

chimneypieces similar to those he designed for Abney Hall, and a design for
the decoration of the entrance hall ceiling with stencilled beams and shields
representing the British monarchs from William the Conqueror to Queen
Victoria.[155] This decoration is still in place.

Crace's reply to Governor Hampton's request for chairs to match some of
his own personal furniture was uncharacteristically rude. He said he was 'morally
unable' to supply 'tasteless and vulgarly commonplace furniture of Louis
Quatorze-style for a Gothic Building.'[156] Governor Hampton had already purchased Rococo-style mirror frames from John Ponzini, a carver and gilder located
at 22 Hatton Garden in London.[157] These are still in Government House. Crace
termed Ponzini's frames the ugliest he ever saw. Instead of the mahogany dining
chairs requested by Hampton, Crace sent simple oak chairs with chamfering and
three carved rosettes for decoration. He said his chairs were 'designed to suit
the House and are handsome – well-made chairs.'[158] They were, in fact, simplified
versions of the chairs he had designed for the bedroom of Prince Albert at Abney
Hall in 1857 [Fig.4:18].

Other items supplied by Crace to the unwilling Governor Hampton included a pair of octagonal oak tables on square bases, small oak side tables of notched beam construction, and a large, extending dining table with stump column legs,[159] all decorated solely by means of chamfering and carved rosettes. Of slightly more elaborate design was a clumsily carved sideboard which resembles that designed by Crace for Lismore Castle. Given his predilection for rich effects, the radical simplicity of this furniture is striking.

Governor Hampton was not pleased with this severe exercise in the Gothic. He said, 'I have received into the New Government House, with great reluctance, several of the articles to be retained, which have been described by all who have seen them, some as paltry, and others as in the worst possible taste.'[160] Had he been alive to witness the dispute, Pugin would doubtless have criticised Crace's designs but applauded his principles in insisting on 'well-made chairs ... designed to suit' the style of Government House.

The controversial commission for Government House in Perth represents the final important episode in J. G. Crace's use of the Gothic style. From the mid-1850s, his eldest son was to play an increasingly important role in the Crace firm, and J. G. Crace began to turn his attention to the Renaissance style as a direct result of his son's profound interest in Italian art. It is therefore now appropriate to examine the career of the final head of the Crace decorating firm, John Dibblee Crace.

J. G. and J. D. Crace

John Dibblee Crace was born in 1838, the eldest and the most artistically talented son of J. G. Crace. A large body of autobiographical material is now among the Mostyn-Crace papers in the V & A. This supplements the substantial numbers of his drawings held there and in the Royal Institute of British Architects and the lectures, essays and pamphlets, both published and unpublished, that he wrote on a wide range of subjects in the decorative arts.

A picture of an accomplished and respected professional man with a self-effacing personality emerges from these. In his obituary it was stated that he 'had a reserve and shyness about his own work which left much of his talent unknown except to the few who were familiar with the delicate colouring and exquisite pencil-work' of his drawings.[161] Mentally, emotionally and professionally, Crace seems to have remained on the closest terms with his father until the latter's death in 1889, when, as he later remarked, he lost his closest friend and advisor, and subsequently much of the pleasure he had found in his work subsided.[162]

J. D. Crace became actively involved in the work of the Crace firm towards the end of 1854, when he was sixteen years old. Owing to his father's partial breakdown he was called home from school in Kent to take over the execution of commissions then under way. These included Abney Hall, Lismore Castle, preparations for the Paris Exhibition of 1855 and, most importantly, a new commission for a suite of state rooms at Windsor Castle. To assist the young man with this daunting task, his grandfather, Frederick Crace, emerged from retirement at the age of 75 to act as supervisor of the work in progress.

Much of the work done in 1854 and 1855 seems to have been under the direction of J. D. Crace himself. In the spring of 1855 his father was abroad. The letters he wrote to his son give a great deal of information about the work under way at Windsor Castle, the most pressing of the commissions. On 16 April 1855 the Emperor of the French, Napoleon III, and his Empress, Eugenie, were to arrive and their suites of rooms had to be ready. It was a first state visit for the Imperial couple, and the Queen remained suspicious about the intentions of Napoleon, whom she had regarded as a usurper.[163] Therefore with such importance attached to the occasion J. D. Crace must have been under enormous pressure.

The Craces decorated no less than eight rooms for the Emperor and Empress at Windsor, in addition to rooms for their servants which Queen Victoria visited and approved.[164] State bedchambers with *en suite* dressing rooms and sitting rooms for Napoleon and Eugenie were created. The former 'Van Dyke Room', which functioned as an unexciting picture gallery in the 1850s,[165] was done over as a luxurious reception room for the Imperial couple [Plate 19]. To transform it, the Craces kept the wooden panelling of the room such as doorcases, window fittings, and the dado panelling, but hung the walls with crimson silk and painted the ceiling with heraldic shields, mostly coloured blue and crimson. A pendant ornament in *carton pierre* was supplied by Jackson & Sons for the centre of the ceiling, from which the chandelier was hung.

A new carpet in a red, gold and maroon colour scheme with a deep floral border was supplied for the room; drawings by J. G. Crace which recently came to light seem to be trial designs for the carpets supplied to Windsor.[166] New carpets and textiles were to be supplied along with re-gilding and the rearrangement of the furniture. Rather than actually designing new interior fittings in a particular historical style, the Craces created an impression of Imperial splendour by using rich red silk on the walls in contrast with green silk upholstery and drapery to unite the different pieces of furniture from the eighteenth and nineteenth centuries that were used in these rooms.

The curtains of the Van Dyke Room, for example, were green Lyons silk with a gilt brocade design in metallic thread. The borders of these curtains were of dark green velvet. In a letter of 27 March from Gibraltar, J. G. Crace wrote to his son, 'The Green velvet to border the Van Dyke room Curtains must not be so dark as in the Original Pattern.'[167] The valances were also green velvet. Green silk curtains were made from Lyons silk for another as yet unidentified room prepared for Napoleon and Eugenie. Apparently Queen Victoria herself requested that the design of these curtains be in the 'first Napoleonic' style in order to reassure her guest of his legitimacy.[168]

Jackson & Sons of Rathbone Place, London, were also at Windsor during 1855. They had worked with the Crace firm on a number of occasions. For the Van Dyke Room, Jackson provided 'window cornices', or pelmets, in *carton pierre*; these are mentioned by J. G. Crace in his letter of 27 March. The firm must have supplied, as well as the central pendant, certain applied foliate ornaments of the Van Dyke Room ceiling, along with four console tables in a revived Rococo style which were sketched by J. G. Crace in a memo to his son.[169]

In the same letter of 27 March, the elder Crace expressed concern for the progress of the 'State Bedchamber' for the Empress Eugenie, now known as the King's State Bedchamber [Plate 20]. He expressed approval of his son's design for the window cornices and instructed him to ensure that this design was compatible with that of the state bed, a late eighteenth-century French Neo-classical bed which has sometimes been attributed to the eminent cabinet-maker Georges Jacob.[170] J. D. Crace's window cornices were indeed an appropriate response to the bed, being architectural and refined in design. His father wrote, 'Weeks will require every gilder that can be got to gild all the Chairs, Sofas, Tables, Window Cornices etc. in time – press on this work and remind Weeks that Carton pierre requires very little preparation.'

In the same letter J. G. Crace continued with his thoughts regarding the state bed, citing the abilities of his various employees, 'I hope that the embroidery for the Bed is going on well. Care must be taken for Mr. Dupeux to mark out on the swags of top Drapery exactly how the flowers are to be placed . . . I hope that Tappolit will make the gold fringe *very close* and of rich good colour and quality – Stansborough knows all about the size and shape and make of the Tassels.'[171] The dome of the bed is still *in situ* at Windsor Castle as prepared by the Crace firm for the arrival of Eugenie in 1855, with its purple silk swags decorated with garlands of embroidered flowers. Purple and green were considered the Napoleonic colours, and at the foot of the bed Crace's staff embroidered an imperial eagle with the monograms of the Emperor and Empress.

On 20 March, the week before he wrote to his son, J. G. Crace had written to Colonel Biddulph of the Royal Household to express his anxieties about finding enough 'competent embroideresses' in order to complete the work on time. He said, 'The embroidery is truly beautiful and I am most anxious to restore it as far as possible to its original beauty.'[172] Here he was referring to the eighteenth-century embroidery on cream silk which was used for the bedcover and inside the dome. It survives today on the state bed. In his letter of 27 March, Crace's final instructions to his son concerned the preparation of velvet tie-backs for the green silk curtains in the Empress's bedchamber. He sketched a sample swag of oak leaves and requested that Haclin make a working drawing of them to enable them to be embroidered by machine. Haclin was the firm's principal artist and had been hired in Paris by J. G. Crace in 1839 to work in the Lower Library at Chatsworth.[173]

Aside from the information they give on the work at Windsor, J. G. Crace's letters to his son give a welcome insight as to how the individuals within the firm operated. Clearly, employees had their respective areas of specialisation, such as Weeks for gilding and Dupeux for drapery. The number of employees working at Windsor in the spring of 1855 must have been in the region of fifteen to twenty, with four or so having particular responsibility, as in the case of Mr. Haclin. It is also evident how closely J. G. Crace and his son supervised every detail of the interiors they created.

This care and attention to detail did not go unappreciated, for on 15 April, the day before Napoleon and Eugenie were to arrive, the Queen and Prince Albert inspected the newly decorated suite of rooms. The Queen described it thus,

> After luncheon we went with all the children . . . all over the rooms beginning with the Imperial couple's . . . The Empress's bedroom, all crimson satin, with the fine old pictures and very handsome furniture, and a really beautiful bed . . . The Emperor's bedroom . . . The bed and furniture are of green velvet, very handsome; all little details are most carefully attended to . . . The Vandyck Room, which looks magnificent, with green and yellow silk curtains and furniture – handsome tables, etc., and the two adjoining Tapestry Rooms, also beautifully done up, are the gentlemen and ladies' waiting-rooms.[174]

On the following day the Emperor and Empress arrived, and the visit was declared a great success by the Queen. On 19 April J. G. Crace wrote to his son from Cadiz, 'It is a great comfort to me to find that you have so well understood all the works in hand and have been able to carry them out with so much expedition.'[175] Their joint effort at Windsor is indicative of the close partnership between father and son which continued for the next thirty years. They were to continue this collaboration at Windsor with the re-decoration of the Waterloo Chamber (now gallery) in 1860, and drawings for this scheme are in the V & A & RIBA [Plate 21].

J. D. Crace's artistic taste was 'carefully encouraged and developed by his

1. William Hodges and Johann Zoffany attrib., The Pantheon, London, c.1772.

2. J. M. Gandy, The Back Parlour at Pitzhanger Manor, Ealing, c.1803.

3. Frederick Crace, design for the Music Room at the Royal Pavilion, c.1817.

4. Edward Crace attrib., design for a painted coach panel, c.1755–60.

5. Frederick Crace, design for a phoenix or ho-ho bird, c.1815.

6.   J. G. Crace attrib., The Morning Room, Arlington Court, 1839.

7.   J. G. Crace, design for the ceiling of the Saloon at Devonshire House, 'as executed, 1844'.

8.   J. G. Crace, design for Lower Library ceiling, Chatsworth, 1842.

10.   Interior of the Large Drawing Room, Taymouth Castle,
decorated by Frederick and J. G. Crace in 1841.

9. Interior of the Lower Library at Chatsworth, decorated by J. G. Crace *c.*1840.

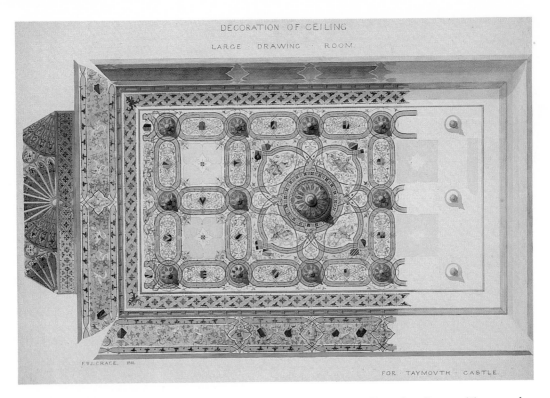

11.   Frederick and J. G. Crace, design for ceiling of the Large Drawing Room, Taymouth Castle, 1841.

12.   J. G. Crace, study of polychromatic decoration in the Ludwigskirche, Munich, 1843.

13.   The ceiling of the first ante-room to the State Drawing Room at Knebworth House (later used as a study by Bulwer-Lytton), c.1844.

14.   The State Drawing Room at Knebworth House, decorated by J. G. Crace in 1844.

15. One of a pair of Gothic side tables in the State Drawing Room at Knebworth House designed by Frederick and J. G. Crace. Carved wood, with marble tops and gilt and polychromatic decoration, 1844.

17. Octagonal table made for the Drawing Room at Abney Hall, now in the collection of the Victoria and Albert Museum. Oak, with walnut veneer and marquetry of coloured woods, designed by J. G. Crace after A. W. N. Pugin, 1853.

16. A detail of the State Drawing Room at Abney Hall with *en suite* console table, J. G. Crace, 1852–53.

18.   J. G. Crace, design for ceiling panel of the Corridor, Abney Hall, *c.*1855.

21.   J. G. and J. D. Crace, design for picture arrangement in Waterloo Chamber (now Gallery),
Windsor Castle, 1860.

19.   The Van Dyke Room at Windsor Castle, from Queen Victoria's Souvenir Album, as decorated by the Crace firm in 1855.

20.   The Empress Eugenie's Bedchamber at Windsor Castle, from Queen Victoria's Souvenir Album, as decorated by the Crace firm in 1855.

22.   J. D. Crace, studies of polychromatic ceilings in Mantua, 1863.

23.   J. D. Crace, design for ceiling of the Saloon, Longleat House, 1874–75.

24. The State Dining Room at Longleat House, decorated by J. D. Crace, 1875–77.

25. Red Library, Longleat House, decorated by J. D. Crace, 1879.

26.   Walnut table with the stamps of Crace and Mazaroz, probably produced for William Waldorf Astor in the 1890's.

27.   A. W. N. Pugin, design for a carpet, Palace of Westminster, 1848.

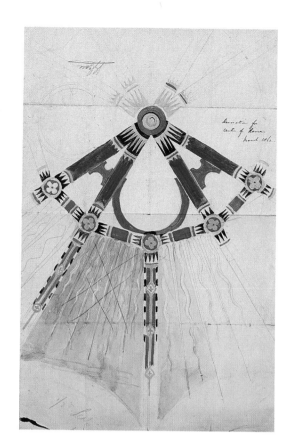

28.   J. G. Crace, design for decoration of the centre of the dome for the 1862 Exhibition building, inscribed March 1862.

29.   Plate XXVIII from W. and G. Audsley, *Polychromatic Decoration . . .* 1882.

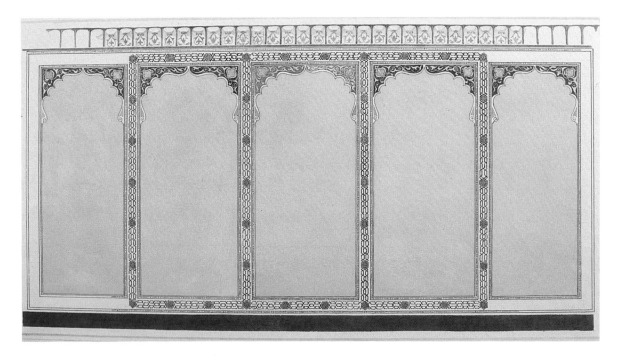

30.   J. D. Crace, design for the North Drawing Room of the Royal Pavilion, 1884.

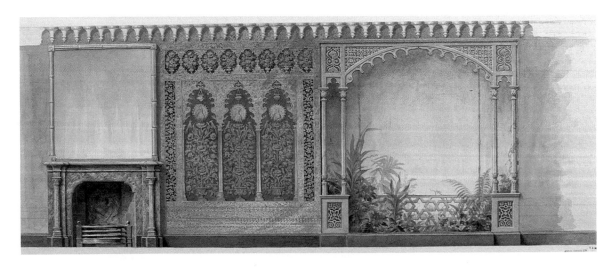

31.   J. D. Crace, design for the South Drawing Room (originally called the Banqueting Room Gallery) of the Royal Pavilion, 1898.

4:19   J. G. Crace, design for the Saloon of yacht, 1858.

father',[176] and he received a thorough training in art, especially in drawing. In his obituary, *The Times* stated that he 'was a most industrious sketcher all through life.'[177] Early in the 1850s he attended King's College School in London, and after 1853 he was tutored by the classics master of the school, an accomplished draughtsman.[178] Despite beginning full-time work during the winter of 1854–55, J. D. Crace continued his studies. In 1855 he

> spent much time in watching work in progress, both in the workshops and in the houses undergoing decoration: some also on one of Scott-Russell's newly built steamers, The 'Pacific', of which the Saloon was being decorated. I also attended Prof. Donaldson's Architectural lectures at University College, studied oil painting with Mr. Haclin, our head artist, and, for a short time, attended the School of Art at Marlborough House, but could not stand the system of 'niggling' finish on subjects to which it was quite inappropriate, so gave that up.[179]

All this was in addition to the work at Windsor Castle.

The reference to the marine engineer J. Scott Russell is significant, since the Crace firm was to decorate the interiors of at least three ships for him. J. G. Crace began such work with Brunel's *Great Western* Steamship in 1838, where he decorated the Saloon in an elegant version of the Old French style.[180] In 1855 the Craces decorated the Saloon of Scott Russell's *Pacific*, and in April 1858 J. G. Crace designed an eclectic Saloon for a private yacht by Scott Russell [Fig.4:19]. The drawing for this commission shows panels of arabesque ornament similar to that employed at Gilling Castle in the 1840s. However, the frieze of Vitruvian scroll around the cornice of the Saloon and the use of brown, black and white, in addition to pink tones, indicates the later, bolder designs of J. G. Crace.[181] Crace used Islamic-style interlace, similar to that of his unexecuted design for the corridor ceiling at Abney Hall [Plate 18], for the ceiling of the yacht, which was for a Turkish client. J. G. Crace did not have as profound an understanding of Islamic art as his son was to develop. However, the choice of an Islamic style for this commission of 1858 indicates the influence upon his work of his visit to the south of Spain in the spring of 1855.

The final ship decorated for Scott Russell by the Craces seems to have been *The Great Eastern* steamship in 1860. J. G. Crace described his Saloon here as in 'a free Renaissance character', and the interior scheme featured the extensive use of ornamental ironwork.[182] During the inaugural journey of the ship, when Crace was on board, the jacket encasing the forward funnel, in which the water for the boiler was preheated, exploded, destroying the Saloon moments after he had left it.

The Exhibitions

After his father returned to England in 1855, J. D. Crace began four years of nearly constant travel, all the time broadening his exposure to the art and architecture of Continental Europe. Later in 1855 he and his father travelled to Paris to view the Exposition Universelle, where the Crace firm's exhibits were enthusiastically received. In the official report of the jury it was regretted that the Crace exhibit was nowhere near as complete as it had been in the 1851 Exhibition in London.[183] This was doubtless due to J. G. Crace's illness earlier in the year. At Paris the firm exhibited a large, carved oak dresser in the Gothic style and samples of the wallpapers and textiles they could supply. The jury awarded the Craces a second-class medal in recognition of 'la superiorité des produits qu'il a présentés'.[184]

In October 1856, J. G. and J. D. Crace travelled to Berlin where they met the architects J. H. Strack and F. A. Stuhler.[185] The latter had worked for the famous architect Karl Schinkel, had published designs for furniture with Strack, and had designed in the Neo-classical, Gothic and Renaissance styles. He was therefore in tune with the Craces' eclectic approach to design. They also met Benjamin Schlick, a follower of the French team Percier and Fontaine who, J. D. Crace later remarked, 'in his younger days had made beautiful drawings of the details of Pompeii'.[186]

On 7 May 1857 Prince Albert opened the Manchester Art Treasures Exhibition after spending the night at Abney Hall in the bedroom J. G. Crace had decorated to receive him. The exhibition was held in Trafford Park, and according to Nikolaus Pevsner, it was 'the first British exhibition ever of works of ancient art on such a scale'.[187] Crace was also the decorator of the interior of the exhibition building itself. The *Illustrated London News* reported that 'The decorations of the building, mainly under Mr. Crace, of London, are highly successful.'[188] The main halls of the buildings had maroon walls complemented by the 'tasteful panels and borders' of Classical scroll ornament to set off the historical portraits exhibited. The same writer praised the decoration of the building because it did not disguise the iron and glass structure. The beams were painted bronze and even the rivet heads were picked out in gold. Crace's use of painting to emphasise the structure of the several large temporary halls he decorated may be one idea that he learned from Pugin, who stressed the importance of revealed structure and appropriate ornament in his *True Principles* of 1841.

The Refreshment Courts were applauded as being 'highly creditable to Mr. Crace', although in 'a very different style of decoration' from the Classical character of the rest of the building. Here the walls were decorated with French paper panels showing Islamic landscapes with birds of exotic plumage. These were installed by the Crace workmen, and the ceiling was painted with designs by J. G. Crace in a 'Moresque' style, 'the prevailing colours being vellum, maroon, and citron'.[189]

There can be no doubt that the success of his interiors for the Manchester Art Treasures Exhibition gave J. G. Crace the confidence to tackle the decoration of the controversial building which was to house the 1862 Exhibition in London. This task, and Crace's role in it, are discussed in the essay by Stephen Wildman.[190] Crace's stencilling of the beams of the building with severe Classical ornament and the use of metallic colours like gold and bronze relate the 1862 Exhibition building to that in Manchester in 1857.

In his work for the 1862 Exhibition, Crace was ably assisted by J. D. Crace, who worked on the site with the men carrying out the painting. They were photographed there in February 1862, surrounded by at least twenty large vats of paint.[191] J. D. Crace stands in the middle of the picture, flanked by eleven Crace employees wearing white artists' smocks [Fig.4:20]. To execute the stencilled decoration, Crace hired about one hundred men, most of whom were completely inexperienced in the technique.[192] However, Crace suggested that stencilled decoration was particularly practical as it did not require highly trained decorative artists.

In addition to the difficult and hurried task of decorating the interior of Fowke's building, sited where the Natural History Museum now stands, J. G.

4:20   Crace workmen on the 1862 International Exhibition site, 20 February 1862.

Crace served as a juror for Class 30, which included furniture and upholstery, as well as exhibiting furniture and wall decoration himself. J. B. Waring illustrated two of the Crace exhibits in his *Masterpieces of Industrial Art and Sculpture at the International Exhibition 1862*,[193] beginning with an enormous Gothic sideboard of oak which resembled that designed by J. G. Crace for Abney Hall in about 1853. The 1862 sideboard measured nine feet in length and was described by Waring as bearing 'the impress of Pugin's peculiar style'.[194] It had a canopied top richly carved with grape vines, with coving underneath the canopy painted in primary colour on a gilt ground. The middle portion of the cabinet featured an open panel which Waring suggested was meant to display a painting, while the two locking drawers of the cabinet were decorated with richly carved vine scrolls and birds, and the short, heavy legs were carved with an ivy design and rosettes.

The whole displayed a degree of richness in its naturalistic carving which was

4:21   Furniture and decoration by J. G. and by J. D. Crace, shown at the International Exhibition, London in 1862, from the *Illustrated London News*.

quite unlike the more chaste cabinet designed by Pugin and made by Crace for the 1851 Exhibition.[195] Waring remarked, 'Mr. Crace is no bigot in art, as was proved by his contributions of furniture in the Renaissance style, which, if anything, we prefer indeed to the somewhat meagre and mannered school of Pugin.'[196] Today, in artistic terms, Pugin's Gothic is considered superior to Crace's more clumsy, three-dimensional use of the style, although Crace's Gothic cabinet seems superior in turn to the 'Medieval Bookcase' displayed by Messrs. Hindley and Sons of London in 1862.[197] It is interesting to observe Waring's preference for Crace's richer, more eclectic use of the Gothic.

At the 1862 Exhibition, furnishings designed by J. D. Crace were publicly displayed for the first time [Fig.4:21]. J. B. Waring praised a polygonal oak cabinet and a walnut escritoire designed by 'Mr. Crace, Jun., whose excellent taste and artistic power we are happy to record.'[198] Even greater praise was lavished upon the 'Raffaellesque' mural decoration and three cabinets in the

Renaissance style exhibited by the Craces, which Waring termed, 'One of the greatest ornaments of Class 30 (Furniture and Decoration)'.[199] Indeed, Waring stated that J. D. Crace's walnut cabinet in the Italian Renaissance style, displayed in the centre bay and flanked by two ebonised display cabinets, formed 'no mean rival' to an ebony cabinet exhibited by the younger Fourdinois, one of the most acclaimed carver-cabinet makers active in Paris in the middle of the nineteenth century, who was well-known for his furniture in the Renaissance style.

Waring's praise of J. D. Crace's furniture in the Renaissance style was echoed in the *Practical Mechanic's* report on the 1862 Exhibition. The walnut cabinet was described as

> well proportioned in all its parts; the design has been carefully studied in its most minute details; there is not a faulty line in the whole of the ornamentation, whether carved or inlaid; and the execution is admirable. Mr. Crace also exhibits a pair of ebonized cabinets in the Italian style, inclosed by glazed doors, which have great merit both in design and execution.[200]

All three cabinets were upright and rectangular in shape, raised upon a plinth, with Corinthian columns used at either side to define their shape. The walnut cabinet had three-dimensional female terms at its base ornamented with shields of lapis lazuli, with two locking doors inlaid with ivory in the upper compartment. The delicacy of its arabesque ornament and carving and the use of precious materials link this early cabinet by J. D. Crace directly to his later commissions, including the spectacular furniture he was to produce for W. W. Astor in the 1890s.

Having decorated the 1862 Exhibition Building, served as a juror and exhibitor in Class 30, and displayed the work of his talented young son, J. G. Crace had one further contribution to make: the design and manufacture of the throne and canopy for the Queen to use when opening the exhibition [Fig.4:22]. His drawing for the throne shows a round-backed, gilt throne with maroon velvet upholstery and an *en suite* canopy with armorial shields which bears a close relationship to that designed by von Klenze for Ludwig I in the Munich Residenz.[201] Crace had seen and admired it in 1843.

By the close of the Exhibition J. G. Crace's career was at its zenith. He was 53 years old, had thirty-two years of professional experience behind him, and his circle of friends and acquaintances was large. It included some of the most important figures of Victorian England. The 6th Duke of Devonshire, Sir Joseph Paxton, Sir Edward Bulwer Lytton, and A. W. N. Pugin and his circle have already been mentioned. J. G. Crace's personal friends also included the novelist Charles Dickens, the composer Sir Arthur Sullivan, and the painter Sir Edwin Landseer.[202] In about 1862 he moved from a comfortable house in St. John's

4:22   J. G. Crace, design for the throne and canopy for the International Exhibition
of 1862.

Wood with gardens laid out by Paxton[203] into 'Springfield', near Dulwich, a large house with a substantial amount of land. Photographs of the house are in a private collection; these show details such as Minton's Gothic tiles in the hall of the house, French chintzes and Rococo-style gilt furniture in the drawing room, and a Gothic-style dining room with a large carved sideboard similar to that shown at the 1862 Exhibition. After his death in 1889, J. G. Crace's son Lewis Paxton Crace, an architect, inherited Springfield and lived there until it was sold early in this century.

Aside from his prosperity and the material comforts he was able to provide for his large family, by the late 1850s J. G. Crace had received great critical acclaim in the leading press of the day. In 1857, for example, the *Illustrated London News* described him as, 'the far-famed Mr. Crace – *the* Crace who has done so much that is in exquisite taste'.[204] In 1863 *The Art Journal* reported that, 'Up to the present time a letter addressed simply to "the Decorative Artists of London" would find its way either to Mr. Crace or to the Dead-letter Office.'[205] His great success in the 1862 Exhibition seems to have allowed Crace to relax somewhat. He continued to design and execute decorative schemes until the year of his death, but during the 1860s and 70s he began to travel more, to participate in learned societies, and to write about the practice of decoration. His eldest son, J. D. Crace, who received considerable attention for his own exhibits in the 1862 Exhibition, began to assume an increasingly important role and began to impart to his father an interest in the arts of Renaissance Italy.

J. D. Crace and Italy

In 1859 J. D. Crace experienced what he later described as, 'the first great event of my life', the visit to Italy that had been recommended by Matthew Digby Wyatt, a family friend. Wyatt delineated a tour for him, and 'it was an excellent and most useful programme, and I have since tried to help others in the same way.'[206] This trip resulted in Crace's design for three cabinets and accompanying wall decoration in the Renaissance style for the 1862 Exhibition.

Unfortunately, an itinerary for J. D. Crace's first trip to Italy does not survive, but two notebooks give detailed information concerning his travels and the buildings which impressed him during his second trip to Italy in October 1863.[207] He travelled in the company of Mr. and Mrs. Charles Barry junior for most of the journey. They were son and daughter-in-law of the famous architect for whom the Craces had worked at the Palace of Westminster. J. D. Crace set out in the morning from Dulwich and arrived in Paris at 8 o'clock on 23 September

1863. He then travelled through Baden, Zurich, and across the Swiss lakes, reaching Milan and the Barrys by 29 September. It was here he began his architectural studies in earnest. His notes from the commencement of the journey to 18 October are in a small, unpaginated green notebook in a private collection.

On the following day J. D. Crace visited the Gothic Cathedral of Milan and made notes concerning the use of colour at Santa Maria delle Grazie, where he remarked upon the use of yellow, green and maroon together, a colouring he was to adopt in later work. On 30 September he noted that Edward Barry, with whom he was shortly to collaborate at the Palace of Westminster, had arrived. He returned several times to S. Ambrogio to sketch the 'ancient mosaics'. On 2 October he arrived at Bergamo, which he thought an 'extremely picturesque' town, and was struck by the refined carving in wood on the stalls of the Duomo. Bergamo was followed by Verona on 4 October, and Mantua two days later.

Crace was immediately taken with the painted interiors at the Ducal Palace and the Palazzo de Tè in Mantua [Plate 22]. These two buildings were to serve as an important source of inspiration during the rest of his life. Some of the drawings he made during the visit in 1863 were published in 1912 in his book, *The Art of Colour Decoration*, a manifesto of design based upon a lifetime of experience designing grand painted interiors.[208] Of the book's twenty plates, he published two of the Palazzo del Tè interiors and two from the Palazzo Ducale, indicating the lasting impression made on him by his visit to Mantua.

J. D. Crace noted the interiors of the Room of Psyche in the Palazzo del Tè, with its decorative paintings by Guilio Romano, in his sketchbook. A corner of the vaulted ceiling is illustrated in Plate IV of *Colour Decoration*, where Crace praised the use of diagonal red panels as a means of marking out the architectural space of the room. He also praised the use of dark blue and red in the painted ceiling decoration to resist the encroachment of the richly coloured wall frescoes below. In the Room of the Caesars, also in the Palazzo del Tè and also painted by Romano, he cited the skill with which white, gilt and bold red was used to emphasise the structural features of the interior.[209]

In the Preface to *Colour Decoration*, Crace stated that his object was to, 'explain how colour affects Architecture, and to show, quite apart from the question of colour harmony, how all-important is the distribution of colour *values* in assisting or marring Architectural effect.'[210] This statement sums up the preoccupation of J. D. Crace during his career – that is, the use of polychromatic decoration to enhance architectural structure. In contrast, the writings of his father during the 1860s centred around the harmonious combination of colours in interiors. In a two-part article for the *Builder*, J. G. Crace set forth his basic rules for decorating a room, which consisted of balancing the 'three masses of colour': walls, curtains and carpets.[211] While his work demonstrates sympathy with his father's ideas, J. D. Crace became deeply interested in the relationship of colour to architecture as a result of his study of Italian Renaissance interiors.

On 8 October 1863, J. D. Crace reached Venice. His taste for paintings by Titian and Correggio, whose work tends to be atmospheric and subtly coloured, was unlike that of his father for the strong colouring and expressive quality of Rubens' work. On 9 October he toured the glass works at Murano and described in detail the process of glass-making he had watched.[212] On 11 October he purchased photographs of monuments in Venice to take back to England, and the following day he sketched the ceiling of the Ducal Palace, which was to be an important source for his work at Longleat House in the 1870s [Fig.4:23]. He also admired the medieval mosaics of St. Mark's Cathedral.

Crace remained in Venice with the Barrys until 16 October, when they visited Giotto's frescoes in the Arena Chapel in Padua, which he described as 'much injured but very beautiful'. Crace was in Bologna on 18 October, followed by Parma, where he admired the arabesques in the interior of S. Giovanni and the Parma Great Theatre, 'a fine interior all white and gold'. On 22 October he arrived in Genoa, where the Palazzo Doria captured his imagination. He remarked that the decoration of the interiors struck him as among the most harmonious and delicately rendered in Italy.[214]

The next two days were spent sketching the interiors of the Palazzo Doria and the decoration of its painted ceilings. He recorded the decoration of the loggia vaulting with particular care and was again intrigued by the distinctly Italian colour scheme of deep red, green and gold. One of his drawings of the Doria vaulting was to appear as Plate XI in *Colour Decoration*. In Chapter 5, entitled 'Treatment by Great Masters', Crace remarked that 'The structural division of the vault is suggested by the deep blue margin', while 'The emphasis of the four rectangular panels in dull red gives a certain firm stability to the whole.'[215]

The facility with which Italian decorative painters of the Renaissance used polychromy to emphasise architectural structure interested J. D. Crace and he was also struck by the way these painters used an overlay of small-scale ornaments, hatching and banding, in order to soften the transitions between solid blocks of strong colour [Fig.4:24]. For example, Crace described the painted borders of the Doria vaulting, visible in Plate XI of *Colour Decoration*, as 'a border of brilliant colours, geometrically blocked out, divided by a fine white line, and ornamented with minutely painted grotesques.'[216] The Loggia of the Palazzo Doria, decorated by Pierino del Vaga, may have influenced his future work in England more than any other coloured interior he examined.

After leaving Genoa on 26 October, J. D. Crace and the Barrys travelled via Nice to Marseilles and then on to Lyons where Crace met his younger brother,

4:23   J. D. Crace, study of ceiling details, Doge's Palace, Venice, 1863.

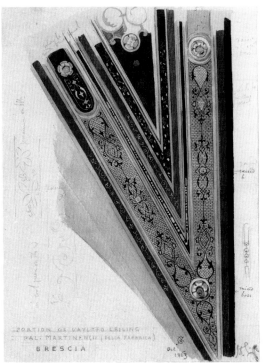

4:24   J. D. Crace, study of architectural polychromy at Parma and Brescia, 1863.

Evrard, who was living at 33 Rue Centrale. His brother was under the supervision of M. Chastel learning about silks and textiles with the firm of Arles Dufour et Cie in Lyons.[217] It is not known when the Craces first came into contact with Arles Dufour, but during the 1860s and 70s they were purchasing some textiles, and almost certainly wallpapers, from the firm.[218]

On 1 November 1863 Crace recorded the arrival of the party in Paris, where the letters awaiting him from his father, 'oblige me to stay'.[219] The numerous errands Crace performed for his father included the purchase of two books on the restoration of the Ste-Chapelle and visits to the cabinet makers Louis Gradé and Jean Paul Mazaroz.[220] The latter was making a 'buffet' for the Craces and further pieces made by Mazaroz for Crace commissions will be discussed later. Gradé, according to J. D. Crace, would have '2 small cabinets finished in a week/2 large in 15 days – Etagère – awaiting reply & dresser – 5 weeks'. Gradé was evidently making this furniture with marquetry of purple wood. Crace sketched the shapes of two tables and noted the cost of the various design options.[225] The circumstances of Gradé's work for the Craces are unknown and open to speculation: this furniture may have been designed by the Craces for a commission, for J. G. Crace himself, or for display in the Wigmore Street showrooms. Further research on Gradé may explain his connection to the leading firm of British decorators.

On 3 November, after a rough crossing, J. D. Crace and the younger Charles Barrys arrived home. For Crace it had been a fruitful trip, and the ideas he received were shortly to appear in an increasing number of commissions.

J. D. Crace's Gothic

The crypt of St. Stephen's Chapel, Westminster, was one of the few medieval structures to have escaped the fire of 1834. The chapel dated to the end of the thirteenth century and was modelled on the Ste-Chapelle. The crypt was structurally restored in 1858 to 1859 by Sir Charles Barry, who died shortly afterwards. His son Edward then undertook the decoration of the chapel there, St. Mary Undercroft, in a medieval style, completing this work in 1869. Edward Barry had met J. D. Crace on several occasions in 1863 in Italy, and the contract held by 'Frederick Crace & Son' for work at the Palace of Westminster had been renewed in 1861,[222] so it is not surprising that J. D. Crace should have been chosen to work with Edward Barry on the chapel.

Barry designed the decoration of the medieval lierne vaults, featuring a gold ground hatched to suggest mosaic on which stylised vine scrolls have been

4:25   J. D. Crace, design for mural decoration, perhaps for the crypt of St Stephen's
Chapel, Palace of Westminster, *c*.1869.

superimposed.[223] However, the scheme for the mural painting seems to have
been the work of J. D. Crace, since two designs by him for very similar schemes
of mural decoration are now in the Royal Institute of British Architects Drawings
Collection [Fig.4:25].[224] One design features *trompe-l'oeil* masonry delineated in
gilt on a chocolate coloured ground, ornamented with lobed medallions. These
features appear on the west wall and the doorway to the Baptistry. The north
and south walls were given a cream ground and suggested masonry by the use
of black outlining and stylised borders of trefoils in blue on a chocolate ground,
alternating with red medallions marked with crosses.

   In combination with Hardman's superb metal fittings and stained glass, Minton's tiles, and Barry's gilt vaulting, the severe cream and brown scheme for
the walls of the crypt chapel by J. D. Crace is striking. It highlights the contrast

between his own decorative style, with its controlled, linear character and brown and gold tones, and the more colourful, lush effects favoured by his father. Crace explained that the crypt chapel at Westminster had been 'decorated in the style of the thirteenth century to which period this fabric belongs.' He said he had deliberately used an earlier medieval style than that of the rest of the Palace of Westminster (the work of his father, Pugin and the elder Charles Barry), where 'the ornament employed has a distinctly "heraldic" character', which he felt was typical of the Late Gothic, or Perpendicular, style.[225] J. D. Crace's Gothic owes far more to Italian monuments such as Sta Maria Novella in Florence, which he illustrated in *Colour Decoration*.[226]

In the late 1860s, J. D. Crace was occupied with several other commissions. In 1867 he had been entrusted with the decoration for a reception held at the India Office on 30 June for a visiting Turkish sultan. At the back of his 1863 travel diary are his notes and sketches for this commission, showing that he carefully planned the lighting of the arcaded, three-storey courtyard of the India Office. For example, the upper storey was to be brightly lit with gas jets, and the middle with 'draperies to all the openings' including embroidered cloths hung over the balconies, while the lower storey was to be decorated with 'rich draperies', mirrors and chandeliers.[227] This part of the Craces' work – that is, decorating for temporary events – is an important aspect of nineteenth-century decorative art which deserves further research.

In the early part of 1868, J. D. Crace designed mural decorations for the stair hall of 142 Piccadilly in London, the residence of J. S. Henry. His design for the hall was Italianate in style, consisting of a painted, arcaded balustrade in brick red with cream mouldings, opening onto an illusionistically painted open sky.[228] Crace also designed bookcases and a writing table for Henry in an equally Italian Renaissance style,[229] with red, lozenge-shaped bosses and slender, baluster-shaped columns on the bookcases which echo the treatment of the stair hall.

In his travel diary of 1863, J. D. Crace frequently remarked that he felt ill and was prone to colds. Late in 1868 he contracted pneumonia, and during the winter of 1868–69 he was sent to the Mediterranean and the Middle East to recover. He later described this journey as, 'the second great event of my life',[230] the first having been his initial visit to Italy in 1859. During his first Middle Eastern journey, he visited Egypt, Turkey, Greece and Palestine, and he sketched continually. Many of his studies of the Middle East are divided between a private collection and the Royal Institute of British Architects [Fig.4:26]. If Crace's study of Italian art provided a formal decorative vocabulary that he was to use for the rest of his life, his study of Middle Eastern art and architecture gave his work the earthy colouring and pearly light that he had so much admired there.

4:26　J. D. Crace, study of panelling in Coptic Church, Fostat, Egypt, 1869.

As a result of this journey he went on to study Greek and to become a founder-member of the Palestine Exploration Fund. In 1866 Crace had become a Contributing Member to the Royal Institute of British Architects,[231] and in 1869, upon his return from the Middle East, he had taken up the Freedom and Livery of the Painter Stainers Company, as had every head of the Crace firm since Edward Crace.[232] In 1872 J. D. Crace first designed decoration in the Islamic style, perhaps tinged with overtones of Italian Gothic. This was at 9 St. James's Square in London, the residence of Henry Hoare. A design in the Victoria and Albert Museum, which appears to be for an entrance hall, features a stencilled design of abstract flowers for the main hall area, with an upper storey decorated with ogee arches and pots holding floral sprays [Fig.4:27].[233] The colours used were deep red and gold with accents of black, white, green and blue.

The overlapping of Gothic and Islamic motifs was common amongst nineteenth-century British designers, since both cultures were products of the Middle Ages. Owen Jones, whose publication *Plans, Details and Sections of the Alhambra* in 1835–45 had made him one of the pioneers in the study of Islamic art, had submitted designs for tiles for the Palace of Westminster which were rejected as being too Islamic in character.[234] Similarly, J. G. Crace had designed an Islamic-style ceiling for Abney Hall which was rejected in favour of a more Gothic design.[235]

The decade of the 1870s encompassed three of the most important decorating commissions of J. D. Crace's career. These were Knightshayes in Devon, Longleat House, Wiltshire, and the Pompeian Room at Ickworth in Suffolk. Only at Knightshayes did Crace work in a medieval style. The house was begun in 1869 for the M.P. John Heathcoat-Amory by the architect William Burges, one of the most eclectic, if not eccentric, of Gothic Revival architects. Burges prepared detailed designs for the interior of the house, but he fell out with Heathcoat-Amory in 1874. According to J. M. Crook, J. D. Crace was engaged in 1874 to decorate the interiors of Burges's massive house of red stone for financial reasons.[236]

In an autobiographical account, Crace remarked that his designs for Knightshayes represent, 'the earlier Gothic style of art', suggesting he was in sympathy with Burges's interest in art of the thirteenth century, and linking his work at Knightshayes to the decoration of the crypt chapel at Westminster. He added that 'the internal woodwork and fittings as well as the coloured decoration' of the house, as executed between 1874 and 1882, were entirely his own designs.[237]

Among the earliest of these designs for Knightshayes must be the ceiling of the Octagon, or Morning Room, with versions now in the Victoria and Albert Museum and RIBA [Fig.4:28].[238] Although the V & A design is undated, the paper is watermarked 1874. This ceiling has recently been restored, although

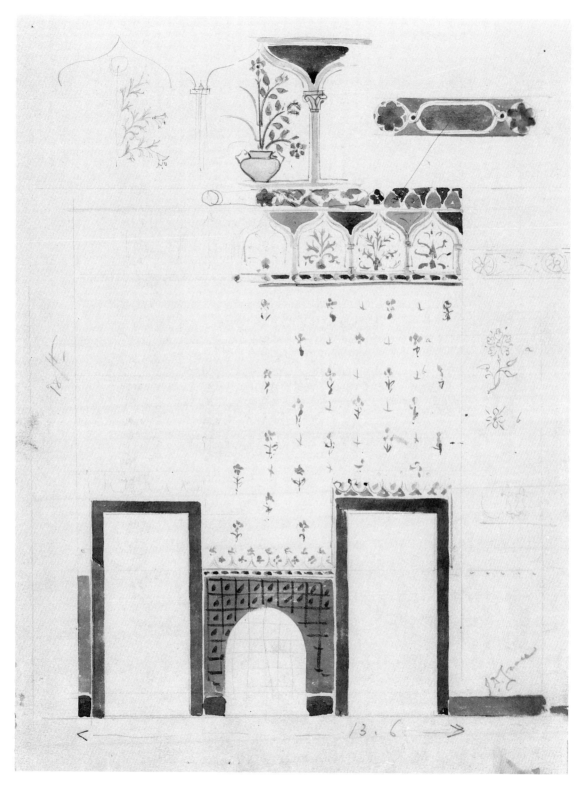

4:27   J. D. Crace, design for the entrance hall, 9 St. James's Square, London, 1872.

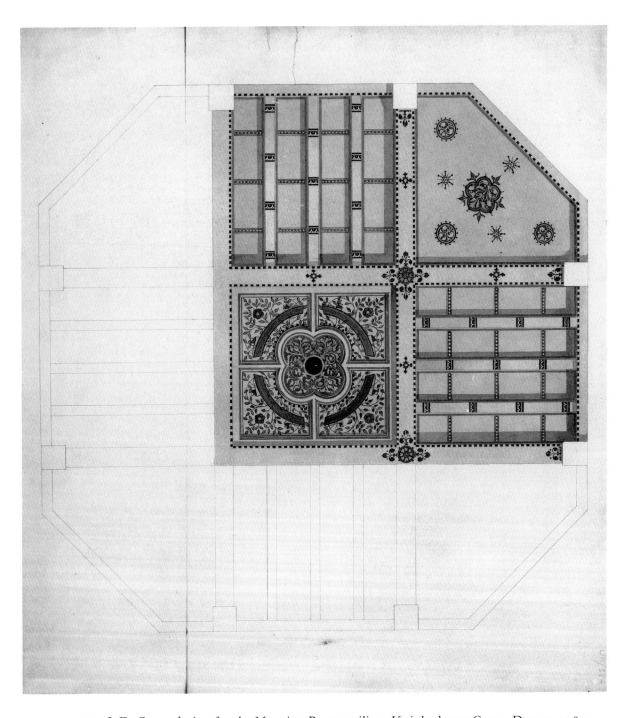

4:28   J. D. Crace, design for the Morning Room ceiling, Knightshayes Court, Devon, *c.*1874.

4:29   J. D. Crace, design for the Dining Room ceiling, Knightshayes Court, *c*.1875, from *The Art of Colour Decoration*.

with a darker ground than Crace intended. His design shows beams and compartments stencilled with quatrefoils, rosettes, and fleur-de-lys outlined in black against a buff-coloured ground, the motifs highlighted by means of red, white and blue. The sparing use of ornament and the linear, even severe, character of J. D. Crace's designs for Knightshayes is strikingly different from the sumptuous Gothic style of his father. The Italian medieval decoration of the interiors of structures such as St. Mark's in Venice which Crace discussed in *The Art of Colour Decoration*,[239] informed his designs for Knightshayes, such as the ceiling for the Dining Room [Fig.4:29].

The use of 'jelly mould' shapes in the ceilings of the Drawing Room and Library at Knightshayes demonstrates that William Burges had been inspired by Islamic art. Crace decorated both of these ceilings with a mixture of motifs. In a drawing for the Library, dated to 1876, the outer border of the ceiling is decorated with a stencilled, 'early Gothic' pattern in black, white and ochre yellow, with Islamic motifs at the centre.[240] This mixing of Gothic with Islamic motifs is seen again in a sketch for the Study ceiling [Fig.4:30], which closely relates to Crace's design for the Entrance Hall at 9, St James's Square [Fig.4:27].

4:30   J. D. Crace, design for Study ceiling, Knightshayes Court, *c.*1876.

4:31   The Library, Knightshayes Court, c.1900.

In 1879 Crace designed Gothic bookcases with linenfold panelling to be fitted around all four walls of the Knightshayes Library [Fig.4:31].[241] Besides allowing ample space to contain books, he incorporated shelves for the display of pottery into his design. He adopted this idea from the unexecuted designs of William Burges.[242] However, Crace's most unusual design for Knightshayes was probably the chimneypiece for the Drawing Room, removed in 1946. A drawing of this indicates that it was executed in carved walnut with small shelves provided for pots. The fire surround was of red Devon marble with an upper panel of alabaster, into which was set a circular mirror flanked by two carved roundels.[243] This design can be linked to contemporary developments among English Aesthetic designers. For example, H. W. Batley exhibited a drawing-room mantelpiece in the Paris Exhibition of 1878 which also featured small shelves for pots and a round mirror above the fireplace.[244]

J. M. Crook has remarked upon the 'sluggish' pace of J. D. Crace's work on the interiors at Knightshayes.[245] This may have been due to the fact that during the exact years of this work, 1874 to 1882, he was involved in another, more extensive project which was of great interest to him. This was the decoration of the principal rooms at Longleat in Wiltshire, including the state rooms on the first floor of the house.

The Italian Renaissance Style

J. D. Crace found a patron who was knowledgeable, wealthy, and congenial in the 4th Marquess of Bath. Their relationship was not unlike that between the 6th Duke of Devonshire and J. G. Crace, in the sense that both client and decorator respected one another's ideas about the interiors to be created. Lord Bath and J. D. Crace had in common an almost single-minded love of the art of Italy. The former had first travelled to Italy in 1854, and in 1867 served as an 'ambassador extraordinary' in Venice on behalf of the British government.[246] It is likely that this appointment provided Lord Bath with the opportunity to purchase a number of paintings by Venetian artists which he brought back to Longleat to be incorporated into its interiors.

Longleat was one of the Elizabethan 'prodigy houses', but the 4th Marquess inherited it after the interiors had been greatly altered by Wyatville early in the nineteenth century. Shortly after 1870 Lord Bath hired the decorator George Fox, the designer of an Italianate library at Eastnor Castle in the 1860s. By 1874, however, Fox had been replaced by J. D. Crace, who saw the Longleat interiors through to completion eight years later. Crace began work on the coloured decoration of the Saloon ceiling, having inherited a rather monotonous structure with alternating square and rectangular compartments designed by Fox. The Saloon was the second of three state rooms on the first floor of the house and had originally functioned as the Long Gallery. Crace coloured the square panels in light blue with an overlay of white arabesques, on which were superimposed classical figures representing, from north to south, War, Power, and Music [Plate 23].[247] These were painted by Henry Scholz, one of the artists who had worked for J. G. Crace at Chatsworth early in the 1840s. The narrow rectangular panels of the ceiling were alternately painted red and green, with superimposed white arabesques. This was exactly the type of decoration J. D. Crace had recorded during his visit to Italy of 1863. In the *Art of Colour Decoration*, Crace praised Raphael's decoration with fine arabesques in white in the Villa Madama in Rome, observing that, 'the minute detail only softens the white without confus-

ing the form'.[248] This observation applies equally well to his own decoration
of the Saloon ceiling at Longleat. His design for the south end of the Saloon
ceiling is in the Royal Institute of British Architects Drawings Collection,[249] and
cartoons for the figures of the ceiling were discovered at Longleat in 1980.[250]

Perhaps at the request of the 5th Marquess of Bath, who inherited Longleat
in 1896, J. D. Crace wrote, 'A Description of the Decorations in the Principal
Rooms at Longleat' in about 1900.[251] A copy of Crace's 'Description', inscribed
to the 5th Marquess, is in the Longleat archives. In addition to designing 'all
the coloured decoration' of the Saloon, which was 'carried out in 1875 by his
staff', Crace states in the 'Description' that he designed the famous chimneypiece
of the Saloon. The lower portion with its muscular caryatids was based on a
sixteenth-century Venetian example by Laonde in the Doge's Palace. The upper
portion of the chimneypiece, including 'the relief ornament above it and the
accessories, as well as the alabaster dressings to the doors', was designed by
Crace.[252] The Saloon chimneypiece was made by George Sinclair at his marble
and stone works in Soho, London who, according to notes in the Longleat archives, received the final design from Crace on 20 April 1875. Crace hung the Saloon
walls with 245 yards of Utrecht velvet, as a ground for the 'fine Brussels tapestries'
purchased by Lord Bath. He also supplied the olive-green and maroon silk
curtains, still *in situ*, 'their appliqué embroidered borders . . . designed and carried
out by Crace'.[253]

The active role played by the 4th Marquess of Bath in the decoration of the
state rooms is revealed in his letters to J. D. Crace. These letters, written between
1874 and 1879, are in the Longleat archives.[254] While the Saloon was being decorated late in 1874 and early in 1875, the State Drawing Room was being planned.
On Christmas Day, 1874, Lord Bath informed Crace that he had sent him the
second volume of Francesco Zanotto's *Il Palazzo ducale di Venezia* (Venice, 1858)
with a plate marked which might be an appropriate model for the ceiling of
the State Drawing Room. Lord Bath wished to incorporate several ceiling panels
he had acquired in Venice. He said, 'If one can only find a drawing at all suitable
one cannot do better than follow it closely. I am fully convinced that for two
hundred and seventy years there has been nothing original that has been really
good except perhaps some of the Adams & such like works.' This statement,
to a great extent, reflects the attitudes of the Victorian 'Establishment' during
the nineteenth century. In 1912 J. D. Crace wrote that the decorative painters
of past ages, 'met the various problems which surface decoration set before them.
They are always the same problems; differing perhaps in extent, or in detail,
but the same in principle.'[255] The idea of attempting to find a new, uniquely
modern style of art in which to express the aims of the later nineteenth century,
as proposed by the French architectural writer and theorist Viollet-le-Duc,[256]

4:32   The State Drawing Room at Longleat House, Wilts, decorated by J. D. Crace,
c.1875.

was never at issue with J. D. Crace or his clients. Instead, he and Lord Bath
viewed the interiors they created at Longleat as belonging to the classical stream
of Western art which had developed since the Renaissance.

The State Drawing Room at Longleat, for which Lord Bath sent Zanotto's
book to Crace, can be viewed as such a room in the European grand manner
[Fig.4:32]. Moreover, this was the most expensive of the three state rooms. Crace
charged £1132 for its decoration in 1877.[257] To set off Lord Bath's collection
of Old Master paintings, Crace installed antique red Genoa velvet which had
been purchased from a church in Italy. Crace dated it to the middle of the seventeenth century. He supplied red silk curtains, still *in situ*, and a red and gold
carpet (subsequently dyed green) which was manufactured 'at Wilton, the design
being taken from an antique Persian carpet' in the South Kensington Museum,

now the Victoria and Albert Museum. Also antique were the marble doorcases of the room, 'of white marble, inlaid in the manner of the Taj at Agra . . . bought, in short pieces, of a dealer'.[258] To surround these exotic mouldings Crace designed grey marble doorcases in an Italian Renaissance style appropriate to the paintings and ceiling of the room.

The richly gilded ceiling dominates the State Drawing Room. In his 'Description' Crace states that Fox's design of 1873 was used. Lord Bath's correspondence to Crace discussed the placement of the painted panels within the ceiling. During Lord Bath's trip to Venice in 1875, Antonio Caldara, a Venetian painter, had been commissioned to copy paintings in the ceiling of the Library of St. Mark's in Venice by Veronese and his pupil Zelotti. These were used to fill the roundels of the State Drawing Room ceiling. Several original paintings were incorporated into the ceiling, and the frieze of the room was attributed to Piero Liberi, a seventeenth-century artist. The decorative painting of the ceiling was designed by Crace in 1876–77, with the classical figures executed by the experienced Mr. Scholz. Crace also designed the upper storey, now removed, for the Italian sixteenth-century chimneypiece installed in the room.[259]

The final state room in the nineteenth-century sequence was the State Dining Room [Plate 24]. This is the only one of the three state rooms which had a ceiling entirely designed by J. D. Crace. The State Dining Room ceiling is richly three-dimensional having a variety of differently shaped panels with gilt scrolled and classical architectural mouldings framing the sixteenth-century paintings which Lord Bath had purchased from a Venetian palace.[260] The painted frieze of the room was also from Venice. The plaster ceiling was made by Jackson & Sons, with whom the Craces had worked on a number of occasions. The painted ornament on the ceiling, chiefly arabesque vine scrolls in grisaille, was designed by J. D. Crace, who chose a black ground 'to throw up the darkened colours of the old paintings'.[261]

The colour scheme of the State Dining Room is a stunning contrast of black and brown, accentuated with the lavish use of gilding and white and silver touches. Crace hung the walls with silvered and gilded seventeenth-century Spanish leather and designed black marble doorcases which echoed the two Franco-Flemish ebony cabinets on stands, of seventeenth-century date, on either side of the door into the Saloon. To continue the black and brown scheme the oak doors and dado were stained dark before being grained, to give them a warm brown colour. The dado was then given black panels framed in gilt onto which arabesques in grisaille were painted by Henry Scholz. Despite the sixteenth-century source for Crace's ceiling, the decoration of the State Dining Room at Longleat owes a debt to Baroque interiors of the seventeenth century and it can be compared to the rich mixture of Venetian and Spanish designs used by

4:33   The Ante-Library at Longleat House, decorated by J. D. Crace in 1878.

Charles Barry in the Spanish Room at Kingston Lacey, Dorset, late in the 1830s.[262]

Two bedrooms on the first floor were also decorated by Crace, one with a ceiling that could almost be described as 'Islamic arabesque',[263] as well as a suite of rooms on the ground floor in the east range, directly underneath the state rooms. These commence with the Ante-Library and include the Red Library, the Billiard Room (now known as the Breakfast Room), and the Lower Dining Room, located below the State Dining Room. On 26 September 1878 Lord Bath wrote to Crace to discuss the planning of these rooms. Work began in earnest in 1879, and the final bills were submitted in 1882. The Billiard Room and Lower Dining Room received splendid gilt ceilings designed after Venetian examples in the Doge's Palace.

The design of the Ante-Library and Red Library are perhaps most original and complete in their decoration. Crace began designing these rooms in 1878.[264] His drawings for the ceilings of the Ante-Library, Red Library, and State Dining Room are in the Royal Institute of British Architects Drawings Collection.[265] The Ante-Library ceiling was designed around a circular painting purchased by Lord Bath in Venice, which has since been removed [Fig.4:33]. The original panel is illustrated in *The Art of Colour Decoration* as Plate XIX. In the notes to this plate, Crace explained, 'The surface has therefore been panelled out by mouldings, the direction of which is expressed more definitely by the dark blue margins with the fine gold interlaced pattern to soften the contrast.' The four panels surrounding the central painting have been decorated with white and gilt scrolling arabesques on a buff coloured ground, with classical mouldings picked out in gilt. Four black and white corner panels contain trophies representing War, Art, Commerce and Music. The quality of execution is outstanding.[266] Between these corner trophies are panels with beautifully painted arabesque figures on a gold ground flanking roundels with classical scenes in grisaille.

The walls of the room were hung with imitation embossed leather in green and gilt with the same material in red and gilt for the Red Library [Plate 25]. While he retained Wyatville's presses in the Ante-Library, Crace designed spectacular marquetry doors and shutters for both rooms, and marquetry bookcases for the Red Library. These feature delicate arabesques in satinwood inlaid in walnut. In his 'Description', Crace stated that he sent his marquetry designs to Florence, where these fittings were made.[267] Crace designed damascened steel lockplates and door handles for the ground floor rooms. These were made by Chesneau, a French craftsman who was not a Crace employee.[268]

4:34   J. G. Crace, design for the Drawing Room ceiling, Grosvenor House, *c.*1872.

4:35   The Drawing Room at Grosvenor House in 1889.

Classicism

Perhaps the most striking feature of J. D. Crace's later interiors at Longleat is
their classical character, as exemplified in the Ante-Library. In about 1885 he
designed a severe, Graeco-Egyptian library for the Marquess of Westminster
at Grosvenor House, London, which had a colour scheme of terracotta and black
stencilled ornament on a white ground.[269] This commission is particularly interesting because J. G. Crace had decorated several of the principal rooms of the
house in the early 1870s. He designed a classical-style ceiling for the Drawing
Room in 1872 in an Italianate colouring of gold, maroon and green, with
arabesque ornaments in white [Fig.4:34].[270] The Grosvenor House interiors, like
those at Longleat, were designed around the Marquess of Westminster's impressive collection of Old Master paintings. The gold coloration of the Drawing Room
was intended to harmonise with yellowed varnish, while the maroon and gold
scheme of the Ante-Room was intended to complement the dark red silk walls
and gilt of the picture frames [Fig.4:35].[271]

Of all the commissions executed by the Craces, the Pompeian Room at Ick-worth House in Suffolk was the most classical. Decorated by J. D. Crace in 1879 for the 3rd Marquess of Bristol, the scheme of the room was organised around wall panels painted after frescos found in the Villa Negroni in Rome in the 1770s. These had been engraved by the well-known French artist Anton Raphael Mengs. The panels were significant to Ickworth, the engravings having once been owned by the 4th Earl of Bristol in Rome. They were appropriated by the invading French troops at the end of the eighteenth century.[272]

In the Pompeian Room, Crace used a scheme of black and white, and terracotta and grey blue, with accents of red, purple, green and blue. The ornament was a combination of stencilled classical motifs and arabesques with carefully observed features from Roman wall painting of the first century B.C. The rela-tively plain wall panels of the Pompeian Room have been crisply defined by means of narrow borders of solid colours and black pilasters with white can-delabra. Crace also designed ebonised bookcases with incised designs and an octagonal table that is visible in early photographs of the room.[273]

In 1884 J. D. Crace began to redecorate the Royal Pavilion in Brighton, where his great-grandfather and grandfather had worked. This intriguing commission is discussed in the essay by Jessica Rutherford.

The redecoration of Leeds Town Hall in 1894 represents a spectacular, late example of J. D. Crace's classicism. Cuthbert Brodrick's Town Hall had been originally decorated by J. G. Crace in conjunction with the sculptor John Thomas in 1857.[274] The *Yorkshire Post* reported in 1894 that, 'Thirty-seven years of Leeds smoke have naturally played havoc with the original work', and J. D. Crace was called in to renew it.[275] Instead of his father's green walls, Crace used a buff and white colour scheme with bold stencilling of classical motifs and accents of black, terracotta and red [Fig.4:36]. His design for the vestibule and part of the Victoria Hall is in the Victoria and Albert Museum,[276] and the rede-coration of his father's scheme can be considered a great success.

The French Renaissance Style

In the 1890s J. D. Crace's most important patron was the American millionaire William Waldorf Astor, for whom he decorated the Astor Estate Office in London; 18 Carlton House Terrace, Astor's London town house; and Cliveden, Astor's country house in Buckinghamshire. In each case, Crace worked in con-junction with the architect John Loughborough Pearson. In 1895 Pearson was designing a library for Astor at 18 Carlton House Terrace,[277] while J. D. Crace

4:36   J. D. Crace, design for the vestibule and Victoria Hall,
Leeds Town Hall, 1894.

4:37   J. D. Crace, design for ceiling, the Long Drawing Room,
18 Carlton House Terrace, London, 1895.

was designing furniture for the room in the following spring. His many designs for Astor in the Victoria and Albert Museum include several drawings for a large library table to be made of mahogany with inlaid vine scrolls of ebonised wood.[278] With its carved consoles, acanthus leaves and bellflowers, the style of this table is a luxuriant French Renaissance, or 'Francois Premier', style. Also for the library were designs for two tables with inlay of pear and holly wood on ebony.[279]

Crace's contribution to Astor's townhouse did not stop there, for in *The Art of Colour Decoration* he illustrated a ceiling he decorated for the Long Drawing Room [Fig.4:37].[280] It is not clear whether Crace actually designed the three-dimensional structure, but he certainly coloured the ceiling in maroon, green, and gold, which he felt would complement the mahogany woodwork of the room and the tapestries hung on the walls [Fig.4:38]. His design for this ceiling is in the Victoria and Albert Museum and shows panels decorated with strapwork ornament typical of French Renaissance design.[281]

The Astor Estate Office on the Victoria Embankment in London was designed by J. L. Pearson early in the 1890s. The style was a robust French Renaissance style, which Astor evidently favoured.[282] J. D. Crace was apparently one of several decorators employed here, and only his drawings for furniture have come to light for this location. Drawings in the Victoria and Albert Museum include an impressive ebony and ivory cabinet on a stand, designed in 1896 [Fig.4:39]. Two photographs of the completed cabinet are with this group of drawings.[283] The cabinet had silver plaques in strapwork designs by Crace in a repoussé technique, and it is an extremely attractive example of French Renaissance Revival furniture at the end of the nineteenth century.

A small drawing by Crace dated 1894 is perhaps of greater significance. This design for a large table for the Astor Estate Office shows four winged lions with open mouths, placed diagonally at each corner on a projecting plinth. Several pieces of furniture with similar designs have come to light in private collections, all of them stamped 'CRACE'. Two are a pair of sofas made of walnut with front legs in the form of open-mouthed lion monopodia, the knees of the legs having oval insets of red marble. The quality of the carving and execution of these sofas is very high, and their similarity to the Crace design of 1894 for the Astor Estate Office suggests that they could have been for this commission.

The presence of a Crace stamp remained puzzling until another piece came to light. This is a large octagonal table of walnut, again superbly carved with winged lion-like figures which closely resemble French Mannerist furniture in the style of Du Cerceau, who worked near the end of the sixteenth century[285] [Plate 26]. In addition to its 'CRACE' stamp, the table bears another, the stamp of 'P. MAZAROZ.R', and the number 2044.[286] In 1863 J. D. Crace had called at the cabinet-making shop of Mazaroz in Paris, regarding furniture he was making

4:38   The Long Drawing Room, 18 Carlton House Terrace, London, in 1966.

4:39   J. D. Crace, design for ebony and ivory cabinet on stand for the Astor Estate
Office, London, 1896.

4:40   J. D. Crace, design for library table for W. W. Astor, probably for 18 Carlton House Terrace, London, 1896.

for the Craces. In the mid-1890s the Frenchman would have been near retirement. However, the great similarity of design between this table, the pair of sofas, and Crace's designs for Astor, almost certainly place them in the mid-1890s as furniture produced for one of the three Astor commissions, most likely the Estate Office.

At Cliveden J. D. Crace designed French Renaissance-style decoration with arabesques and putti for the ceiling of the staircase. This was to set off a central panel painted by A. L. Hervier.[287] His drawing for this ceiling decoration is in the Royal Institute of British Architects, as are designs for a carved ivory writing table he was designing for Astor [Fig.4:40].[288] *Country Life* illustrated the stair hall of the house, with the Crace ceiling visible, in 1912.[289]

The Closure of the Crace Firm

In 1899, when he was 61 years old, J. D. Crace sold the Wigmore Street premises. They were demolished the following year by the new owner. He retired to 15 Gloucester Place, where he had already been living, and let go his remaining workmen. This might seem puzzling in light of the numerous and prestigious commissions he had undertaken in the decade of the 1890s, not only at Leeds Town Hall and the three Astor locations, but also the Royal Pavilion, the Royal Exchange and the Royal Standard Music Hall both in London and Tillyra Castle in Ireland. The last was rebuilt for the poet and playwright Edward Martyn in 1882, and Crace worked there nine years later [Fig.4:41].

Crace seems to have decided to close the firm after his father's death in 1889. He explained:

4:41   J. D. Crace, design for stair hall, Tillyra Castle, Co. Galway, Ireland, 1891.

From that time until 1899, I gradually reduced the extent of country work, and in December of the latter year, closed the Business, and sold the premises, and confined myself to 'consultative' work; one reason being the harassing anxiety attached to the employment of men, caused partly by Trades Union action, and finally by the Employers' Liability Acts. I was then nearly 61 years of age, and had no partner. The responsibility became too heavy. It was the practice of both my Father and myself, to personally direct, and supervise by frequent visits, every work – large or small.[290]

The fact that he had begun to reduce his workload from the time of his father's death suggests that this was the single most important reason for his retirement. His son, J. F. Crace, was not interested in continuing the business of decoration, and this factor, along with his worry concerning employees, resulted in the decision to close the firm of decorators founded by his great-great-grandfather in 1768.

Documents of J. D. Crace in a private collection shed some light upon the number of his employees during the 1870s and 80s. A letter of presentation to him and his bride, Caroline Foster, on the occasion of their wedding in 1873, was signed by 101 employees: possibly the highest number of employees in the history of the firm. Near the top were Mr. Haclin, the chief decorative artist of the firm, and Mr. Scholz, who had painted the State Rooms at Longleat. These two men had been hired by J. G. Crace in 1839. Another signatory was A. B. Jolly, who became foreman of the firm towards the end of the nineteenth century. In 1898 Jolly wrote on behalf of the Crace employees to wish J. D. Crace a happy 60th Birthday. This letter listed nineteen employees who had been with the firm for more than thirty years. Jolly had been employed with the Craces for thirty-nine years, while a Mr. Randall had remained the longest, at forty-seven years. The decision to close the firm must have been a difficult one, but many remaining employees would have been close to retirement. Jolly went on to perform decorative work at Arundel Castle in 1901, where he represented himself as a former Crace employee and remarked that he could supply wallpapers, carpets and hangings 'used at Windsor Castle and the Houses of Parliament'.[291]

The Crace firm must have been at its largest in about 1873, the year J. D. Crace became a partner with his father and the Record of Partnership was drawn up.[292] The Record of Partnership lists outstanding credits and debits between the years 1872 and 1886. For example, accounts due to J. G. Crace & Son on 31 December 1872, totalled £37,289, a healthy amount. Payments were owed by Lord de Lisle for the Library at Penshurst, the Marquess of Westminster for the rooms at Grosvenor House, and E. W. Pugin, perhaps for work at Scarisbrick. Small amounts were due from clients in Montreal, Macao, and Calcutta.

4:42   The Drawing Room, Gungahlin, near Canberra, Australia, furnished by Crace
for E. K. Crace in *c.*1883.

These must have been for textiles and wallpapers, or even furniture, like that
shipped to J. G. Crace's son E. K. Crace for his house, 'Gungahlin', Canberra,
Australia [Fig.4:42].[293] Outstanding debts numbered £11,088, owed to familiar
firms such as Gillows, Mintons, Wedgwood, Jacksons, Cope and Collinson, and
Jeffry & Co. French firms appear in these accounts, including Arles Dufour,
to whom Evrard Crace had been attached, Gillon Fils and Josse & Fils.

   Perhaps of greater interest are the inventories for the close of each year. In
1876 the firm's premises were at 36 and 38 Wigmore Street (38 was formerly
14 Wigmore Street), 4 and 5 Little Welbeck Street, and 11 and 12 Welbeck Mews.
This represented the Crace firm at its widest extent. In the showrooms at 36–38
Wigmore Street, the breakdown was as follows:

Paperhangings	£1240
Silks & stuffs	3040
Carpets	2045
Cabinets furn. & chairs	835
	7160

The inventory of the workshops at Little Welbeck Street and Welbeck Mews contained:

Uphost.'s shops	£ 430
Joiners & cab mkrs	180
Painters & gilders	480
Scaffolding	185
Plate Glass	15
Ironmongery	440
Gothic Showrm	70
Cement Shed & basement	110
	1910

and

Timber in yd & shops	
D⁰ Millbank	1690

The total amount of the inventoried goods for the year 1876 was £10,760, indicating a substantial amount of stock. The greatest amount of money was tied up in textiles, whilst the smallest sum was represented by the stocks of furniture. The relatively large amount of raw timber in stock may mean that the firm tended to wait for orders before making up more than a sampling of the furniture it could produce.[294]

After 1899 J. D. Crace took on a 'consultative' role and became increasingly involved in writing and lecturing on art subjects. Shortly before his retirement, he had published 'Heraldic Drawing and Its Adaptation',[295] 'Household Taste',[296] and an important if brief article on the achievements of A. W. N. Pugin.[297] After giving up the firm in 1899, J. D. Crace proceeded with a number of articles and books which indicate the intellectual side of his abilities. He published 'Plaster Decoration' in 1904,[298] 'Painted Decoration' in 1906,[299] *Gleanings in the Field of Ancient Art* in 1907,[300] 'A Week in Picardy' in 1910,[301] and 'Medieval Mural Painting', and *The Art of Colour Decoration* both in 1912.[302] Many of these are sound art historical writings which stand up to scrutiny today. J. D. Crace certainly has more publications to his credit than the rest of the family of decorators but he represents only the final episode in a long-standing tradition of scholarship and collecting on the part of the Craces.

5

J. G. Crace and A. W. N. Pugin

by Alexandra Wedgwood

THE CLOSE professional relationship which existed from *c.*1842 to 1852 between J. G. Crace and A. W. Pugin is unique in J. G. Crace's career. He did not work consistently with any other architect and his work in the Gothic style was produced almost exclusively from Pugin's designs. It is clear from his own account and from that of his son, J. D. Crace, that he admired Pugin greatly.[1] Their relationship is also closely documented; from 1844, almost all Pugin's letters to Crace survive in the RIBA Library and most of the designs that he sent to J. G. Crace are preserved in the Victoria and Albert Museum. In addition, many examples exist of their joint production, such as furniture, wall-papers and stained glass.

It is not known exactly when the two men met. John Talbot, 16th Earl of Shrewsbury and Waterford (1791–1852), had been in contact with Pugin since the autumn of 1836, becoming his main patron. According to J. G. Crace they were introduced by the Earl, and he implies that this happened in 1842.[2] There is documentary evidence that they were working together at Lord Shrewsbury's seat, Alton Towers in Staffordshire, from 1844.

It is possible that their families may have been acquainted earlier, when Frederick Crace was working on the internal decoration at the Brighton Pavilion and Pugin's father was making the illustrations for Nash's book of the building.[3] Taymouth Castle, Perthshire, also brought J. G. Crace and A. W. Pugin into proximity, although the circumstances of this commission, where Pugin's contribution to the design was hidden by the acknowledged architect, J. Gillespie Graham, meant that the two did not meet there. Pugin was connected with work at Taymouth between 1837 and 1842, and J. G. Crace was responsible for internal decoration there in 1841.

By the beginning of 1844, however, Crace was in charge of decorative work at Pugin's own house, The Grange, Ramsgate, and there is clear evidence from their correspondence that Crace had a high opinion of Pugin and that Pugin in return valued his friendship. Soon he addressed Crace as 'My dear Sir', and there were never any quarrels between them. Pugin wrote, 'Your man is like his master, everything that can be desired.'[4] He also found Crace to be an extremely useful friend in London who was prepared to do odd jobs, which ranged from finding a suitable piano for Pugin's children to arranging an embroidered christening mantle to be made in a hurry for one of Pugin's clients.[5]

Pugin's drawings were always made at great speed and included little precise detail. He therefore trusted Crace's ability to interpret and develop his designs, and often asked him to choose suitable colours. He wrote on 2 June 1846, regarding a carpet for the great dining room at Chirk Castle, '. . . and make any improvement you can, keeping to the principle.'[6] Crace would also work out technical details and add necessary information like the heraldry. In spite of their close relationship, Crace sometimes questioned Pugin's more radical Gothic designs, and Pugin would not spare his words in their defence. He called Crace's idea for an X-frame chair, apparently that for his own church of St. Augustine, Ramsgate, which was probably made during the autumn of 1850, 'the very acme of bad construction. I hope no-one will spy it out and bring it up against my true principles.'[7] It seems Crace was not offended and would finally accept Pugin's judgement.

Their most important joint project was that for the internal decoration of the Houses of Parliament. Pugin's second phase of working for Charles Barry began in September 1844 with his designs for the fittings of the House of Lords. J. G. Crace started work there in 1845 on the painted panels of the ceiling of the Chamber and his appointment must have been due to Pugin's recommendation.[8] Barry appreciated that Pugin had to work with colleagues who understood his methods. Pugin's correspondence clarifies the working relationship of Pugin, Crace and Barry. In a letter of 1846 he writes:

Things will be very active at the New Palace forthwith. I am preparing sketches which Mr B. will forward to you for pounces for another ceiling & I have strongly urged the necessity of getting all the patterns ready for the cove in the house [of Lords]. They will be done a good deal like the rough sketch I leave but I will send you up a detail sketch and then I think you better do one *at once*. You will be obliged to draw out FS the various shields that are to be painted about the throne and the sooner these are done the better, it will be all so much advanced. The ceiling &c in the chamber next the House of Lords [either the Prince's Chamber or the Peer's Lobby] will be next done. I remarked to Mr Barry about you making the carpet for the throne which he seemed to approve of & I will send you a sketch to get out a coloured drawing full size for him to see.[9]

5:1   A. W. N. Pugin, design for wallpaper, Palace of Westminster, late 1847.

5:2   A. W. N. Pugin, letter to J. G. Crace with sketch for chair, November 1850.

Barry always had the last word.

Crace's participation began with painting decorative panels, and this remained his main activity at Westminster. As has been shown, however, he supplied the carpet for the throne, and in the autumn of 1847 Pugin started designing wallpapers for Crace to supply [Fig.5:1]. From 1848 they were producing papers for the Houses of Parliament. A large number were designed, not all of which were used, and at the same time some textiles were produced, including a pattern for blinds and several for carpets.[10] From late 1850 Crace added furniture to his other work at Westminster. Pugin wrote:

Mr. Barry wants a Pattern chair made for the commons lobbies [Fig.5:2]. His idea is a light but strong chamfered chair like the above sketch covered with green leather & [sketch of a crowned portcullis] stamped on the back. Will you get one of them for Mr. Barry to see forthwith. Of course the nails must show. [sketch of a large dome-headed nail in the shape of a cinquefoil flower]

As a postscript he wrote: 'The stamp will not be on the back of the model chair. That must be done after the order is got.'[11] After Pugin's early death, no further new designs for decorative painting, wall-papers or textiles were made for the Houses of Parliament. Crace appears to have continued to supply these items from existing patterns.

The accounts[12] show that after the Houses of Parliament their major joint work was at Chirk Castle, Clwyd, for Colonel Middleton Biddulph in 1846–47. Very little of their substantial alterations, internal decoration and fittings have survived. Pugin decorated the eighteenth-century entrance hall and probably all the eighteenth-century reception rooms in the north wing, his only attempt at decorating classical rooms. The strong colours of the saloon were unusual and criticised at the time.[13] Other important private clients included Captain W. H. Hibbert at Bilton Grange, Warwickshire, in 1846–48, John Allcard at his summer house of Burton Closes, Bakewell, Derbyshire, in 1847–48, and Earl Somers at Eastnor Castle, Herefordshire, in 1849 and 1850 [Fig.5:3]. The details of such work gave Pugin a great deal of trouble and he expressed his annoyance to Crace: 'I could make a church as easy as a grate ... Such a job as Chirk is enough to drive any man mad. All little things and as difficult to get properly done as the greatest. It is worse than the House of Lords.'[14]

One of Crace's major patrons was, of course, the 6th Duke of Devonshire, and for him Crace fitted up the Irish castle at Lismore, Co. Waterford. This had been restored and gothicised by William Atkinson from 1811. As with all commissions for work in the Gothic style, Crace turned to Pugin, who was clearly unhappy at what he was being asked to do. In a letter dated 16 April 1850, he wrote:

> I assure you I have no idea what sort of paper to make for Lismore, I feel quite in the dark about it. I am not in the possession of any data. You could have made a better job yourself without me, for you know what is wanted & I do not. I wish you would let [me] give you sketches of what I think & and not make a business transaction of it, for I cannot make a job of it.[15]

Pugin did, however, provide designs for wall-papers, ceiling decorations and carpets at Lismore, but it seems likely that much of his detail was altered in execution. The work was supervised by Crace, using his own men, and took some time to complete, much of it being done after Pugin's death. The Castle does, however, contain a splendid range of furniture, mostly made from designs that Pugin had sent Crace for general use.[16]

Crace worked principally for rich private clients and for them produced sumptuous designs, as at Chatsworth, whereas Pugin, in his rôle as propagandist for his 'true principles' of design, always wanted to appeal to a wider public.

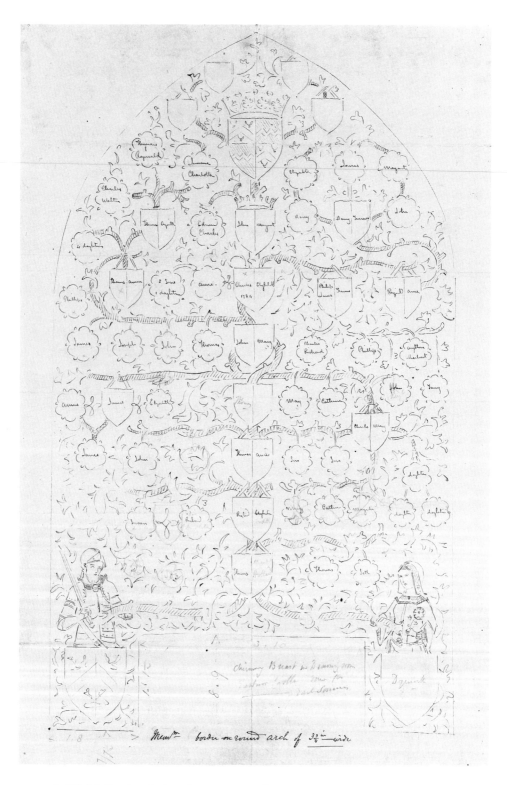

5:3   A. W. N. Pugin, design for overmantel at Eastnor Castle, with inscription by
J. G. Crace, 1849.

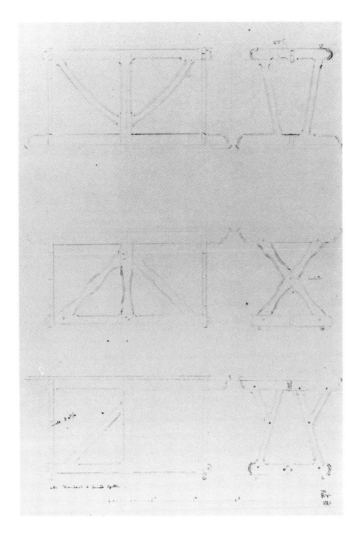

5:4 A. W. N. Pugin, design for three tables, 1849.

This was also allied to his business sense, which told him that there was a substantial market for domestic interior decoration waiting to be tapped. Early on in their relationship they produced a textile which they called 'Gothic tapestry'. Pugin wrote: 'I am delighted with the stuff. I think it is the best thing that has been done & I think I can get it extensively used for vestments. Now have you any objection to invest a little capital & keep about 50 to 100 yards.'[17] By the end of 1847 he was designing wall-paper patterns for Crace to sell: 'I am very anxious to get lots of good Patterns for papers. I am sure they will answer your purpose but when you get a stock you should make this known. We must have a turn at *carpets* next. Let us reform them altogther.'[18] He did, indeed, send Crace a number of carpet patterns in early 1848 [Plate 27].

5:5   A. W. N. Pugin, oak cabinet shown in the 1851 Exhibition, made by J. G. Crace.

In 1849, following his third marriage and consequent emotional tranquillity, Pugin spent considerable time supplying Crace with designs for furniture to be made up and sold by Crace. He was continually emphasising the importance of simplicity:

> I am extremely anxious about this plain furniture & send you at once a lot of drawings. Rely on it, the great sale will be in articles that are within the reach of the middling class, clergymen furnishing parsonage homes etc . . . I am so anxious to introduce a sensible style of furniture of good oak, & constructively put together that shall compete with the vile trash made & sold. These things are very simple & I am certain with a little practice can be made to pay & sell well [Fig. 5 :4].[20]

Pugin was always aware of the importance of advertising and he sent Crace a copy for the lettering of an advertisement in a letter of February, 1850. It must have become obvious, however, that the greatest publicity would come from participation in the Great Exhibition of 1851 and this took precedence over all their other projects for at least one year. All Pugin's close colleagues, Crace, John Hardman, the Birmingham metalwork and stained glass manufacturer, George Myers, his builder, and Herbert Minton, the pottery manufacturer in Stoke-on-Trent, combined to produce the 'Mediaeval Court'. Crace supplied textiles, wall-papers and furniture, including the splendid inlaid octagonal table now in Lincoln's Inn, and an oak cabinet now in the Victoria and Albert Museum[21] [Fig.5:5]. The Mediaeval Court received much critical acclaim and Crace was awarded a Prize Medal. While the Exhibition was open, an advertisement labelled 'Ancient House Furniture' appeared in *The Builder*, drawing attention to mediaeval style furniture, textiles and wall-papers available at Crace's shop.[22] The impact of the Mediaeval Court was considerable and major commissions followed, of which Leighton Hall, Welshpool, Powys; Abney Hall, Cheadle, Cheshire; and Horsted Place, Little Horsted, Sussex, are the chief examples. Within a year of the Great Exhibition, however, Pugin was dead, and the commercial enterprise which he had hoped would revolutionise Victorian taste could not take place without him.

Crace returned to his grand clients, who mostly preferred classical styles, but he kept Pugin's letters and designs. He used the designs, largely unaltered, from time to time throughout his working life when he needed to produce Gothic furniture, wall-papers or textiles. J. D. Crace gave Pugin's letters to his father to Paul Waterhouse in 1898 when he was writing his important articles on Pugin's work for the *Architectural Review*.[23] J. D. Crace clearly recognised the historical interest of Pugin's designs when he presented them to the Department of Prints and Drawings at the Victoria and Albert Museum in 1908 and 1912. In this way the details of the fascinating professional relationship between the two men have been preserved.

6

J. G. Crace and the Decoration of the 1862 International Exhibition

by Stephen Wildman

THE INTERNAL decoration of the 1862 Exhibition building was both a triumph and a failure for J. G. Crace. Against all expectations, he succeeded in supervising the painting of this vast edifice in less than four months. His elaborate colour scheme, however, suffered the same widespread criticism as Francis Fowke's building itself, despite his own belief that it had achieved an effect appropriate for an undertaking which in many ways proved to have surpassed its predecessor, the Great Exhibition of 1851.

Little attention has been paid to the decoration of international exhibition buildings, their architecture and contents literally over-shadowing the colouristic impact of their interiors.[1] This is partly due to the paucity of visual evidence: written descriptions alone are hard to judge, and contemporary coloured engravings tend to be somewhat unreliable. However, a meticulous chromolithograph by Vincent Brooks, together with commentaries from the copious literature on the Exhibition, provide the means to recall Crace's scheme more accurately than any other.

A simple background to Crace's thankless task needs to be given. The 1862 Exhibition is hardly remembered today, chiefly because it was transitory, at least in an architectural sense – few physical traces survived more than a decade.[2] It was also deemed to have been a failure, but this popular opinion was based on two subjective matters alone – the design of the building, and the comparison with all aspects of the Great Exhibition. On the question of its overall purpose, which was specifically to display and judge improvements in design and manufacture since 1851, there was grudgingly uniform agreement as to its success. With the memory of the Crystal Palace permanently maintained in the rebuilt version at Sydenham, there was never a possibility that the new exhibition building would stand comparison, and it was largely for this reason that the beleaguered 1862 Commissioners gratefully accepted Henry Cole's proposal of Francis

6:1   View of orchestra under one of the domes of the International Exhibition
building, April 1862.

Fowke, the Royal Engineers architect of the South Kensington Museum site,
as architect, thereby avoiding a messy entanglement with more august names
eager to put Paxton (himself an 'amateur') in his place.[3]

The 1200-foot brick façade to Cromwell Road (on the site of the Natural
History Museum) must indeed have come as a disappointment to those who
were naively expecting a second Crystal Palace – but it must be remembered
that this was intended to remain as a permanent picture gallery in the event of
a financial surplus (which did not materialise). The four huge iron and glass
courts behind, with a nave 800 feet long and two transepts, gave some echo
of 1851, but bore wooden pitched roofs; light came from clerestory windows,
supplemented in darker hours by gas. Fowke's most original contributions were
also the most derided: two enormous glass domes at either end over the transepts,
at 160 feet in diameter the largest ever constructed in this country [Fig.6:1].
Although they gave the building a distinctive skyline, they were ridiculed as
being like dish-covers or even crinolines, and very few voices were raised in

support of what can now be considered one of the most extraordinary pieces of Victorian architecture. The *Athenaeum* did at least realise the architect's dilemma:

> His critics never seemed to have considered that he was building the one thing commissioned from him – a huge shell – fit to contain thousands and thousands of objects, useful and beautiful – part of which shell was certainly temporary . . . With the means at his command, and the restrictions under which he laboured, we do not see that our architectural engineer could have done much more.[4]

The same critic went on to point out how

> It is not fair, in estimating the building, as a building and apart from the decorations, to compare it with the Crystal Palace. The mere fact of being open to the sunny day, and having the gorgeous sky-canopy for a roof, with all its islanded white clouds and sweeping masses of shadow to boot, gave charms which Capt. Fowke cannot be blamed for not equalling.

The internal decoration of the building was another matter. In 1851, Owen Jones needed to do little to enhance the impact of the Crystal Palace, but nevertheless put much thought into a very simple and understated scheme of decoration concentrating on blue, red and yellow lines (each flanked by white) following Paxton's endlessly repeated modules. Conscious of the myriad colours to be provided by the exhibition's contents, he fought shy of anything more elaborate: 'Parti-colouring may become the most vulgar, as it may be the most beautiful, of objects'.[5] Succeeding exhibition buildings either repeated Jones's basic formula (as at New York in 1853) or played safe by using a single tint throughout, and relying solely on the objects to attract the eye, as occurred at Paris in 1855.[6]

As a display of Fine Art rather than a true international exhibition, the Manchester Art-Treasures Exhibition of 1857 was on an altogether smaller scale, but it did offer Crace his first attempt at such a job. He used a greenish-grey throughout the three-nave iron and glass building (by Edward Salomons), with relieving lines of red and white, and gold columns – a scheme 'universally admitted to be most appropriate and successful'.[7] The critic John Beavington Atkinson went further in declaring it 'a great triumph' and 'a defeat of that flaunting manner of obtrusive decoration with which this country is now threatened – a manner worthy only of shops and casinos'.[8]

Fowke's 'Brick Palace' finally got under way in April 1861. Its internal decoration was giving cause for concern by the autumn, as no decision had been reached. Presumably on Cole's advice, Fowke recommended Octavius Hudson, a lecturer in ornament at the Art Training School, for the job. One of the more shadowy figures of the South Kensington circle, he had slim credentials through work in Salisbury, Ely and Chester cathedrals. A trial portion of his proposed scheme (possibly using a 'rich salmon colour' against a pale background) seems to have been painted in December, along with others by one of the contractors, John Kelk (buff and green), and Fowke himself (employing 'the fashionable "mauve" in the columns, with the same fast colour alternately with white in the ceiling').[9] None was thought satisfactory, the *Illustrated London News* taking particular exception to one treatment of the roof 'in alternate bands of white and pale blue, running parallel but diagonally' (probably Fowke's scheme).[10] 'We repeat again', urged the magazine, 'let the chromatic treatment of this interior be as simple and unpretending as the structure itself.'

Urgent calls now came to approach bigger names, such as Matthew Digby Wyatt (responsible for most of the decoration in the Sydenham Crystal Palace) and Owen Jones who, the *Building News* thought, knew 'more about colour than all the officials of South Kensington put together'.[11] Unwilling to lose face, the Commissioners turned to Crace, who accepted. 'I had not too much time to think', he said later, 'the work must be done; it was January the 23rd when I received the authority from the Royal Commissioners to assume the decoration of the building with the entire responsibility of the results, and the work was to be completed by March.'[12] The magazine *Fun* came up with this amusing jingle for the occasion:

> Said FOWKE to COLE,
> "This you'll control."
> Said COLE to FOWKE,
> "You surely joke!"
> Said FOWKE, "I opine
> You've a School of Design
>   At the famous Brompton Boilers!"

> Said COLE to FOWKE,
> "It's ended in smoke!"
> Said FOWKE to COLE,
> "Upon my soul,
> I thought Design
> Was the special line
>   Of the School at Brompton Boilers!"

Said COLE to FOWKE,
"We must aid invoke."
Said FOWKE to COLE,
"Well, it's rather droll
That a house-decorator
Should set things straighter
       Than the School at Brompton Boilers!"[13]

Given the enormousness of the task, and the speed with which it was to be executed, it is all the more remarkable that Crace decided on a more elaborate scheme of decoration than any previously used in an exhibition building. Instead of simple architectonic lines of primary colour, he proposed the use of stencilled ornament, gilding and variegated colour (although concentrating on red, blue and grey) in order to attain what he termed 'softness, richness and glow'. It is certainly true that this conformed with the more 'High Victorian' flavour that 1862 had in comparison with 1851, but there was also a practical underlying purpose.

Faced with Fowke's ingeniously constructed but irredeemably barn-like building, Crace's basic idea was the daring one of richly ornamenting the austere wooden roof – thereby turning the building's greatest apparent liability into an asset – and leaving the lower exhibition spaces plain, to be enriched by individual displays. Vincent Brookes's coloured lithograph, probably based on Crace's own drawings and reproduced in Thomas Harris's short-lived periodical *Examples of Architecture of the Victorian Age*,[14] shows every detail of the 'kind of Raffaelesque decoration'[15] which was to be applied to the roof. The boards and window surrounds would be warm grey, with a 'vellum' colour used on the horizontal purlins and on the trusses of the roof ribs, the latter relieved with red and grey piping. On the huge ribs themselves Crace deployed alternate bands of red and blue, and further alternating the rhythm on each rib (red-blue-red, then blue-red-blue, and so on): this, he decided, would avoid a monotony of effect over the long vista of each nave. Black and white chevrons were added to the leading edges of the ribs. On the roof panels he applied 'an upright scroll ornament in red, with gold, star-like rosettes, sparingly introduced', and on the ribs the novel decoration of plain black circles at the intersections of each joint, with gold stars and more scrollwork on either side.

The iron columns of the nave were painted pale bronze, relieved with vertical gold lines, and culminated in capitals which Crace chose to gild, over an alternate ground of red and blue. At gallery level were railings containing rose, shamrock and thistle motifs: again painted light bronze, with the emblems gilt, these were backed with deep red cloth. Each of the necessarily darker courts beneath the galleries was treated simply; Crace adopted 'a quiet maroon colour, made with venetian red and purple brown', with light grey ceilings. Although too late to have much effect, Crace urged the exhibitors, especially those of brightly-coloured fabrics, to look to the harmonious arrangements of their goods. In his opinion, 'the effect of many rich and valuable stuffs was seriously impaired at the Exhibition of 1851, by injudicious arrangement of them. Brocaded silks of gay colours, or printed woollens or cottons, are best exhibited if somewhat shaded from the light; it would be well, too, if they were contrasted with deep tones of velvet or other plain material.'

It was in the decoration of the domes that Crace was to have his ultimate fling [Plate 28]. This is impossible to describe succinctly, not least because of the internal effect created by Fowke's dodecagonal domes sitting over a four-point (and thus more naturally octagonal) crossing. Red was used for the main ribs, maroon for the lower columns (gilded again at the capitals). In the spandrels of the four main arches appeared medallions on a red ground by another South Kensington man, Richard Burchett, 'emblematic of Manufactures, Commerce, and the various arts and sciences which lend their aid', and over the four subsidi-ary angle arches more panels, this time green, bearing the names of the continents and 'the initials of those, so beloved by us all, Victoria and Albert' [Fig.6:2]. In the entablature beneath the drum of each dome were placed, in gold letters three feet high on a blue ground, two texts (in Latin) from the Book of Chronicles. One, David's exordium, was fully appropriate for a great international exhibi-tion: 'Thine, O Lord, is the greatness, and the glory, and the victory, and the majesty: for all that is in the heaven and the earth is thine.' To cap it all, the focal point of each dome became a light blue 'umbrella', 'gold colour and gilt rays diverging from the centre and streaming a considerable way down the blue, the shaped outline of which is bordered with red and gold ornament'. Two sketches for this coup de Crace, in his own hand, survive in the Office Scrapbook (sold at Christie's, 13 December 1988), but it is difficult to know whether he would have been aware of a similar treatment, by Signor Monte Lilla, given to the interior of the dome of the 1853 New York exhibition building, where 'rays from a golden sun at the centre descended between the projecting latticed ribs'.[16]

It should be borne in mind that scaffolding still encumbered most of the interior, especially beneath the domes, when the commission was undertaken, and Crace, 'who honestly admits that he never had courage to climb the ladders higher than a hundred feet, was drawn to the top of the domes in a snug box by means of ropes.'[17] Here he found how rough-hewn the timbers were through-out the building, and settled on the use of a single coat of distemper for the whole work. In visual terms this would be as effective as four coats of oil paint,

6:2 Decoration of spandrels and upper wall beneath east dome of International Exhibition building, April 1862.

with the disadvantages of being neither preservative nor washable; Crace was made aware, however, 'that the important principle of "the greatest effect at the least cost" should be strictly attended to', with a budget not to exceed £2000.[18] Once painting had begun, there were never fewer than a hundred men at work.[19]

The painting of the Picture Galleries, in the 'permanent' Cromwell Road frontage, was achieved with astonishing speed. Here, Crace chose sound, uncomplicated colours: sage green for the walls, with a vellum cornice and lighter green in the ceiling cove, and the end walls maroon as a background for the display of sculpture. 'To show with what energy it was necessary to carry out the works, I will mention that the whole of the picture galleries on the east side were painted and decorated in five days. I was asked on Saturday if my designs were ready – I decided the colours on Monday morning, the work was commenced at midday, and completed mid-day the following Saturday.' The final part of the painting campaign, of the tympana over the nave end walls, was undertaken on 19 April, and all was complete in time for the Opening Ceremony on 1 May.

Writing in the *Quarterly Review*, the ecclesiologist A. J. Beresford Hope encapsulated a fairly common overall opinion of the decoration: 'as a whole, when the railway-speed at which he had to work, and the impossibility under which he laboured of obtaining a fair sight of his own work, are considered, we must say that Mr. Crace has very honourably and ably aquitted himself of a work which, in less willing hands, would have been both thankless and impossible.'[20] The more popular commentators applauded Crace for his 'taste and judgement in the surmounting of inherent difficulties'[21] and considered this scheme 'generally satisfactory.'[22]

Many other critics did not. A prevailing view was that although the individual elements were tasteful in themselves, they simply failed to work on a large scale. In the *Saturday Review*'s opinion, 'as to Mr. Crace's "graceful colouring", we are constrained to admit that the more we see of it the less we like it. Not unsuitable to a small structure, it is destructive of scale as well as of aerial tint in such a large building as this'.[23] The alternating blues and reds of the roof ribs, which Crace was at pains to defend in his Society of Arts paper by referring to precedents as Assisi, Orvieto and Florence, attracted the most criticism. The *Athenaeum*'s reviewer judges that 'while the roof itself is delicately bright with pearly grey and tastefully decorated, there is much unreposing character in the doubly counter-charged markings of its ribs. Thus coloured, the markings of the ribs, instead of aiding the long vista of the roof, fritter its effect into a sparkling glitter, where there should be rest for the eye.' 'So strongly are these shortcomings felt,' continued the writer, 'that every one acknowledges the unpainted machinery annex to be the most beautiful and satisfactory part of the edifice, excepting of course the picture galleries, which have been decorated on a wiser principle.'[24] The annexes were, in fact, slightly coloured in lavender and stone-yellow, under the direction of Fowke, who himself felt obliged to complain about Crace's colouring of the roof, which he thought only served to 'completely spoil what is really a good piece of timber work'.[25] Robert Mallet, writing for the *Practical Mechanic's Journal*, gave further reasoned argument: 'To us it seems that this breaking up of the length of these curved ribs into transverse blotches of colour has been an error of judgement. . . . The decoration should have coincided with and enforced the structural arrangement, and not marred it, as this alternate chequer work has done.' He did allow, nevertheless, that the decorations beneath the domes were 'grand, harmonious and rich; and could we shut out from eyesight, along the vistas of the nave and transepts, the to us most disagreeable effect of the chequering of the roof ribs, the *ensemble* would be perfect'.[26]

Quite the most devastating negative review came, appropriately enough, from the magazine *The Critic*. After picturing 'Mr. Crace, the great colourist, waiting, with his romantic palette, ready to whitewash the very heavens, if that were

6:3   View of nave, International Exhibition building, from the *Illustrated London News*,
30 August 1862.

demanded of him', the reviewer launched into a detailed critique. Crace's pale
bronze 'many persons would call dirty green streaked with dirtier yellow'; the
roof ribs, 'with a *hardiesse* most astounding', were painted 'with a perfect
harlequinade of crosses, dots, chequers, scrolls, and nondescripts, touching every
note on the gamut of colour from black to white, with all the confidence and
the cruelty of a handsome pianist with a prodigious hand and no ear for music';
the use of gilding 'never was so out of place and so thrown away as in the National
Building'; the blue ground on the entablature beneath the domes 'is uncommonly
gaudy, and in vulgar keeping with the red of the spandrels'; and the effect of
the interior of the domes 'is truly ponderous'. While some of these criticisms
may have foundation, the ultimate comment seems unduly vindictive: 'The result
of Mr. Crace's scheme is that his interior has positively no general effect; it is
a succession of crude discords'.[27] One would like to know who was wielding
the savage critical knife.

Crace does not seem to have responded to these public criticisms, and was happy enough to have 'stuck to his own colours' (his joke). Even in the rather muted discussion following his Society of Arts paper, it was recognised that 'it required no artistic knowledge to see that in the decoration of this building the great thing to be kept in view was the uses to which it was to be put rather than the ornamentation of the building itself. Mr. Crace had very clearly stated that as the principle on which he had acted and which had induced him to adopt the style of ornament he had introduced.'[28]

His involvement with the Exhibition was not confined to the decoration alone. He was an exhibitor in Class XXX (Furniture and Upholstery), and a Juror in that Class, as he had been in the Great Exhibition: this precluded him from consideration for a Prize Medal. On one opulent three-bay stand were two ebonized cabinets and another, heavily carved, in Italian Renaissance style; while nearby were three pieces in Puginian Gothic, including a nine-foot sideboard overladen with decoration.[29] Crace was also responsible for several of the cases erected by the bigger manufacturers throughout the British Court, including one in a quasi-Indian style for the North British India Rubber Company.[30]

It is impossible to know what the interior of the 1862 Exhibition building actually looked like, with only the crudely-coloured popular engravings – such as the *Illustrated London News* supplements[31] – to give an indication [Fig.6:3]. It need only be said that Crace's scheme of decoration was the most interesting experiment of its kind – whether or not it succeeded – ever undertaken on such a scale in this country during the nineteenth century.

> It's a wonderful place is the Great International,
> > And – although discontent somewhat dashes our pride,
> Thanks to Royal Commissioners' conduct irrational, –
> > We justly may boast of the marvels inside.
> > > And the things that are filled in,
> > > And CRACE's fine gilding,
> > > Make us pardon FOWKE's building
> > > To some slight extent.[32]

7

Polychromatic Decoration as Applied to Buildings of the Nineteenth Century

by Clive Wainwright

T HE HISTORY of interior painted decoration in Britain is a long and complicated one and several aspects of it will be illuminated elsewhere in this book because of the Crace firm's involvement in them. Two modern publications have pioneered the study of aspects of the subject. The remarkable scholarly achievement of Edward Croft-Murray in bringing order to such a large and difficult subject is embodied in his two volumes *Decorative Painting in England 1537–1837*, the second volume being published in 1970. Then in 1984 appeared Helen Smith's *Decorative Painting in the Domestic Interior in England and Wales c.1850–1890*.

Many areas of the subject are not covered in any modern publication, the Middle Ages for instance, which are important and interesting not only in themselves, but as the inspiration for so many Gothic Revival architects. Some articles have, of course, been published on aspects of medieval painted decoration in specific buildings but no modern comprehensive book on the subject exists and the best sources are often the nineteenth century books, several of which I will quote from. The crucial period of the 1840s, which falls between the two books mentioned above, saw a lively debate on how best to apply polychromatic decoration to modern interiors. Then there are the many varied schemes carried out in public buildings and churches from 1837.

The decorative schemes of a few individual artists, designers and architects have been analysed in books, exhibition catalogues and articles devoted to their work, for instance William Burges (1827–1881).[1] In other instances publications on specific buildings which contain painted decoration describe the work of particular designers like Thomas Willement (1786–1871)[2] or groups of artists as was the case with the New Palace of Westminster.[3] In one case, that of the celebrated firm of Campbell Smith who worked for Burges and are still in business, a history of the firm has been published.[4]

There is the whole question of the history of the subject in Continental Europe which so often provided the inspiration for British designers. Here the modern published sources are rather less sparse than for this country and again we also have the extensive nineteenth-century literature to fall back on. Indeed, these are the very publications which inspired the Craces and their contemporaries. Here, as with this country, much valuable material is buried in monographs, articles, and exhibition catalogues on individual artists, architects and designers like Quatremère de Quincy, Viollet-le-Duc, Hittorff, Gau, Semper, Schinkel and von Klenze.

Both here and on the Continent so many actual schemes of decoration have been destroyed or painted over that most people are unaware of how widely such decoration was applied to buildings. As scholarly research relating to the restoration or re-creation of such schemes in surviving buildings proceeds, more is being discovered and published each year. The re-appraisal of nineteenth-century architecture and design is such a recent phenomenon that the money and the skills to investigate and restore surviving schemes of painted decoration have only recently become available. In Germany pioneering work has been done in this field. Here in Britain the Council for the Care of Churches is, through its Wall Painting Committee, funding the restoration of the elaborate Owen Jones decoration in the church at Sutton Waldron in Dorset. Then in Yorkshire the Pevsner Memorial Trust is restoring the Clayton and Bell scheme in the church at Garton-on-the-Wolds. As such projects multiply the whole history and practice of nineteenth-century painted decoration will slowly be understood once again.

As Croft-Murray so ably describes, throughout the eighteenth century, secular and ecclesiastical buildings both Classical and Gothic were decorated with both figurative and abstract painted schemes. The library at Strawberry Hill was painted in the Gothic style by Clermont in 1754 whilst the library at Osterley three miles away was painted in the Neo-classical style in the 1770s by Cipriani. In the nineteenth century the work of archaeologists and scholars brought both Classical and Gothic polychromy to the attention of artists, architects and designers who followed this research with great interest. There was no argument concerning the widespread use of both internal and external painted decoration in medieval buildings, although in the eighteenth century this practice was rarely followed either in church restorations or in Gothic Revival buildings. Strawberry Hill was an exception and even here painted decoration was not widely used. Eighteenth-century theorists as diverse as Winkelmann and Kant argued that Neo-classical sculpture and architecture should be white despite the growing evidence from the excavations at Pompeii and other Classical sites that ancient architecture had been a riot of colour. As the evidence accumulated architects and artists increasingly wished to emulate the classical originals.

Interestingly much of the early archaeological work was carried out by British architects. C. R. Cockerell excavated painted sculpture from the famous Greek temple on the island of Aegina in 1811 and published his findings in 1819.[5] Then in 1816, after carefully examining buildings in Athens, William Wilkins published his *Atheniensia ; or Remarks on the Topography and Buildings of Athens* which describes their polychromy. But it was the Continental scholars who argued persuasively for the use of polychromatic decoration in modern Classical buildings. The celebrated German architect Leo von Klenze played a key role in this campaign in publications[6] and in colouring his own buildings. He was later to display the actual Aegina marbles in the polychrome interior of his Glyptothek building in Munich.

In France J. I. Hittorff also published on the subject and applied the principles in his buildings. Architects throughout Europe were inspired by the splendid coloured plates depicting his reconstruction of the polychromatic decoration of the Greek temple of Empedocles at Selinus published in his *Restitution du temple d'Empedocle à Selinonte, ou l'architecture polychrome chez Grecs* of 1851. At this same date Hittorff was putting these principles into practice in his seminal church of St.-Vincente-de-Paul in Paris which, though completed in 1844, was not decorated internally with its 'encaustic frescoes' until 1849–53. He was a considerable scholar as well as architect and in 1820 came to London to examine the Elgin Marbles for any traces of their original painted decoration. Fortunately the whole fascinating story of Hittorff and polychromy has recently been told.[7]

The theory and practice of this phase of polychromy as applied to Classical interiors was transmitted from the Continent to this country partly by the published books but also by personal contact between the architects themselves. Hittorff was a friend of T. L. Donaldson, Owen Jones and several other English architects. One very important conduit for this information was, however, the great German scholar and architect Gottfried Semper who arrived in England as a political refugee in 1849 and stayed until 1855. He had published in 1836 his *Die Anwendung der Farben in der Architectur und Plastik* (The Use of Colour in Architecture and Sculpture) which has splendid colour plates. Semper was immediately taken up by Henry Cole and his circle and became a teacher at the Government School of Design. Then in 1851 he published his *Uber Polychromie und ihren ursprung* and the copy he presented to Cole is inscribed 'with the author's fullest respects May 17 1852'. He was involved with many of Cole's projects including the 1851 exhibition and the setting up of the collections which were to become the South Kensington Museum.

Semper was thus able to teach a wide range of students in the applied arts and make them familiar with the latest continental theories, particularly those of German artists and architects. As we have seen (pp.68–73), Crace was very influenced by the polychromatic decorations carried out in Munich. Semper also became friendly with all the British architects and designers and was able to introduce them to foreign visitors who were in London. For instance in January 1851 he accompanied Owen Jones and Hittorff to a meeting at the RIBA concerned with colour in ancient Greek architecture at which Donaldson gave a paper concerning Hittorff's research on polychromy. Semper certainly met Crace – if he did not know him before – when the interior of the Crystal Palace was being decorated.

Thus by the early 1850s the application of polychromatic decoration to the interiors of Neo-classical buildings had been placed upon a firm new footing created by the archaeological work and publications of both British and Continental architects and scholars.

In one aspect of polychromy this country was the pioneer and that was in the study of surviving medieval painted decoration and the application of these principles to Gothic Revival interiors, both secular and ecclesiastical. Several Georgian antiquaries noted and described surviving painted decoration. The combative architect and antiquary John Carter published in 1780 his *Specimens of ancient sculpture and painting now remaining in this kingdom from the earliest period to the reign of Henry VIII*. Then Joseph Halfpenny published his *Gothic Ornaments in the Cathedral Church of York* in 1796. The necessary scholarly evidence for the growing use of correctly blazoned heraldic devices in both secular and ecclesiastical buildings was provided by Thomas Willement in his *Regal Heraldry. The Armorial Insignia of the Kings and Queens of England from coeval authorities* published in 1821.

One of the earliest instances of the accurate and scholarly application of polychromatic medieval-style ornament in a domestic context was at Goodrich Court. The castle was created in the early 1830s by Sir Samuel Rush Meyrick the celebrated antiquary and collector. In March 1830 Meyrick wrote to his friend the scholar and collector Francis Douce of his '. . . intention of painting in two of the recesses of the drawing room in Goodrich Court subjects from the old romances'.[8] These paintings were executed and included the legend of Sir Tristram, a subject to be used more than twenty years later by William Dyce in his frescoes in the Robing Room of the House of Lords.

Just as advanced were the painted decorations in the Asiatic Armoury at Goodrich; sadly only a black and white engraving survives [Fig.7:1]. They were Islamic in style and partly inspired by the decorations of the Alhambra: 'The ceiling which has gilt stars on a blue ground, the cornice and the papering of the room are from ancient Persian illumination'.[9] This is twelve years before Owen Jones published his book on the Alhambra.

Whilst Goodrich was being decorated, the Regency architect and antiquary

7:1   The Asiatic Armoury at Goodrich Court in 1830 from Joseph Skelton, *Engraved Illustrations of Antient Arms & Armour . . . 1830.*

T. F. Hunt (1791–1831) became one of the first to analyse fully the historical evidence relating to medieval polychromy in print:

> Painting on walls may indeed be traced in England to high antiquity. Henry III, a great encourager of the fine arts, kept several painters in his service ... One chamber at the palace at Winchester was painted green, with stars of gold and the whole history of the old and new testament ... So great and general was the taste for painting in Edward the Third's time that even the walls of the bed-chambers of private gentlemen were ornamented with historical pictures. Chaucer in his famous 'Dream' fancies himself in a chamber, 'ful wel depainted, and al the walles with colours fine were painted in the text and glose, and all the Romaunte of the rose' ... [10]

Soon Pugin was arguing for the use of polychromatic decoration in all Gothic Revival buildings following medieval prototypes. In 1841 he wrote of medieval open timber roofs, 'Every portion of these roofs was enriched with painting, and when in their glory must have formed splendid canopies to the temples of the living God ... How many have been daubed over by the remorseless whitewasher!'[11] He illustrates [Fig.7:2] the ceiling of the Clopton Chantry at Long Melford in Suffolk which he describes thus, 'The ground of this ceiling is azure; the stars are of lead, gilt; the inscription on the rafters is IHU Mercy, and Gramercy; the arms on the shields are those belonging to different branches of the Clopton family, with their names inscribed beneath. The scripture on the large scroll is extracted from the Psalter, the whole richly painted.'[12]

In 1844 Pugin published his book *A Glossary of Ecclesiastical Ornament* which in 1846 went into a second edition. It is impossible to overestimate the worldwide impact of this book on Gothic Revival architecture, combining as it does a very scholarly text and splendid chromolithographic plates. Although every aspect of the church interior is covered, from tiles to metalwork and vestments, nowhere had so many coloured designs for polychromatic decoration been published before. Then in 1849 Pugin followed this up with his *Floriated Ornament*, which is completely devoted to chromolithographic designs for flat pattern derived from the natural world. In these two books architects and designers had the raw material to decorate any Gothic Revival building.

Pugin by no means had the field of polychromy to himself. He learned a great deal from Thomas Willement with whom he had worked at Alton Towers. Willement had been in business as a stained glass painter and decorative painter since 1812, having inherited the business from his father who in 1787 described himself on his trade card as 'Coach, Herald and House painter 22 Green Street Grosvenor Sq. & every other denomination of ornamental & plain painting'.[13] Until Willement retired from business in the 1860s he was one of Crace's most successful competitors.

7:2   The Clopton Chantry in Long Melford Church from A. W. N. Pugin, *True Principles . . .* 1841.

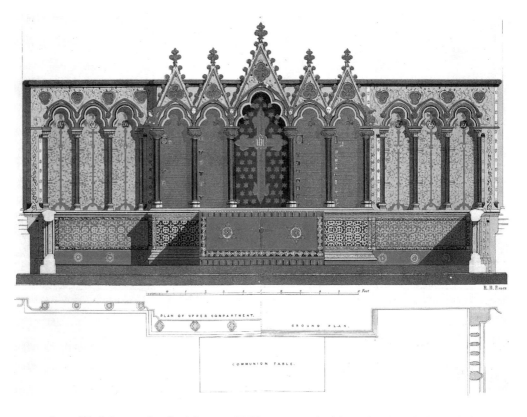

7:3   Stencilled decoration by Thomas Willement at the Temple Church from Sidney Smirke, *Illustrations and Architectural Ornaments . . .* 1845.

Willement carried out all the painted decoration in London and designed and made the stained glass for the restoration of the Temple Church in the early 1840s. This scheme was the most scholarly and elaborate scheme of Gothic Revival polychromatic decoration to have been carried out up to that date. It attracted tremendous interest at the time and influenced a whole generation of architects, not least Pugin. Today it is less well known than it should be, perhaps because it was bombed in the war along with all Willements' design drawings for the work. Fortunately it was published in colour in 1845[14] and [Fig.7:3] from the book illustrates much of the Willement work there.

The 1840s saw a spate of publications which helped to reinforce Pugin's advocacy of polychromy. Owen Jones published in 1846 his *The Polychromatic Ornaments of Italy* and in 1847 E. L. Blackburne his *Sketches graphic and descriptive, for a History of the Decorative Painting applied to English architecture during the middle ages* both of which had chromolithographic illustrations. As well as the architects' there were the practical decorators' books (the Crace publications have been dealt with elsewhere); the most prolific author amongst them was David Ramsay Hay, the Edinburgh decorator, who had played such an important part in decorating Abbotsford.[15] Hay published a number of important theoretical works on the subject and in 1844 his *Original Geometrical Diaper Designs* appeared. His most influential book was, however, *The Laws of Harmonious Colouring adapted to interior decorations, manufactures and other useful purposes*. This was first published in 1828 and by 1847 was in its sixth edition, in 1848 it was translated into German. Although Crace did work north of the border Hay was very successful and took most of the Scottish commissions.

Pugin's interiors, whether secular like the New Palace of Westminster or ecclesiastical like St. Giles, Cheadle, closely followed the medieval precedent and were brilliantly painted throughout. But interestingly it was Pugin himself who undermined the use of polychromy on every surface within a building, having stated that 'All plaster, cast-iron, and composition ornaments, painted like stone or oak, are mere impositions . . . Hence yet the rubble wall and oaken rafter of antiquity yet impress with feelings of reverent awe . . .'.[16] Pugin was not in fact opposed to polychromatic stencilling or figurative paintings covering wood, stone or plaster, but was against graining a cheap wood to look like an expensive one or painting plaster to mimic stone, or marbling it. But the concept of leaving stone as stone or oak as oak and not painting them at all was avidly taken up by the younger generation of Gothic Revival architects like Street, Butterfield and Shaw. The 'Truth to Materials' concept which was to be so crucial to the Arts and Crafts movement was launched. Thus even before Pugin died in 1852 the unrestricted use of polychromatic decoration which he favoured was out of fashion in Gothic Revival buildings.

Although in 1845 the architect John Whichcord could still write advocating that architects should emulate the Middle Ages, 'It often happened that throughout the whole interior of a church the materials were nowhere discernible. In Rochester cathedral, even as far back as the work of the thirteenth century, the Petworth marble columns have been entirely hid with colour.'[17] Whichcord's views were to be increasingly controversial and the whole question was argued out at length in the architectural periodicals of the 1850s and 1860s. For instance under the headline 'Natural Colour in Sacred Architecture' an anonymous letter was published: 'It may be that we are entering on the "reign of polychromatic terror" . . . Colour must, if used in much profusion, create different feelings from those which ought to exist in an edifice dedicated to the worship of god. And by this I mean colour artificially and artistically employed. The contrary effect is produced by the use of *natural-coloured* stone in preference to *coloured pigments*.'[18] The architect William White, a leading protagonist of the 'Reformed Gothic' school, leapt to the defence of polychromy prompted by this letter '. . . as affording me a fitting opportunity of laying before you some defence of the position which I desire to maintain in favour of a more profuse employment of colour in sacred art'.[19]

These arguments led to most Gothic Revival architects, and indeed many working in other styles, leaving materials like metal, stone and wood uncoloured or largely so. If colour was used motifs were stencilled on the bare stone, metal or wood so that most of the natural material was exposed. To paint plaster, although of course actually equally dishonest, was acceptable, but to paint wood and stone was not. Although even in the later 1860s some ecclesiologists were still arguing logically on medieval precedent for total polychromy, the battle was largely lost, 'And if anyone should think it unnatural to gild or colour stone or oak, let us remind him that the application of colour attaches no more unreality to the material than carving its surface into foliage or animals does. Our old church architects had none of that mistaken respect for bare oak or stone that has prevailed so much in later years.'[20]

During the 1870s William Burges ploughed an almost lone furrow in painting far more surface within his buildings than his contemporaries, but even he sometimes left stone as stone [Fig.7:4]. The most important guide to the current designs and attitudes of the Gothic Revivalists of the closing decades of the century, when polychromy was giving way once again to the bare stone and plaster of the Arts and Crafts movement, was published in 1882. The authors were the Liverpool architects W. and G. Audsley and the book was *Polychromatic Decoration as applied to buildings in the Medieval Styles*. They deplored partial polychromy but accepted it as a fact.

7.4   The Summer Smoking Room at Cardiff Castle showing painted decoration and
bare marble.

> During the middle ages colour was freely applied to sculpture of all descrip-
> tions, but in the present day there appears to be great reluctance to follow
> this ancient practice in its full development. There seems to be too great value
> laid on stonework nowadays ... Usually the decoration is confined to the
> plastered surfaces, the stonework and woodwork being left untouched. That
> such was not the case in the great periods of Christian architecture we have
> ample proof.[21]

The splendid chromolithographic plates depict stencil designs of the most
advanced Gothic character [Plate 29]. The Audsleys however built in and published on a number of styles, for example George's splendidly illustrated *The
Ornamental Arts of Japan* came out in 1882–84. Then in 1892 George with his
son Maurice published *The Practical Decorator and Ornamentist* which illustrates
in lavish colour designs for polychromy in a wide range of styles. These Audsley
volumes comprise a wonderfully inventive and colourful climax to the whole

polychromy movement and give us an excellent impression of the movement just as it was about to decline.

I have in this short essay attempted to sketch out the basic outline of the polychromatic movement in the nineteenth century. As will be apparent from the exhibition which accompanies this book and the other essays published here the firm of Crace played an important part in this movement both as craftsmen and through their publications. Most of the aspects of the subject which I have touched upon badly need more research and publication but the bare bones of the subject and the identity of the main theorists and designers are established.

8

Redecoration and Restoration: the Crace firm at the Royal Pavilion, Brighton, 1863–1900

by Jessica Rutherford

As a result of the sagacity and vision of the Commissioners of Brighton the Royal Pavilion can claim to be amongst the earliest municipally owned houses to be preserved and opened to the public as an historic interior. Before it was sold to Brighton in 1850 the Pavilion's magnificent rooms had been completely stripped and left in a dilapidated state; 'Scarcely more than the bare walls remained, for the chimneypieces had been torn down; the chandeliers, the organ, and even the grates removed; the Music Room stripped of its beautiful Chinese paintings, and the whole place dismantled and disfigured, as though its doom had been fixed'.[1] Within a year of purchase, however, the main ground floor rooms had been completely redecorated and opened to public view. The subsequent history of the Royal Pavilion is one of successive redecoration and restoration, forming a fascinating study of Victorian attitudes to period refurbishment.

The various schemes proposed by the Crace firm for the interior of the Royal Pavilion in the period 1863–1900 ranged from pure decoration, or redecoration in a style considered to be in harmony with the spirit of the original designs, to straightforward restoration as then conceived. The treatment of various rooms was dependent on the degree to which original surface decorations and features remained *in situ* and on their grandeur; for example in the Music Room and Banqueting Room, with their magnificent ceilings intact and incorporating certain decorations returned from Kensington Palace in the mid-sixties, restoration was the favoured approach. The Drawing Rooms, however, which were devoid of original wall decorations and modest in scale, were completely redecorated, albeit in a style deemed sympathetic; in the case of J. D. Crace this was tempered by his preference for the Moorish style rather than the more appropriate Chinese idiom.

Although members of the Crace firm worked extensively in the Royal Pavilion until the early 1820s, they were not employed there by later royal owners, namely William IV and Queen Victoria. It was not until some time after Brighton acquired the Pavilion that the Crace firm once again took part in new decorative and restoration schemes. In 1850 the Pavilion had been sympathetically redecorated by Christopher Wren Vick, a Brighton based decorator who had done much work in the Pavilion for both William IV and Queen Victoria. His scheme, based on the original Regency decorations, included the installation of new stone chimneypieces designed by John Thomas. By 1863 the ground floor rooms required redecoration and the Borough Surveyor was instructed by the Pavilion Committee to obtain estimates; a few months later John Gregory Crace (1809–89) submitted proposals for the approval of the Committee.[2] Why the Crace firm became involved again in the Pavilion after some forty years is unknown; presumably, as the project was not put out to tender, the Surveyor contacted J. G. Crace direct. By 1862 Vick had ceased to work as a 'painter, plumber, glazier and house decorator'; in the absence of a reliable, established contractor it seems likely that Crace was considered to be the most appropriate firm to undertake such works in the Pavilion.

Crace felt that Vick's decorative scheme was 'derogatory to the building'[3]; the annotation he (or his son) made to his pencil sketch of the South Drawing Room reads 'nothing to preserve in this room'. He dismissed Vick's knowledge of the history of the building and his involvement with its decoration since the 1830s. Crace executed some 'before and after' pencil sketches, showing elements of Vick's scheme and his own proposals [Fig.8:1]. Although he recommended the restoration of the ceilings of the Music Room, Saloon and Banqueting Room he proposed a new style of decoration to the walls which 'without attempting richness yet shall appear suitable and in good taste'.[4] For these State Rooms he suggested a very high dado (5′6″), presumably to match the height of the tallest Thomas stone chimneypiece, which was in the Music Room. This dado would 'take the wear and be so finished as to be handsome in itself as well as a means of ventilation'.[5] His designs for the wall surfaces, more or less uniform for all rooms regardless of their scale or original purpose, comprise panels of Moorish character divided vertically by pairs of *trompe l'oeil* columns [Fig.8:2]. It is probable that Crace developed the form of the pairs of columns from Thomas's chimneypieces as any new decorative scheme would have to incorporate such existing permanent features. [Fig.8:3].

The adoption of a Moorish style was possibly the result of Crace's visit to Spain in 1855 and his appreciation of the architecture and decoration of buildings in the southern part of the country: he had already experimented with Moorish motifs in a ceiling design for Abney Hall in the late 1850s. No doubt this style

8:1   J. G. Crace, design for the Banqueting Room in the Royal Pavilion, c.1863. The left side, coloured, shows part of Vick's existing 1850 scheme; the right, in pencil only, Crace's proposed scheme.

would have seemed to him sympathetic to certain aspects of the Pavilion's architecture. However, despite Crace's avowed concern for the original decoration of the Pavilion (so intimately associated with his father) in this scheme he showed little respect for, or sympathy with, the original 1820s interior.

As a consequence of a row between Crace and the Pavilion Committee, which seems to have been the result of a genuine misunderstanding regarding Council working procedures, the designs were, perhaps fortunately, never executed. Crace had been requested to produce designs and a specification for the works, but became unhappy regarding the amount of detail initially required by the Committee. In a letter dated 8 October 1863, he refused to prepare coloured drawings that other craftsmen could execute, or to work in competition.[6] Although he understood that the realisation of his designs would be subject to public tender, Crace believed that this was simply a matter of form to comply with the appropriate Act of Parliament and that he would receive the contract

8:2   J. G. Crace, design for the North Drawing Room (originally called the Music
Room Gallery), *c.*1863. The *trompe l'oeil* double columns echo the design of the John
Thomas stone chimneypieces still in situ in 1863 (see fig. 8:3).

8:3   Photograph, post 1865, of the North Drawing Room showing Tony Dury's
scheme, and Thomas's stone chimneypiece on the west wall.

regardless. When informed that the works would have to be formally put out
to tender, he withdrew from the project.

Regrettably, the whole matter was publicly discussed at a Council meeting,
and Crace's correspondence with the Surveyor Lockwood (including the above-
mentioned letter) was published in the *Brighton Guardian* (28 October 1863) along
with a report on the debate. The comments of members of the Council concerning
Crace's understanding of his position regarding the tender procedure were unfor-
tunate, implying that Crace's behaviour was corrupt and that he must consider
the Pavilion Committee 'a set of thieves or stupids'; words such as 'imprudent',
'bamboozle', 'knavery' echoed across the Council Chamber. Understandably
Crace was upset by the publication of his letters and the subsequent debate in
the Press and withdrew all previous offers to serve the Council in the future.

In January the following year, a Mr. Pantaenius submitted designs and specifications for the lower suite of rooms, introducing 'such of the original fittings
and decorations which have been presented by Her Majesty to the Corporation
as can be used with propriety'.[7] Given the previous misunderstanding between

Crace and the Pavilion Committee, Pantaenius clearly defined his role, namely to produce designs and specifications for which contractors could submit tenders in competition in accordance with Council regulations. The contract was subsequently awarded to Tony Dury whose estimate was £2750.

Some twenty years later concern was expressed at the condition of decorations of the North Drawing Room (known in the 1820s as the Music Room Gallery). The Surveyor, Philip Lockwood, considered that the style which Dury had adopted in 1864 'was not so much in accordance with the Oriental Character of the Pavilion as it should have been',[8] and proposed that it should be redecorated in accordance with the original design as seen in Plate 18 of E. W. A. Brayley's *Illustrations of Her Majesty's Palace at Brighton*, 1838, (the early chinoiserie Yellow Drawing Room): 'The walls should be panelled with painted and gilt bordering of an Oriental Character ... yellow should be the prevailing colour and the draperies to the windows etc should be of striped yellow pattern'.[9]

In his report Lockwood seems to have confused the two Regency schemes, referring to the later 'Music Gallery' design (Plate 19 in Brayley) as elaborately Chinese, and the earlier 'Yellow Drawing Room' design as 'altered and simpler in character'; whatever the confusion it was clearly an attempt to redecorate the room in sympathy with an original scheme of the Regency period. Perhaps for this reason the firm of Crace was approached to design and superintend the work. In a letter dated 27 June 1884, J. D. Crace agreed to submit designs and offered to provide skilled workmen or artists to execute them.[10]

Crace was forced to devise a ceiling design that would incorporate Dury's raised flock borders and panel design, which could not be removed without damaging the plaster. He submitted an elevation [Plate 30] and a ceiling design [Fig.8:4]. His proposals were as follows:

Wash off and paint the ceiling which [sic], with tinted grounds in the large panels, and colour and ornament in the smaller panels. Paint the raised flock borders relieved with colours picked in to the design and with a little gilding.

Wash off the paper decorations from the cornice and paint the leaves a light tint with ornament as shewn, clean the gilt stems and pendants and renew the gilding where necessary, and pick in colours to the back ground.

Prepare the walls for painting, wash out the paper decoration from the raised flock margins: remove the centre vertical margin from each of the two long wall spaces and divide the space left into three panels (in place of two) by two similar margins. Paint the panels pale buff with ornamental heads as shown in design, and decorate the margins in black and white with some relief of gilding.

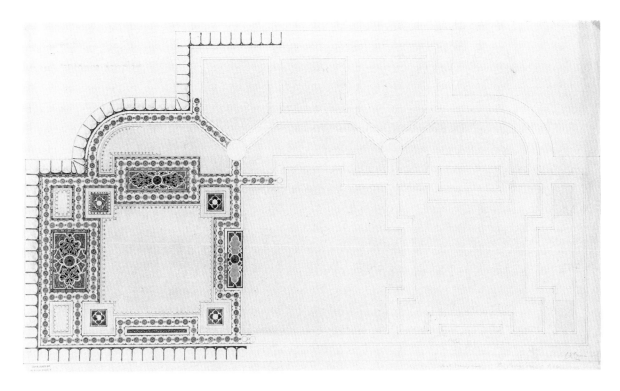

8:4   J. D. Crace, design for the ceiling of the North Drawing Room, 1884.

Paint the columns pale bronze colour relieved with gilding, and the doors to rich brown with relief of ivory color and gold.[11]

The elevation shows the sections of west wall flanking either side of the chimney. The scheme is richly coloured, predominantly yellow and Moorish in style; Crace recommended a design of 'oriental character of rather purer style than what prevails in the adjoining room, and free from Chinese eccentricities'.[12] He followed the Dury scheme of floor to ceiling panels with no dado, but simplified the design, painting over Dury's profusion of wreaths, garlands, monkeys, and butterflies on both the ceiling and walls. He considered this approach appropriate for a small, low room, where elaborate detail, being close to the eye, might be too prominent and wearisome. His treatment of the ceiling, with geometric pattern and borders, neatly concealed the fussy and over-detailed Dury scheme and bound the room into harmony with the new wall decorations. A contemporary historian and critic considered Crace's scheme to be 'one of the finest specimens of decorative Art in Brighton. Although differing widely in style from the embellishments of the other rooms in the building, it is quite in keeping with them so far as brilliancy and elaboration are concerned.'[13]

A group of original sketches, working drawings and pounced designs for the

8:5   The North Drawing Room, 1914–18, in use as a hospital for Indian soldiers, and showing Crace's 1884 scheme still in situ.

ceiling, wall and door decorations have survived which illustrate the working procedures for the execution of this scheme. From Crace's approved design full scale working drawings were produced and pounced by artists; trials were then submitted to Crace for his approval. As part of the redecoration the room was partially lit with electricity; also the gas standards were replaced with gas wall brackets designed by Crace. As is invariably the case, the cost of the project considerably exceeded its estimate. Crace's decorations remained *in situ* until the early 1950s [Fig.8:5] when they were replaced with a scheme based on fragments of the original flake white and gold fret pattern.

In 1896 the Borough Engineer and Surveyor, Francis May, reported to the Pavilion Committee on the restoration of the Saloon. He proposed that the work should be 'a restoration of the original designs of the Architect, rather than a re-decoration after any modern style'.[14] Three firms were invited to submit designs, specifications and estimates: Messrs. Graham and Biddle, Messrs. Collinson and Lock, and Messrs. J. G. Crace and Son. Prior to submitting his specification Crace visited the Pavilion and made many working sketches of details of the Saloon [Fig.8:6]. The contract was awarded to Crace, provided that all the gilding in the Saloon was renewed and that he agreed to 'ornament the pilasters

8:7   J. D. Crace, design for the restoration of the Saloon, 1896.

8:6   J. D. Crace, sketch of the mirror frame
in the Saloon, March 1896.

8:8   J. D. Crace, sketch for an
electric lighting system on the
palm tree columns in the South
Drawing Room, 1898.

in accordance with the original design'.[15] The work carried out was indeed an attempt to restore rather than redecorate [Fig.8:7]. A comparison of the Crace painted paper dado recently discovered under the original painted and gilt mahogany dado (returned by George V in the 1930s) shows a scheme closely related to the original by Robert Jones, although clearly differing in colour treatment, style, and techniques.

Crace's next project, some two years later, was for the South Drawing Room (originally called the Banqueting Room Gallery). This was pure decoration, with no attempt at either restoration or reinterpretation of past schemes. It was a lavish, richly decorative design in the Moorish style incorporating existing features such as the alcove and chimneypieces. The design for the west wall shows a colour scheme softer in tone than the earlier North Drawing Room [Plate 31]. The heavy embossed linen paper comprised a design of Moorish arches in bronze against a dull red background surmounted by a frieze in gold and blue. The arched recess is embellished with lush vegetation in a gold setting; the stone chimneypiece was marbled green, with sage green skirting. The Committee approved Crace's designs in principle, but considered some of the colours in the ceiling decoration too pronounced and suggested the introduction of more subdued tones.[16]

With the new ceiling design the positions of the electric lights had to be amended. As the South Drawing Room had a low ceiling Crace proposed the use of standard pillar lights, concealed lights in the large recess and the addition of lights round the upper stem of the palm tree columns.[17] A small sketch by Crace shows his proposal for adding lights beneath the palm leaves [Fig.8:8].

A contemporary account describes the South Drawing Room's exotic appearance:

> The walls of the apartment are hung with a novel and somewhat unique Tyne-castle canvas of Oriental character in relief, richly treated in colours and lacquer gildings, which at once attracts attention, as it invests the room with a special charm. But perhaps the most striking feature of the decorations is the tasteful recess formed in the wall of the western side of the room. This is filled in with an ornamental fretted arch of wood, which, with the columns and skirting and ornamental balustrade suitably painted and decorated, looks like some Indian window; and the more so, by reason of the back being lined with looking glass (divided in panels by gilt bamboo moulding) which reflects not only the decorations of the room but portions of the foliage of the trees which adorn the Western Lawn.[18]

Crace's design for this room survived until the mid-1930s.

J. D. Crace's rich Moorish designs no doubt influenced the Council's Surveyor

May in his project to remodel the Museum and Library (1901–3) in the adjacent buildings on the Pavilion Estate. Here, particularly in the entrance hall, Moorish designs flourished in richly tiled columns and wall decorations; the influence of the Royal Pavilion, characterised by Crace's preferences in the 1880s and 1890s, was predominantly Moorish rather than Chinese.

Through his work in the Pavilion J. D. Crace became accepted as an important adviser to the Pavilion Committee. He was consulted on a variety of matters such as the restoration of the Music Room or the designs of new carpets and curtains. In 1898 Crace was asked by the Town Clerk to inspect the original decorations from the Pavilion, stored at Kensington Palace, with a view to their return, as without experienced professional advice decisions could not be made as to a selection of appropriate objects. Following a visit by Crace more original decorations were returned as a gift from Queen Victoria. No list of the objects returned to Brighton has been located, but there are in the Royal Pavilion Archives some notes made by Crace whilst visiting Kensington Palace on 29 April 1898; these comprise rough sketches and lists of items including doors, glass, panels and trimmings.

Following extensive works to the Music Room, J. D. Crace undertook his last major project in Brighton in the spring of 1899: the restoration of the Banqueting Room. In his report to the Committee following his inspection of the interior he assumes that the intention is to 'retain its original features by restoring the more artistic portions of the work and cleaning and renovating what is in a condition to be preserved with advantage'.[19] He recommended considerable repainting, notably of the sky ceiling and palm leaves, glass, the wall paintings and the pendentives, and the regilding of much carved ornament; the dragons supporting the chandeliers would be 'either partially gilt or entirely silvered and then glazed with transparent colours'. His primary concern was, however, to restore the room according to the original designs with appropriate techniques. He proposed reprinting the frames to the wall paintings using the original blocks which had survived. He was aware of the original colour of the background paper (blue and gold) and considered restoring or replacing the green and gold paper then *in situ*. The room underwent further 'improvements' with the installation of radiators, a new oak floor, and curtains. The total project cost nearly £2500, which was generously financed by Councillor G. W. Willett.

Historians this century generally denigrate the Victorian phase of the Pavilion's history; undoubtedly by today's standards Victorian restoration works tended to be crude and insensitive. In the 1890s, however, they were much admired by contemporaries and as a result civic pride in the Royal Pavilion was maintained, so ensuring its future. Enthusiastic reports in the local papers followed each project; whilst restoration to the Music Room was still in progress in 1898, the *Brighton Herald* commented that 'ere long the Music Room will become one of the most beautiful rooms in the Kingdom, and one of which the town may well be proud'.[20]

J. D. Crace's contribution towards the long term preservation of the Royal Pavilion was invaluable. With his experience and knowledge he guided the Pavilion Committee during the latter decades of the nineteenth century towards formulating a policy of restoring the interior. Through his influence the foundation of a philosophy of restoration was established which has subsequently been pursued with more academic and scientific rigour in this century.

Conclusion

by Megan Aldrich

Apart from Frederick Crace's designs for interiors at the Royal Pavilion, Brighton, and J. G. Crace's collaborative work with Pugin, the reputation of the Crace firm of decorators has faded into obscurity since the 1930s. This may, in part, be due to the conventional wisdom of the twentieth century, where the use of revived historical styles has been viewed as an indication of weakness in design indicating a lack of inspiration on the part of the designer. The Craces, for example, cannot be viewed as 'reformers' and placed within the context of modernism, as delineated in the seminal book by Nikolaus Pevsner, *The Sources of Modern Architecture and Design*.[1] In order to gain a complete picture of decorative art and design in Victorian Britain, it is important to consider not only *avant garde* designers but also practitioners like the Craces, who may be viewed as progressive designer-decorators and ultimately as more representative of the art of the nineteenth century than the self-proclaimed reformers.

The five generations of Crace decorators were active in seeking out the newest and best developments in decorative art and in translating these developments into fashionable interiors for important clients. This is particularly true of the two Victorian Craces. Throughout their long careers J. G. and J. D. Crace displayed a willingness to adapt the progression of styles of the nineteenth century, as these evolved, to their executed work with thoughtful deliberation. For example, there were two instances where they were called upon to decorate buildings by William Kent: the Saloon of Devonshire House, London, *c.*1840 by J. G. Crace, and the Council Chamber of Burlington House, for the Royal Academy, *c.*1890 by J. D. Crace. Both responded with decorative schemes that used recognisable features from Kent's Palladianism. J. G. Crace created a suite of Gothic rooms at Knebworth House, Hertfordshire, because the owner wished to reflect the late medieval date of the house and his own interest in the Middle Ages. At Longleat, J. D. Crace created a suite of rooms in an Italian Renaissance style because of the wishes of his patron, who recognised the house as among the earliest of classically inspired English country houses. Hence a strong element of common sense informed the Craces' eclectic use of past styles, and the appropriateness of these styles was carefully considered. J. G. Crace refused to provide furniture in the Rococo style for Government House in Perth, Australia, a Jacobean-style building.

The work of the Craces was well received in the contemporary press. By 1880 they had achieved considerable fame and were considered as unusual amongst decorators for their active participation in design. In 1881 *The Journal of Decorative Art*, one of the leading periodicals on the subject, described the Craces as 'the oldest and most distinguished firm of decorators in the country'.[2] In 1884 *The Little Journal* remarked that they were 'sufficiently remarkable to warrant special notice', and published an article on the history of the Craces and their work, beginning with Edward Crace.[3] On the occasion of Queen Victoria's Jubilee, a hint that the grand European styles practised by the firm were becoming slightly out of date is contained in an 1887 notice in *The Journal of Decorative Art*. This cited the Craces' knowledge of polychromy, 'as in their instance, combined with a consummate knowledge of harmonious draping and furnishing' giving rise to 'the highest development of decorative art and effect'. However, the article continued: 'The tendency of recent years has been gradually pointing to a different conclusion'.[4] By the end of the nineteenth century a number of designers had established themselves with recognisable, personal styles. However, *Furniture and Decoration* remarked in 1891 that, 'Twenty years ago . . . the prominent English decorator, with the exception of such established names as Crace, was a *rara avis*'.[5] Therefore, as nineteenth-century decorators whose interiors displayed a distinctive 'Crace' quality, they may be considered as innovators.

Appreciation of the grand, historically inspired interiors created by the Craces lasted until the Second World War. In 1906 Hubert Corlette contributed a lengthy study of J. D. Crace's work to *The Art Journal*, in which he described the last and most conservative Crace as a 'skilled colour designer' in the grand tradition of Renaissance Italy,[6] a comparison which must have pleased J. D. Crace. After his death, several ceiling designs by him were illustrated in *The Modern Painter and Decorator*, a practical guide to interior decoration, which was published in about 1930. However, the 1930s saw the popularisation of white interiors and furniture of tubular steel created by modernists such as the Bauhaus designers and the Swiss architect Le Corbusier. The sumptuous, painted interiors of the Craces were temporarily eclipsed.

Notes

Abbreviations

V & A: Victoria and Albert Museum, London, National Art Library
C-H: Cooper-Hewitt Museum, New York
RIBA: Royal Institute of British Architects

1 The Georgian Craces pp.3 to 32

1. It is in a private collection.
2. These are the Department of Prints and Drawings at the V & A; the Drawings Collection at the RIBA, London; the Department of Drawings, Prints and Photographs at the Metropolitan Museum of Art, New York; the Department of Drawings and Prints at the C-H, the Smithsonian Institution's National Museum of Design, New York; The Royal Pavilion, Art Gallery and Museums, Brighton.
3. This distinction was first made by Mrs. Elfrida Mostyn in the 1960s when she compiled a large amount of information on the Craces. The documents she collected form the bulk of the Mostyn-Crace collection, now in the MSS collection of the V & A.
4. These are found in the Mostyn-Crace collection, acquired by the V & A in 1977.
5. Thomas Crace married Mary Gregory in 1718; John Crace married Ann Eastham, niece of Henry Gregory, in 1776; and Frederick Crace married Augusta Gregory in 1804.
6. Three drawings attributed to Charles Crace for coach panels are in C-H, 1948-40-184, 185, 187. In 1750 Charles Crace published a set of plates for coach designs (Metropolitan Museum of Art, see *The Carriage Journal*, IV, no.3, 1962). A book of coach panel designs by Edward Crace is in a private collection.
7. See V & A, JFC-19.
8. See an account of his grandfather by Frederick Crace, V & A, EC-1.
9. The original building burned in 1792, and the site is now occupied by Marks and Spencer. See London County Council, *Survey of London*, 31, *The Parish of St.*

James Westminster, Sheppard, F.H.W., gen. ed. London, 1963, pp.268–273.
10. As quoted in Wells, William 'The Pantheon, Oxford Road', *Leeds Art Calendar*, 5 (Winter 1952), p.11.
11. In the collection of the Leeds City Art Gallery.
12. Trotter, William Edward, *Select Illustrated Topography of Thirty Miles round London*, 1839, p.107; as cited in Edward Croft-Murray, *Decorative Painting in England, 1537–1837*, 2, *The Eighteenth and Early Nineteenth Centuries*, Feltham, Middlesex, 1970, p.196.
13. *Survey of London*, 31, p.273.
14. Public Record Office, London; PRO C12/2003 28.
15. J. G. Crace, 'Early History', typescript, C-H, Department of Drawings and Prints, n.d.
16. This was before 1778, the publication date of Crace's catalogue of the pictures in Kensington Palace, Hence the date of 1781 given by Frederick Crace (V & A, EC-1), which has been repeated in more modern accounts of the firm, is wrong.
17. V & A, EC-1, p.3.
18. *A Catalogue of the Pictures, etc. in His Majesty's Royal Apartments, Kensington Palace*, 1778; V & A, EC-31; and 'Queens Palace' (now Buckingham Palace) V & A, EC-28.
19. Notes by John Dibblee Crace in the V & A, EC-20, p.4.
20. V & A, EC-1, p.1.
21. Painted *c.*1800, the portrait is in a private collection.
22. Two certificates for their marriage, dated January 1776 in Gretna Green and August 1776 in London, are in the V & A, JC-11, 1 and 2.

23. V & A, JC–3, notes by Frederick Crace.

24. In the account of John Crace by his son Frederick Crace (JC–3); the certificate of John Crace's Freedom of the Company is in the V & A, JC–7.

25. C-H, 1948–40–103.

26. V & A, JC–8.

27. *Ibid.*, JC–8.

28. See Collard, Frances, *Regency Furniture*, Woodbridge, Suffolk, 1985, p.333.

29. V & A, JC–12.

30. V & A, Department of Furniture and Woodwork, Information section for Althorp.

31. V & A, JC–3, unpaginated.

32. *Ibid.*

33. Now in the Sir John Soane Museum. See Stroud, Dorothy, *Sir John Soane, Architect*, London, 1984, p.65.

34. See Rosoman, Treve, 'The Pitzhanger Story', *Traditional Interior Decoration*, 2, October/November 1987, p.127; and Binney, Marcus, 'An Extension to the Soane Museum', *Country Life*, 151, May 25, 1972, p.1307.

35. C-H, 1948–40–72, 180 & 181.

36. V & A, JC–3, unpaginated.

37. In Walpole, Horace *Anecdotes of Painting in England*, 4, Strawberry Hill, 1771, pp.162–66.

38. Britton, John and Pugin, Augustus, *Illustrations of the Public Buildings of London*, 2, London, 1828, pp.193–201.

39. See Croft-Murray, Edward, *Decorative Painting in England 1537–1837*, 2, *The Eighteenth and Early Nineteenth Centuries*, Feltham, Middlesex, 1970, Catalogue of Painters.

40. London, 2, p.199. See also Watkin, David, *The Royal Interiors of Regency England*, London, 1984, p.112.

41. Scottish Record Office, Edinburgh GD147/54/1/1 and GD147/56/1/11. In both documents he is listed as 'Mr. Grace', a misspelling which occurred with regularity in early documents pertaining to the firm.

42. For further information see Stroud, Dorothy, *Henry Holland, His Life and Architecture*, London, 1966.

43. V & A, FC–41, unpaginated.

44. These were Woburn Abbey, Althorp, 12 Lincoln's Inn Fields, Pitzhanger Manor, the Bank of England, and Aynhoe Park. The accounts in the Soane Museum are yielding further information on John Crace's work as they are catalogued by Susan Palmer.

45. C-H, 1948–48–157, 163, 164.

46. C-H, Department of Drawings and Prints; Crace, J. G. 'Early History', typescript, n.d., p.4.

47. *Ibid.*, p.5.

48. Mr. Sotheby, *A Catalogue of the English Historical Library of the Late John Crace, Esq.*, July 7, 1819; V & A, JC–1.

49. See Stroud, *Henry Holland*, London, 1966, and

Sheraton, Thomas, *The Cabinet Maker and Upholsterer's Drawing Book*, third edition, revised 1793–94, London, 1802, Plate 32.

50. See Stroud, Dorothy, 'Woburn Abbey, Bedfordshire, The Last Phase', 2, *Country Life*, 138, July 15, 1965, p.159.

51. C-H, 1948–40–65.

52. Morley, John, *The Making of the Royal Pavilion, Brighton*, London, 1984, p.106.

53. V & A, JC–17.

54. Accession no.1948–40–46.

55. In 'Regency Styling: The Prince and the Decorator Frederick Crace (1779–1849) [sic] at the Royal Pavilion, Brighton', *The Connoisseur*, 131, June 1953, p.130. Drawings attributed by Bloch to 'Anonymous Designer I' can, for the most part, be assigned to Frederick Crace.

56. 'Copies of ledger entries from the Books of Messrs. Crace & Sons [sic] now in the possession of Messrs. Cowtan & Sons Ltd. of 18 Grosvenor Gardens, London. SW1, and of New York, who acquired them on taking over the business of Messrs. Crace in 1899', typescript, n.d., The Royal Pavilion, Art Gallery and Museums, Brighton.

57. As John Dinkel has remarked, the Craces collected 'every conceivable type of article of Chinese workmanship' from the East India wharves in London. See Brighton Borough Council, *The Royal Pavilion, Brighton*, London, 1983, p.38.

58. *The Royal Pavilion, Brighton*, p.38.

59. The Royal Pavilion, Art Gallery and Museums, typescript of Crace accounts, p.31.

60. *Ibid.*, pp.32–39.

61. *Ibid.*, p.43.

62. *Ibid.*, pp.50–1.

63. *Ibid.*, p.4. Edward Gray Saunders worked chiefly in the capacity of a builder at the Pavilion early in the nineteenth century. See Roberts, Henry D., *A History of the Royal Pavilion, Brighton*, London, 1939, pp.58–61.

64. Temple Williams Antiques, in *Country Life*, 143, April 4, 1968, supplement, p.51, attributed to Frederick Crace.

65. C-H, 1948–40–26, see Morley, *Brighton*, p.221.

66. The Royal Pavilion, Art Gallery and Museums, Brighton, typescript of Crace accounts, p.49.

67. *Ibid.*, pp.54.

68. C-H, 1948–40–39, see Morley, *Brighton*, p.154, plate 148.

69. C-H, 1948–40–26, illustrated in Morley, *Brighton*, p.221.

70. Cited in 'The Pavilion A Hundred Years Ago', *The Herald*, January 5, 1907; V & A, FC–24.

71. See, for example, C-H, 1948–40–67, illustrated in Morley, *Brighton*, p.116, plate 94.

72. V & A, FC–12, 16, 22; in addition, a bill of 1819 from Frances Bernasconi to Frederick Crace for plasterwork at the Pavilion, is document FC–18.

73. V & A, Department of Furniture and Woodwork, W.1–1966.

74. The rest of the suite comprised a secretaire and a daybed which appeared on the London art market in 1961 and 1975, respectively.

75. C-H, 1948–40–9A & B; see Morley, *Brighton*, cover illustration.

76. This may be an example of Crace borrowing decoration directly from Oriental sources.

77. The Royal Pavilion, Art Gallery and Museums, Brighton, no.102649, illustrated in Morley, *Brighton*, p.191, plate 227.

78. Morley, *Brighton*, p.270. Preliminary designs for the Brighton corridor are contained in a sketchbook in the V & A, FC–28.

79. C-H, 1948–40–11, 12, 13, 14, 22.

80. See Roberts, *Brighton*, p.134 and plate 38, and Collard, *Regency Furniture*, p.330.

81. For further information on Lambelet, see Croft-Murray, Edward, Catalogue of Painters.

82. As quoted in Roberts, *Brighton*, p.133.

83. Several of his drawings are among the Crace drawings in the C-H. See Dinkel, *Brighton*, p.71ff.

84. See Dinkel, Morley, Roberts.

85. Public Record Office, Work 1/16, 20 December 1827. See Linstrum, Derek, *Sir Jeffry Wyatville, Architect to the King*, Oxford, 1972, p.202.

86. C-H, 1948–40–96a and b, 97.

87. As cited in the *Sunday Observer* (11 December 1927), V & A, FC–11.

88. Robinson, John Martin, *Royal Residences*, London, 1982, p.164.

89. Now with the Mostyn-Crace papers in the V & A.

90. This cutting is now in the V & A, JC–6.

91. 24 September 1859; V & A, FC–10.

92. Linstrum, *Sir Jeffry Wyatville*, pp.185–86.

93. As quoted in Fitzgerald, Shaunagh, 'Designs for Decoration in the Private Apartments of Windsor Castle', the *Connoisseur*, 175, December 1970, p.222.

94. It is illustrated in Plumb, J. H., *Royal Heritage: The Story of Britain's Royal Builders and Collectors*, second edition, London, 1984, p.222.

95. 'Sketches, designs and studies by John G. Crace/ 1825 to 1880', RIBA, Drawings Collection.

96. *Ibid.*, folio 12 nos.1 and 2.

97. *Ibid.*, folio 15, no.6. This study, a caricature of the Prince Regent, contains a note on the back by Frederick Crace which has been partially cut down. It was evidently the draft of a thank-you letter for hospitality extended to his son, presumably J. G. Crace, 'during his stay at Kilboy,' a seat near Tipperary. See V & A, FC–28, especially pp.11–14. Despite the fact that several pages bear a watermarked date of '1799', the majority of drawings seem to date to the 1820s.

98. Sotheby Park Burnet (9 April 1970), *London, Catalogue of Designs for the Private Apartments at Windsor Castle by Sir Jeffry Wyatville, The Property of D. Lowsley-Williams, Esq.*

99. de Bellaigue, Geoffrey, and Kirkham, Pat, 'George IV and the Furnishing of Windsor Castle', *Furniture History* (1972), pp.1–34.

100. An autobiographical account by J. G. Crace, written in 1881; V & A, JGC–21, unpaginated.

101. *Ibid.*

102. Linstrum, *op. cit.*, p.193.

103. Mordaunt Crook, J. and Port, M. H., *The History of the King's Works*, 6, 1782–1852, London, 1973, p.284.

104. The collection was catalogued in 1878 by J. G. Crace, exhibited at the South Kensington Museum in 1879, and purchased by the British Museum in 1881. See Crace, J. G. 'Old London', *Society of Arts Journal*, 15 (December 1866), pp.53–62; and Crace J. G., ed. *A Catalogue of Maps, Plans and Views of London*, London, 1878.

105. For example, a watercolour by Shepherd of c.1837 shows the Crace premises at 14 Wigmore Street, London. The front showroom with its Renaissance-style decoration is clearly visible through the window from the street. (C-H, 1948–40–98.)

106. Augusta Gregory, the daughter of John Gregory of Chelsea had married Frederick Crace in 1804.

107. See V & A, JG–55, 58 and 64. In addition, JG–54 is a document giving power of attorney to Frederick Crace in 1813, so that he could manage the properties and investments of the widow of John Gregory.

2   Charles and Edward Crace and Rococo Coach Painting pp.33 to 41

1. Humphreys, A. L., 'Long Acre and the Coach-makers', *Notes and Queries*, CLXXXI, p.215. There is no recent comprehensive work on English eighteenth-century coachmaking, but see Felton, W., *A Treatise on Carriages*, London, printed and sold by the author, 1794, and Watney, M., *The Elegant Carriage*, London, 1961 (with bibliography).

2. 'Whereas it is customary for all Gentlemen to see

Draughts of Coaches, &c. before they fix or bespeak the same: This is to inform as well such Gentlemen as those of the Trade that by enquiring at Jacob Smith's Birmingham Warehouse, over against the White-Bear in Long-Acre, near Drury Lane, they may be supplied with Draughts of all the different sorts of Carriages . . . all of which are drawn in the newest and Genteelest Taste, and perfect by Scale to work after, by CHARLES CRACE, who has designed and drawn for the Trade several years, and has just finish'd a complete Collection of the same, particularly some new Designs in the French and Chinese taste. Apprentices, or those designed for the Trade, taught Drawings as above' (newspaper cutting from an unidentified journal dated by hand 1756, formerly attached to a Crace design at the C-H, 1948-40-185).

3. See trade cards of John Bromley, James Theebridge, Augustus Sims, Thomas Tillinghast and others in the Heal and Banks collections, British Museum. The design of Bromley's card is close to the Crace coach decorations. These cards suggest that the decorative part of coach painting was, or could be, separated from the plain body painting. Mortimer confines coach painters 'to those artists alone, who paint History, Landscape, Figures, and Flowers, on State and other Coaches, which are often executed in as masterly a manner as any other Paintings' (*Universal Director*, 1763, p.6). He lists only Charles Catton. The painting of coats of arms was the cause of a long conflict between the Painter Stainers Company (to which most coach painters belonged) and the Herald Painters of the College of Arms.

4. e.g. Charles Catton, G. B. Cipriani, John Crome, J. F. Herring, John Martin, Peter Monamy, J. H. Mortimer and Clarkson Stanfield. See Stewart, B. and Cutten, M., *The Shayer Family of Painters*, 1981, pp.1–3. William Shayer worked as a heraldic artist to a coachmaker. I am indebted for this reference to David Coke.

5. *Rococo, Art and Design in Hogarth's England*, 1984, pp.30–32, cat.E.20, 21 and *passim*. George Edwards's and Matthew Darly's drawing school was for 'artificers and mechanics of all Branches, and that Kind of Drawing that is proper for their different callings' (*Daily Advertiser*, 12 December 1755).

6. The design book (Private collection, cover size 215 × 277mm) contains 35 drawings, 34 of which are pasted onto 16 leaves of late eighteenth-century laid paper. One of the pages has been cut and the remnant used as a guard for another sheet of paper of the same type. The remnant shows oxidised metallic paint, suggesting that the book had very briefly been intended to have designs executed on the pages themselves. Traces of blue sugar paper in the binding show that such a paper cover originally protected the roughly

stab-bound pages, which were probably assembled in the late eighteenth century. About 1830 the pages were given marbled paper boards and perhaps the wove paper and end papers (one watermarked 180...). It is possible that the drawings were pasted in at that date. During the second half of the nineteenth century a morocco spine was added which is lettered in gold 'Drawing of Ornament for Coach Panel, by Edward Crace' with the date in gold '1764' on a separate piece of leather applied. This spine was probably pirated from a mid-nineteenth-century portfolio. The drawings are executed on thin sheets of laid paper in pencil and wash, body colour and metallic paint. Some of the colours, especially the greens, have faded and sunk into the page in an oily halo (there are also other oil stains). It is possible that the draughtsman was using oil-medium paint to replicate accurately the colours of the coach panels. Most of the sheets show signs of having been folded into four. Two designs have been silhouetted and mounted onto thin secondary sheets. The subjects are: 7 designs for full panels, 17 designs for panel decoration in the form of imaginary structures, 7 designs for the decoration of sides of *carrosses coupés* and 3 for Berlin coaches. The remaining drawings are for the surrounds of armorial decoration, and a coat of arms. There are four Crace designs for coach painting at the C-H, all of which correspond closely to the designs in the book. Indeed, the two smaller drawings may have been cut from the book, which contains the remnants of several cut-out pages. 1948-40-186, 187, are large fully-worked sample sheets, related to panel designs in the book. One is inscribed on the back in a nineteenth-century hand 'a Drawing by Charles Crace'. A silhouetted design for a *carosse coupé* (1948-40-184) is inscribed in a pencil in a late hand 'C. Crace 1756' while a design for a Berlin (1948-40-18), linked to the series in the design book, is inscribed in pencil in a later hand 'Charles Crace 1754'. This last design, and several in the design book, bear rough sketches of family crests. It is probable that these are imaginary. (I am indebted to Stephen Calloway and Jim Murrell for the technical aspects of this note.)

7. Waterhouse, E., *The Dictionary of British 18th-Century Artists in Oils and Crayons*, 1881, p.81. See also Croft-Murray, E., *Decorative Painting in England, 1537–1837*, vol.II, 1970, pp.185–190. For the Avery book see Harris, J., *A Catalogue of British Drawings for Architecture . . . in American Collections*, Upper Saddle River, 1971, p.72. A sketch of a standing figure of Justice is probably related to a similar figure painted on the Lord Mayor's Coach (1757). Several of the drawings are for sign boards. A drawing by Cipriani, not in the volume, of the birth of Venus, is surrounded with mantling of coach-painting type (Christie's, 15.11.1988, lot 6).

8. Francois Boucher, *Recueil de Fontaines*. Frederick Bloemaert after Abraham Bloemaert, 'Lente' copied by Cipriani on p.1 (*Konstryk Tekenboek van Abraham Bloemaert*, Amsterdam, 1740, *Troisième Partie*, pl.76).

9. e.g. *Livre d'Ornements*, c.1740 (Berliner, R., and Egger, G. *Ornamentale Vorlageblätter*, Munich , 1981, 1280–1283).

10. cf also the simple foliage-clasped vases in many of the Crace designs with the strikingly similar vase in the title plate of Babel's *Cartouche représentant fontaines et jardinages*. Close to several of the Crace compositions are the wall decorations of a doll's house at Haarlem (Pijzel-Dommisse, J. *'t Is poppe goet esanders niet*, Haarlem, 1983, p.73). Very similar imaginary structures are to be found in *A New Drawing Book of Ornaments, Shields . . . &c*, a set of six plates, one of which is dated 1752 (Heckscher, M. 'Lock and Copland: A Catalogue of the Engraved Ornament', *Furniture History*, XV, 1979, p.17).

11. Hayward H., and Kirkham, P., *William and John Linnell, 18th-century furniture makers*, 1980, vol.II, no.314.

12. Girouard, M. 'The Apotheosis of Rococo, The Lord Mayor's Coach', *Country Life*, CL, 16 November 1978, pp.1596–1598.

13. Described as a coach painter's crest book, it shows whole coats of arms with the bearers named and dates between 1755 and 1758. Also inscribed are the names of the (?) makers Poole, Beach and Lancaster.

14. D.358–360, 363–366–1886. They are clearly sample patterns, being inscribed with numbers on the back. Two are in the Cuvilliés-like style used by Cipriani. One is signed and dated (?) J1791, a plausible date in view of their handling.

15. Title and twelve plates. The only complete set known to me (and it is hand-coloured) is at the Yale Center for British Art (L 397.8 (4°). It was published by A. Webley who also published in the same year *The Nobleman and Gentleman's Director and Assistant, in the True Choice of their Wheel-Carriages*, (title and 35 plates) the plates of which resemble the Crace book of 1750 in their treatment, and show no decoration.

16. A fashion lifted directly from Continental precedents (c.f. R. Wackernagel, *Fransösische Kronungswagen von 1695–1825*, Berlin, 1966, pl.xxivd.

17. e.g. in such prints as 'The Scald Miserable Masons' by J. Benoist of 1742 (Phillips, H., *Mid-Georgian London*, 1964, fig.226). Panels were also painted with simple diaper patterns as in the satirical print 'Stand Coachman, or the haughty lady well fitted' of 1750 (Phillips, *op. cit.*, fig.116). The Darnley Chariot of 1715, formerly at Cobham Hall (*The Carriage Journal*, vol.2, no.2, 1964, p.47, ill.49) has elaborate armorials augmented with naturalistic floral decoration. The Trewinnard Coach of c.1735, at Truro Museum, is painted with small cartouches of early English Rococo type (*The Carriage Journal*, vol.2, no.4, 1965, p.135, ill.57). Against this must be set the elaborate Rococo decoration of c.1750 on the Baskerville Dress Landau of c.1700, at the Nottingham Industrial Museum (*The Carriage Journal*, vol.6, no.1, 1968, p.6, ill.126), and that on a number of sedan chairs painted with putti and Watteauesque scenes in scrollwork, which have presumably escaped the frequent repaintings to which coaches were subject. Felton (1792), who shows only the simplest armorials and a small range of field patterns, interestingly states:

> The ornament painting is merely to beautify the carriage, which it does materially, when it is well executed; but when otherwise, it hurts the appearance of it. This depends on the capacity of the artist: the pannels had better be entirely plain, than daubed as many of them are, in imitation of painting; and in particular that of Heraldry, which requires some merit to execute properly. (*Op. cit.*, p.107)

suggesting that fully decorated coaches were more common than the surviving evidence would lead one to expect.

18. C-H, 1948–40–185 (*Rococo*, 1984, cat.L76).

19. cf the vase treatments with those of Maurice Jacques's set of c.1765, *Vases Nouveaux*. Pillement's *Fleurs de Caprice* and *Fleurs de Fantaisie*, were published in London in 1760, but flowers in his style were used on trade cards c.1755–60 (*Rococo*, 1984, cat.R6, 7e).

20. Six pages without title, each lettered 'C Crace Delin. F. Patton Sculp' and with a publication line dated 1750. The only copy known to me is at the Metropolitan Museum of Art, New York (2723.64).

21. I have been unable to find French coaches painted in the Crace manner.

3   The Royal Pavilion, Brighton: Chinoiserie Designs by Frederick Crace
pp. 42 to 50

1. See Medley, Margaret, *A Handbook of Chinese Art*, London, 1977, p.95.

2. See Brankston, Archibald, *The Early Ming Wares from Ching-te-chen*, 1938 (reprinted Hong Kong, 1970), p.76.

3. See Medley, *op. cit.*, pp.49 and 99.

4. See Lang, Gordon, *The Wrestling Boys*, Stamford, Burghley House, 1983, no.245.

5. Wirgin, Jan, *Song Ceramic Designs*, p.179.

6. See Wilson, Verity, *Chinese Dress*, London, 1986, p.41, no.26.

7. Morley, John, *The Making of the Royal Pavilion, Brighton*, London, 1984, p.192.

8. See Wilson, *op. cit.*, p.102, no.87.

4   The Victorian Craces pp. 53 to 136

1. V & A, JGC–15.

2. See Gow, Ian, 'The First Intellectual Housepainter', *The World of Interiors*, May 1984, pp.18–19. For further information on Hay, see Wainwright, Clive, *The Romantic Interior*, London, 1989, p.167.

3. This branch of the family was redeemed by Dr. Frederick Crace-Calvert, the son of Alfred Crace, who became an internationally known expert on the dyeing of textiles. (Frederick Crace-Calvert, *Dyeing and Calico Printing*, Manchester, 1876.)

4. V & A, JGC–37; dated 1829. Crace travelled in the company of an older family acquaintance, Mr. Buchan.

5. V & A, JGC–37; notes made on 25, 26, and 27 June 1829.

6. This is evident in the titles applied by the publisher John Weale to re-issues of eighteenth-century designs. See Aldrich, Megan, 'Looking Glasses in the Chippendale Style', *Antique Collecting*, 21 October 1986, p.77.

7. V & A, JGC–37.

8. *Ibid.*

9. *Ibid.*

10. Christie, Manson & Woods, *Fine Architectural and Decorative Drawings*, London, 13 December 1988, lots 82 and 84, and 89–90, respectively.

11. London County Council, *Survey of London*, 30, *Parish of St. James Westminster*, Part 1, *South of Piccadilly*, F. H. W. Sheppard, gen. ed. London, 1960, p.301.

12. V & A, JGC–37.

13. *Ibid.* Entry for 4 July.

14. *Ibid.*

15. *Ibid.* 20 July.

16. *Ibid.* 21 July.

17. *Ibid.* 23 July.

18. *Ibid.* 7 August.

19. See the entry in Jervis, Simon, *The Penguin Dictionary of Design and Designers*, Harmondsworth, 1984, pp.360–61.

20. V & A, JGC–21.

21. V & A, FC–1.

22. At 31 North Street.

23. V & A, JGC–21; this was in 1827. There are several portraits of members of his family by F. H. Crace in a private collection.

24. V & A, JGC–21.

25. *Ibid.* JGC–20.

26. *Ibid.*

27. *Ibid.*

28. *Ibid.*

29. Two examples of these invitation cards are in public collections. In the V & A is JGC–27, while the C-H has another example, 1948–40–101, addressed to Mr. Chawner and dated 3 June 1839. Chawner worked in the Office of Sir John Soane and was a friend of John Crace.

30. C-H no.1948–40–98.

31. *Ibid.* 1948–40–102.

32. In Cornforth, John, 'Arlington Court, Devon', 1, *Country Life*, 169, 30 April 1981, p.1180.

33. See Nouvel, Odile, *Wall-papers of France, 1800–1850*, trans. Timmers, Margaret, London, 1981, pp.52–55.

34. The letter is in the Devon Record Office and is quoted in Cornforth, 'Arlington Court', p.1180.

35. V & A, JGC–21.

36. V & A, Department of Prints and Drawings, E.746–1981, 746–1981, 744–1981, 716–1981.

37. *Ibid.* 1832–1912.

38. Chancellor, E. B., *The Private Palaces of London*, London, 1908, p.246.

39. V & A, JGC–38.

40. Reference no.C/165/B.

41. 'Devonshire House, Chiswick, Chatsworth and Brighton Household, 1848'.

42. See note 40.

43. See note 41.

44. As described by the 6th Duke of Devonshire in his 'Handbook' to Chatsworth of 1844. A watercolour of the room before Crace decorated it is reproduced

in Cornforth, John, *English Interiors, 1790–1848: The Quest for Comfort*, London, 1978, p.32.

45. The Duchess of Devonshire, *The House, A Portrait of Chatsworth*, London, 1982, p.156.

46. RIBA Album, folio 32.

47. As quoted in *The House*, p.155.

48. In 'John G. Crace & Son', *The Little Journal*, 1, May 1884, p.142. V & A, JGC–22.

49. See Chatsworth Household Accounts, Ref. no.C/165/B, and the volume for 1848.

50. As noted by James Macaulay, it is highly likely that Graham had the assistance of the young A. W. N. Pugin at Taymouth. See 'The Architectural Collaboration Between J. Gillespie Graham and A. W. Pugin', *Architectural History*, 27, 1984, p.410.

51. Rowan, Alistair, 'Taymouth Castle, Perthshire', 2, *Country Life*, 136, 15 October, 1964, p.980.

52. *Ibid*.

53. V & A, Department of Prints and Drawings, E.2743–1914.

54. Scottish Record Office, Ref.GD112/20/1/46/1.

55. V & A, Department of Prints and Drawings, E.1827–1912. It is illustrated in Darby, M. & J., Physick, J., *Marble Halls*. London 1973, p.156.

56. See Rowan, 'Taymouth', 1 and 2, *Country Life*, 136, 8 and 15 October 1964, pp.912–16 and 978–81.

57. SRO GD112/20/146/1.

58. See Thornton, Peter, *Seventeenth-Century Interior Decoration in England, France and Holland*, London, 1978, p.35, fig.41.

59. V & A, JGC–3; seven letters, 7 September to 7 October 1843.

60. Crace's lecture has been published in the *R.I.B.A Papers*, 4, 1835–45, unpaginated.

61. Boase, T. S. R., *English Art, 1800–1870*, Oxford, 1959, pp.208–09.

62. Hobhouse, Hermione, *Prince Albert, His Life and Work*, London, 1983, p.85.

63. See V & A MSS 86.MM.44, Pugin's notes on travels to Munich, Augsburg, Ulm and Lucerne in 1838.

64. The principal artist was Julius Schnorr von Carolsfeld. See Nowald, Inken, *Die Nibelungenfresken von Julius Schnorr von Carolsfeld im Konigsbau der Munchner Residenz, 1827–1867*, Kiel, Schriften der Kunsthalle, 1978.

65. See RIBA, *Catalogue C–F*, pp.51–52.

66. *RIBA Proceedings*, 1st series, 1850–51, unpaginated.

67. In *Ibid*., p.1.

68. *Ibid*., p.1.

69. In Anon., 'John G. Crace and Son', *The Little Journal*, p.142.

70. The increasing interest in using interiors as a means of displaying groups of objects can be linked to the Romantic Movement as a whole. See Wainwright, *The Romantic Interior*.

71. Crace, 'Buildings at Munich', p.3.

72. See Nowald, *Die Niebelungenfresken*; and Brunner, Herbert, and Hojer, Gerhard, *Residenz Munchen: A Guide to the former Royal Palace Munich*, Munich, Bayerische Verwaltung der staatlichen Schlosser, Garten und Seen (1982), pp.114–117.

73. See Flower, Sibylla Jane, 'Knebworth House, Hertfordshire', 1, *Country Life*, 177, 31 January 1985, pp.244–48; and 2, 7 February 1985, pp.320–23.

74. Girouard, Mark, *The Victorian Country House*, London, 1979, p.108 and p.447, n.9.

75. Flower, 'Knebworth', p.322.

76. See Flower, Sibylla Jane, *The Stately Homes of Britain*, Devon, 1982, p.185.

77. Crace, 'Buildings at Munich', p.5.

78. This device was used by Pugin in designs for Abney Hall, executed by J. G. Crace, *c*.1853.

79. Crace Album.

80. In the Hertfordshire County Record Office, but on loan to Knebworth House.

81. Collard, Frances, *Regency Furniture*, Woodbridge, The Antique Collectors' Club, 1985, p.179. An example of this suite can be seen in the Robing Room at the Palace of Westminster.

82. In 'Augustus Welby Pugin, and Furniture', *R.I.B.A. Journal 1*, 3rd series (1894), pp.517–19.

83. Especially in *The True Principles of Pointed or Christian Architecture*, London, 1841, considered by some to be his definitive manifesto on the principles of nineteenth century design.

84. See pp.137–145 of this book.

85. Crace MSS, Box 1, RIBA Library.

86. For further information see Hussey, Christopher, 'Alton Towers, Staffordshire', 2, *Country Life*, 127 (9 June 1960), pp.1304–07.

87. *Ibid*., PUG 1/2, 1/4, 1/5 and 1/7. See Wedgwood, Alexandra, *A. W. N. Pugin and the Pugin Family: Catalogues of Architectural Drawings in the Victoria and Albert Museum*, London, 1985, pp.175–76.

88. See Wedgwood, *Pugin and Family*, pp.231–34.

89. RIBA Library, Crace MSS, Box 1, PUG 13/4.

90. *Ibid*. PUG 1/30.

91. *Ibid*. PUG 3/14.

92. See Mordaunt Crook, J., and Port, M. H., *The History of the King's Works*, 6, *1782–1851*, London, 1973, p.614; and RIBA Library, Crace MSS, Box 1, PUG 13/3.

93. See Port, M. H., ed., *The Houses of Parliament*, London, 1976, especially chapters 8 and 9. See also Wedgwood, *Pugin and Family*, pp.203–28.

94. Stanton, Phoebe, *Pugin*, London, 1971, p.183.

95. Crace, John G., 'The Decorations of Chirk Castle',

The Builder, 13, 22 September 1855, p.449.

96. *Ibid.*

97. Grüner, Ludwig, *Fresco Decorations and Stuccoes of Churches and Palaces in Italy, during the 15th and 16th centuries*, London, 1844.

98. Crace, 'Chirk', p.449.

99. V & A, Department of Prints and Drawings, E.2746-50-1914. An additional drawing by Crace for the House of Lords ceiling is in the RIBA Library, see *Catalogue, C–F*, p.49.

100. See Wedgwood, 'Crace and Pugin' (in this book), p.138.

101. See Fig.5:1.

102. 'An Account of the Palace of Blois and Palace of Chambord, France', *The Builder*, 5, 5 June 1847, pp.263–64.

103. *Ibid.*, p.264.

104. Charlton, L. E. O., ed., *The Recollections of a Northumbrian Lady, 1815–1866, being the Memoirs of Barbara Charlton*, London, 1949, p.175.

105. 'Gilling Castle, Yorkshire', *Country Life*, 24, 26 September 1908, p.423.

106. *The Buildings of England: Lancashire 1, The Industrial and Commercial South*, Harmondsworth, 1969, p.128.

107. The Picture Gallery ceiling is illustrated in, Hussey, Christopher, 'Ince Blundell Hall, Lancashire', 1, *Country Life*, 123, 10 April 1958, p.876. Crace's wall decoration had been painted over by this date.

108. A discussion of the individual designs by Pugin for Eastnor and Lismore, as executed by Crace, is contained in Wedgwood, *Pugin and Family*, pp.192–94 and 197–200.

109. *Ibid.*, p.194. The Drawing Room is illustrated in Barker, Godfrey, 'Eastnor Castle', *Connoisseur*, 208, October 1981, pp.97–100.

110. Metropolitan Museum of Art, Department of Drawings, Prints and Photographs, 67.736.49; for Pugin's designs, see Wedgwood, *Pugin and Family*, pp.192–94.

111. *Ibid.*, pp.194–95.

112. The library table was recently shown in Washington, D.C. See *The Treasure Houses of Britain: Five Hundred Years of Private Patronage and Art Collecting*, Jackson-Stops, Gervase, ed., New Haven and London, 1985, p.609.

113. Girouard, Mark, 'Lismore Castle, Co. Waterford', 2, *Country Life*, 136, 13 August, 1964, pp.389–93.

114. Wedgwood, *Pugin and Family*, pp.199–200.

115. Department of Prints and Drawings, X626/3815-1953.

116. 'Messrs. John G. Crace & Sons, 1887'; V & A, JGC–24.

117. A watercolour of Crace's panel, prepared for M. D. Wyatt's publication on the exhibition, is seen here. V & A, Department of Prints and Drawings, E.731-1950.

118. The Art Journal, *The Crystal Palace Exhibition Illustrated Catalogue, London 1851*, facsimile edition, intro. Gloag, John, New York, 1970, p.318.

119. Wedgwood, *Pugin*, pp.191–92.

120. Art Journal, *Catalogue*, p.317; V & A, W.25-1852.

121. *An Illustrated Cyclopedia of the Great Exhibition of 1851*, London, n.p., 1851, p.218.

122. V & A, Department of Prints and Drawings, E.1831-1912.

123. J. G. Crace, 'Munich', p.6.

124. Hobhouse, *Prince Albert*, p.134.

125. For further information see Aldrich, Megan, 'Gothic Interiors of the 19th Century: John Gregory Crace at Abney Hall', *V & A Album*, 5, 1986, pp.76–84.

126. Wedgwood, *Pugin*, pp.188–89.

127. This phenomenon is discussed in Girouard, Mark, *The Victorian Country House*, pp.10–13.

128. Wedgwood, *Pugin*, p.189; V & A, Department of Prints and Drawings, E.1518-1912.

129. *Ibid.*, p.188, cat. no.259.

130. *Ibid.*, cat. no.252 and 254, left-hand design only.

131. See V & A, Department of Furniture, Mostyn-Crace Boxes I–V. These photographs were acquired by Mrs. Elfrida Mostyn from a descendant of James Watts during her research on the house. See Mostyn, Elfrida, 'Abney Hall, Cheshire, 1, *Country Life*, 18 April 1963, pp.846–49; and 2, 25 April 1963, pp.910–13.

132. Kelly, Frederic, *The Post Office London Directory for 1854*, London, 1853, p.809.

133. The furniture was moved to Callally Castle, Northumberland, and sold in 1986. See Christie, Manson & Woods, *Callally Castle, Alnwick, Northumberland*, 22–24 September 1986, pp.85–99. Lot 133 (p.90) is especially close to the Abney furniture.

134. See *The Treasure Houses of Britain*, p.609.

135. Department of Furniture, Circ.334-1958.

136. The library bookcases, in store at Bramall Hall.

137. See Wedgwood, *Pugin*, pp.192–94.

138. For other furniture from Abney Hall, see Sotheby's *Applied Arts from 1880*, London, 19 December 1986, lots 367–72.

139. V & A, JGC–20.

140. *Ibid.*, JGC–4, 5, and 7.

141. V & A, Department of Furniture Mostyn Box III.

142. V & A, JGC–7.

143. 9 May 1857.

144. See Wedgwood, Fig.5:1.

145. V & A, Department of Furniture Mostyn Box III.

146. See Wainwright, Clive. 'The Speaker's State Bed',

V & A Album 2 (1983), pp.67–73.

147. See the essay by Alexandra Wedgwood, p.137 in this book.

148. Christie's, *Callaly*, lots 134 and 137.

149. See pp.96–98 of this book.

150. See Metropolitan Museum of Art, NY, 67.736.55.

151. See 'Her Majesty's Visit to the Marquis and Marchioness of Breadalbane', *The Illustrated London News*, 24, 17 June 1854, pp.579–80.

152. The design is now in the V & A, Department of Prints and Drawings, E.2751–1914.

153. *Ibid.*, E.1753–1914. 'Illustrations of the Royal Visit to the City: The Guildhall – The Decorations', *The Illustrated London News*, 42, 20 June 1863, p.678.

154. Stewart, Noel, 'Government House, Perth', *Historic Houses of Australia*, Melbourne and Sydney, 1974, pp.132–39.

155. Crace's signed drawing for the ceiling is at Government House, Perth.

156. See Government House, Perth, 'The Crace Affair', typescript, n.d. I am indebted to Mr. Hugh Samson, Official Secretary in 1986, for supplying me with a copy of the manuscript, which is based upon extracts from the nineteenth-century correspondence.

157. Kelly, Frederic, *The Post Office Directory of London*, London, 1885.

158. 'The Crace Affair', p.2.

159. Illustrated in Aldrich, 'Abney', p.83. Crace's Gothic chimneypiece and a chair are visible to the right of the table.

160. See note 158.

161. *The Times*, 22 November 1919; V & A, JDC–19.

162. C-H, Department of Drawing and Prints, 'John Dibblee Crace', typescript, p.21.

163. For further information see Aldrich, Megan, 'Fit for an Emperor at Windsor', *Country Life*, 8 December 1988, pp.56–59.

164. Queen Victoria, *Leaves from a Journal: A Record of the Visit of the Emperor and Empress of the French . . . 1855*. intro. Raymond Mortimer, London, 1961, p.27.

165. The Van Dyke Room, before its re-decoration in 1855, is illustrated in Mackworth-Young, Robin, *The History and Treasures of Windsor Castle*, rev. ed. Andover, 1988, front cover.

166. Christie, Manson & Woods, *Fine Architectural and Decorative Drawings*, London, 13 December 1988, lots 112, 114–15.

167. V & A, JGC–7.

168. See 'The Cult of the Obscure', *House and Garden*, 11 May 1985, p.119. These curtains, now in a private collection, are illustrated.

169. V & A, JDC–50.

170. Aldrich, 'Windsor', Figure 4.

171. V & A, JGC–7.

172. Windsor, Royal Archives Add.PP VIC 135.

173. See pp.63–64

174. Queen Victoria, *Journal*, p.27.

175. V & A, JGC–5.

176. *Ibid.*, JGC–14, Notes by J. F. Crace.

177. *Ibid.*, JDC–19.

178. *Ibid.*, JDC–39, p.18.

179. *Ibid.*, p.22.

180. It is illustrated in 'The "Great Western" Steamship', *The Mirror of Literature, Amusement, and Instruction*, 31, 1838, pp.242–53. I am indebted to Clive Wainwright for this reference.

181. V & A, Department of Prints and Drawings, E.1834–1912.

182. V & A, JGC–14.

183. Exposition Universelle de 1855, *Rapports du Jury Mixte International*, 2, Paris, Imprimerie Imperiale, 1856, pp.465–66.

184. *Ibid.*

185. See Jervis, Simon, *The Penguin Dictionary of Design and Designers*, Harmondsworth, 1984, p.470.

186. V & A, JGC–20, an account of J. G. Crace by J. D. Crace, unpaginated.

187. *The Buildings of England: Lancashire 1. The Industrial and Commercial South*, Harmondsworth, 1969. p.405.

188. Anon., 'The Art-Treasures Exhibition at Manchester', *The Illustrated London News*, 30, 2 May 1857, p.400.

189. *Ibid.*

190. See pp.146–155 in this book.

191. V & A, Department of Prints and Drawings, Photographic file for the 1862 Exhibition, 67.194.

192. Crace, J. G. 'On the Decoration of the International Exhibition Building', *Building News*, 8, 11 April 1862, p.260.

193. vol.3, London: Day & Son, 1963, plates 205 and 247.

194. *Ibid.*, plate 205.

195. V & A, Department of Furniture, W25–1852.

196. *Industrial Arts*, plate 205.

197. *Cassell's Illustrated Family Paper Exhibitor*, London, 1862, p.140.

198. *Industrial Arts*, plate 205.

199. *Ibid.*, plate 247.

200. *The Practical Mechanic's Journal, Record of the Great Exhibition 1862*, London, 1862, p.492.

201. V & A, Department of Prints and Drawings, E.2752–1914. Von Klenze's throne, in turn, is clearly based upon the throne of Napoleon at Fontainebleau, designed by Percier and Fontaine.

202. Correspondence from these men is in a private collection.

203. It is illustrated in Crace's personal photographic album, V & A, Department of Prints and Drawings,

X626/3815–1953.

204. 30, 14 March 1857, p.400.

205. 'Painters' Hall: the Third Exhibition of Works of Decorative Art,' 1863, p.145.

206. V & A, JDC–39, unpaginated.

207. One of these is in a private collection, and the other is in the V & A JDC–63.

208. London, B. T. Batsford.

209. *Ibid.* Plate X; however, this drawing is dated April 1906.

210. *Ibid.* p.ix.

211. Crace J. G., 'On Colour', *The Builder*, 25, 30 November 1867, pp.874–75; and 7 December 1867, pp.888–89.

212. In the green sketchbook, private collection.

213. V & A, JDC–63, p.4.

214. *Ibid.* p.9

215. Notes to Plate XI.

216. *Ibid.*

217. V & A, JDC–63, pp.39–40.

218. As indicated in the Record of Partnership between J. G. and J. D. Crace, owned by a private collector. See Nouvel, *Wall-papers of France, 1800–1850*, where a number of papers manufactured by Dufour are illustrated.

219. V & A, JDC–63, pp.41–47.

220. See Ledoux-Lebard, Denise, *Les Ebénistes Parisiennes du XIXeme Siècle*, Paris, Les Editions de l'Amateur, 198, rev. ed. of 1965, pp.235–36 (Gradé) and p.477 (Mazaroz).

221. V & A, JDC–63, p.45. It is tempting to speculate whether Gradé could have made the suite of library furniture for the 6th Duke of Devonshire at Chatsworth in about 1840.

222. Port, *Parliament*, p.176. Frederick Crace had actually died in 1859, however.

223. *Ibid.*, p.180.

224. They have been mistakenly attributed to J. G. Crace and described as 'Unidentified chapel decoration' in RIBA, London, *Catalogue of the Drawings Collection, C–F*, London, 1972.

225. V & A, JGC–14, notes on J. G. Crace by J. D. and J. F.

226. p.72.

227. V & A, JDC–63, pp.55–62.

228. V & A, Department of Prints and Drawings, E.1836–1912.

229. *Ibid.*, E.1922–1912 (bookcases) and E.1921–1912.

230. C-H, Department of Drawings and Prints, 'John Dibblee Crace', typescript, p.20.

231. V & A, JDC–7, a letter of 29 May 1866 from J. P. Seddon and C. F. Hayward to J. D. Crace.

232. *Ibid.* JDC–9, receipt dated 26 July 1869.

233. Department of Prints and Drawings, E.1911–1912.

234. Jervis, Simon, *Dictionary of Design and Designers*, p.257.

235. See p.90 in this book.

236. 'Knightshayes, Devon: Burges versus Crace', *National Trust Yearbook* (1975–76), p.46.

237. V & A, JDC–65.

238. V & A, Department of Prints and Drawings, E.1887–1912; and RIBA, U11/35A.

239. p.19.

240. V & A, Department of Prints and Drawings, E.1886–1912.

241. *Ibid.* E.1896–1912.

242. The National Trust, *Knightshayes Court, Devon*, rev. ed., Hertfordshire, 1984, p.27.

243. V & A, Department of Prints and Drawings, E.1895–1912.

244. Aslin, Elizabeth, *The Aesthetic Movement, Prelude to Art Nouveau*, London, 1981, p.76.

245. 'Knightshayes', p.45.

246. Lee, Sidney, ed., *The Dictionary of National Biography*, 56, London, 1898.

247. See Aldrich, Megan, 'The Marquess and the Decorator', *Country Life*, 183, 7 December 1989, Figures 8 and 10.

248. Notes to Plate VII.

249. Box U11/29/3.

250. I am indebted to Kate Harris, Librarian and Archivist to the Marquess of Bath, for this and other information.

251. V & A, JDC–61.

252. *Ibid.*, p.3.

253. *Ibid.*

254. These were catalogued by Kate Harris in 1989.

255. *Colour Decoration*, p.18.

256. *Entretiens sur l'Architecture*, Paris, 1863, vol.1.

257. In the Summary of Accounts, Longleat archives.

258. Crace, 'Description', p.2.

259. *Ibid.*, p.1.

260. Crace, 'Description', p.4.

261. *Ibid.*

262. Aldrich, 'The Marquess and the Decorator', p.166.

263. It is now known as the 'Prince of Wales Bedroom'.

264. 'Description', p.5.

265. Box U11/27 to 29.

266. A detail of the trophy of War is illustrated in Aldrich, 'The Marquess and the Decorator', figure 2.

267. p.5. Unfortunately he did not record the name of the firm of cabinet makers who executed them.

268. Crace, 'Description', p.5.

269. V & A, Department of Prints and Drawings, E.1857–1912. This house has been demolished.

270. *Ibid.* E.1830–1912.

271. See Crace, J. D. *Colour Decoration*, p.84.

272. For the complicated background to the room, see Flower, Sibylla Jane, *Debrett's the Stately Homes of Britain*, Exeter, 1982, pp.203–05.

273. Avray Tipping, H., 'Ickworth, Suffolk', 2, *Country Life*, 58, 7 November 1925, pp.698–705.

274. Linstrum, Derek, *Historic Architecture of Leeds*, Newcastle, 1969, p.56. J. G. Crace had worked with Thomas at Bestwood Lodge, Nottingham, 'The Cedars', South London, and at the Manchester Assembly Rooms.

275. 'The Re-decoration of the Victoria Hall, Leeds', *The Yorkshire Post*, 15 April 1894, p.6.

276. Department of Prints and Drawings, E.1850–1912.

277. Quiney, Anthony, *John Loughborough Pearson*, London, 1979, pp.218–20.

278. Department of Prints and Drawings, E.1877–1912.

279. *Ibid.* E.1883 and 1884–1912.

280. p.84.

281. Department of Prints and Drawings, E.1854–1912.

282. Quiney, *Pearson*, pp.211–20, 281.

283. Department of Prints and Drawings, E.1862 to 1875–1912.

284. With a group of miscellaneous sketches in the Crace Archive, V & A.

285. See Jervis, Simon, *Dictionary of Design*, p.158–60.

286. This stamp was used after 1865. See Ledoux-Lebard, *Ebénistes*, p.477.

287. Pevsner, Nikolaus, *The Buildings of England: Buck-inghamshire*, Harmondsworth, 1960, pp.198–99.

288. Drawings Collection Box U11/46/1–3, and RAN 9/D/26.

289. 'Cliveden, Bucks.', 1, vol.32, 7 December 1912, pp.808–18; and 2, 14 December 1912, pp.854–59.

290. V & A, Department of Furniture, memorandum by J. D. Crace of March 1911; folder 34, Symonds and Whinneray file.

291. Wainwright, Clive, 'Arundel Castle from 1850', *The Connoisseur*, 197, March 1978, pp.172–85.

292. Private collection.

293. See typescript, C-H, Department of Drawings and Prints.

294. Conveniently, J. G. Crace had a cousin, Charles Napoleon Crace, who was a 'timber and mahogany merchant'. Kelly, *Directory*, 1854, p.809.

295. *Journal of the R.I.B.A.*, 5, 3rd series, 1897–98, pp.265–77.

296. *The Furniture Gazette*, 17, 11 March 1882, pp.151–52; 18 March 1882, pp.167–69; 1 April 1882, p.203.

297. 'Augustus Welby Pugin, and Furniture', *Journal of the R.I.B.A.*, 1, 3rd series, 1894, pp.517–19.

298. *Journal of R.I.B.A.*, 11, 3rd series, 1904, pp.253–70.

299. *The Art Journal*, 1906, pp.47–53.

300. London, 1907.

301. *Journal of R.I.B.A.*, 3rd series, 1910, pp.730–34.

302. Paper read before the Society of Mural Decorators and Painters in Tempera, Painters' Hall, London 29 November 1912; and London, 1912.

5 J. G. Crace and A. W. N. Pugin pp.137 to 145

1. V & A, Mostyn-Crace bequest, JGC–20 and JGC–21.

2. V & A, Mostyn-Crace bequest, JCG–21.

3. John Nash, *The Royal Pavilion at Brighton*, 1827.

4. RIBA Library MSS PUG5/20.

5. Wedgwood, A. *A. W. N. Pugin and the Pugin Family, Catalogues of Architectural Drawings in The Victoria and Albert Museum*, 1985, cat. nos.284–5, p.191.

6. RIBA Library MSS PUG3/6.

7. RIBA Library MSS PUG8/68.

8. The official appointment was made through Charles Barry (V & A, Mostyn-Crace bequest, JGC–20).

9. RIBA Library MSS PUG3/11.

10. Wedgwood, A. *op. cit.*, cat. nos.504–572, pp.220–8. The question of who was responsible for the manufacture of these wall-papers and carpets has not yet been resolved. It is unlikely that it was Crace himself.

11. Wedgwood, A. *op. cit.*, cat. no.481, pp.216–8.

12. RIBA Library MSS PUG13/1–14.

13. *The Builder*, XIII (1855), p.449.

14. RIBA Libary MSS PUG3/20.

15. RIBA Library MSS PUG7/24.

16. For example, a dwarf bookcase for which three designs of 1849 exist, see Wedgwood, A. *op. cit.*, cat. nos.693–5, p.251.

17. RIBA Library MSS PUG1/43.

18. RIBA Library MSS PUG4/26.

19. Wedgwood, A. *op. cit.*, catalogue nos. 840–871, pp.270–4. An example of no.848 was found at Holy Trinity Church, Leighton, Powys, in 1981.

20. RIBA Library MSS PUG10/6.

21. V & A no.25–1852.

22. *The Builder*, IX 1851, p.473.

23. Waterhouse, Paul 'Life and Work of Welby Pugin', *Architectural Review*, III, 1897–8, pp.167–175, 211–221, 264–273 and IV, 1898, pp.23–27, 67–73, 115–118 and 159–165.

6   J. G. Crace and the Decoration of the 1862 International Exhibition pp.146 to 155

1. Luckhurst, Kenneth W. *The Story of Exhibitions*, 1951, remains the standard work on the subject. Allwood, John, *The Great Exhibitions*, 1977, and Friebe, Wolfgang, *Buildings of the World Exhibitions*, 1985, are also useful.

2. *Survey of London*, vol.XXXVIII, 'The Museums of South Kensington and Westminster', chapter IX, offers a succinct account of the history of the 1862 Exhibition Building.

3. See Bradford, Betty, 'The Brick Palace of 1862', *Architectural Review*, CXXXII, July 1962, pp.15–21.

4. *Athenaeum*, 3 May 1862; quoted in Kempt, Robert, *What Do You Think of the Exhibition?*, 1862, p.82.

5. From a lecture given at the Institute of British Architects, 16 December 1850; quoted in Tomlinson, Charles (ed.), *Cyclopaedia of Useful Arts & Manufacturers*, 1852, p.xlvi.

6. See Mallet, Robert (ed.), *The Practical Mechanic's Journal: Record of the International Exhibition, 1862*, pp.22, 28

7. *Ibid*, p.32

8. *Blackwood's Magazine*, LXXXI, June 1857, p.760.

9. *Survey of London*, *op. cit.*, p.144, notes 113–4.

10. *Illustrated London News*, XL, 4 January 1862, p.10.

11. *Building News*, 7 February 1862, p.84; quoted in *Survey of London*, *loc.cit.*

12. Crace, J. G. 'On the Decoration of the International Exhibiton Building', a paper read at the Society of Arts, 9 April 1862; printed in the *Journal of the Society of Arts*, X, 11 April 1862, pp.339–43. All further quotations by Crace are from this source.

13. 'How They Painted the Exhibition' in *Fun*, II, 29 March 1862, p.19.

14. *Examples of the Architecture of the Victorian Age, and Monthly Review of the World's Architectural Progress*, vol.I, May 1862, plate II.

15. *Times*, 28 January 1862, p.6.

16. *The Practical Mechanic's Journal*, *op. cit.*, p.22.

17. *Fraser's Magazine*, LXV, June 1862; quoted in Kempt, *op. cit.*, pp.75–6.

18. *Report of the Commissioners for the Exhibition of 1862*, 1863, p.54.

19. *Illustrated London News*, XL, 22 March 1862, p.282, contains a engraving of the Exhibition's Painting Shop.

20. *Quarterly Review*, 112, July 1862, p.191.

21. *Blackwood's Magazine*, XCII, July 1862, p.72.

22. *Sixpenny Magazine*, III, 1862, p.4.

23. *Saturday Review*, 3 May 1862; quoted in Kempt, *op. cit.*, p.92.

24. *Athenaeum*, *loc.cit.*

25. *Survey of London*, *op. cit.*, p.145, note 120.

26. *The Practical Mechanic's Journal*, *op. cit.*, pp.42, 53.

27. *Critic*, 12 April 1862; quoted in Kempt, *op. cit.*, pp.96–8.

28. Lord Taunton, Chairman; *Journal of the Society of Arts*, *loc. cit.*

29. *The Practical Mechanic's Journal*, *op. cit.*, pp.491–2.

30. See, for example, the *Art Journal Illustrated Catalogue of the International Exhibition, 1862*, p.181.

31. The coloured Supplement to the *Illustrated London News*, 18 October 1862, gives perhaps the best idea.

32. *Fun*, II, 19 July 1862, p.173.

7   Polychromatic Decoration as applied to Buildings of the Nineteenth Century pp.156 to 166

1. Crook, J. Mordaunt, *William Burges and the High Victorian Dream*, London, 1981.

2. Wainwright, Clive, 'Davington Priory Kent' *Country Life*, December 9 1971, 1650–1653.

3. Boase, T. S. R., 'The Decoration of the New Palace of Westminster, 1841–1863' *The Journal of the Warburg & Courtauld Institutes* XVII, 1954, 319–358.

4. Campbell, Kenneth, *Campbell Smith and Company 1873–1973*, 1973.

5. Cockerell, C. R. 'On the Aegina Marbles' *Journal of Science and the Arts*, VI, 12, 340.

6. von Klenze, Leo, *Versuch einer Wiederstellung des toskanischer Tempels nach seinen historischen und technischen Analogien*, 1822.

7. Middleton, Robin, 'Hittorff's polychrome campaign' in *The Beaux Arts and Nineteenth-Century French Architecture*, ed. Robin Middleton 1982.

8. Wainwright, Clive, *The Romantic Interior: The British Collector at Home 1750–1850*, London, 1989, 256.

9. *Ibid.*, 251.

10. Hunt, T. F. *Exemplars of Tudor Architecture adapted to modern habitations: with illustrative details selected from Ancient Edifices*, 1830, 14–15.

11. Pugin, A. W. N. *True Principles of Pointed or Christian Architecture: Set forth in two lectures delivered at St. Marie's Oscott*, London, 1841, 34–35.

12. *Ibid.*, 37.

13. I am indebted to Michael Snodin for this

information.

14. Smirke, Sidney *Illustrations of the Architectural Ornaments and Embellishments and Painted Glass of Temple Church*, London, 1845.

15. *Romantic Interior, loc. cit.*, 167–168.

16. *True Principles, loc. cit.*, 45.

17. Whichcord, John 'Observations on the Polychromatic Decoration of the Middle Ages', *Quarterly Papers on Architecture*, IV, 1845, pt.vii, 9.

18. *The Ecclesiologist*, XXII, 1861, 67–68.

19. *Ibid.*, 141.

20. 'Wall painting or whitewash?', *The Church Builder* 1867, 16.

21. Audsley, W. & G. *Polychromatic Decoration as applied to buildings in the Mediaeval Styles*, 1882, 32.

8   Redecoration or Restoration: The Crace Firm at the Royal Pavilion, Brighton, 1863–1900. pp.167 to 179

1. Fleet, Charles, *A Handbook of Brighton*, Brighton, 1854, p.54.

2. Letter from J. G. Crace, dated June 20th, 1863, transcribed in the *Proceedings of the Pavilion Committee*, vol.3, p.326–7, Royal Pavilion Archives. (In future notes the volumes will be referred to as PPC, with the appropriate volume and page numbers.)

3. Letter from Crace, dated October 26th, 1863; PPC, vol.3, p.386–7.

4. Crace letter, see (2) above.

5. Crace letter, see (2) above.

6. Letter from J. G. Crace, October 8th, 1863; PPC, vol.3, p.376–7.

7. Letter to the Town Council of Brighton from T. Pantaenius, dated January 6th, 1864; PPC, vol.3, p.411–3.

8. Surveyor's report, dated June 9th, 1884; PPC, vol.13, p.344–5.

9. *Ibid.*

10. PPC, vol.13, p.348–9.

11. Letter from J. D. Crace, dated August 7th, 1884; PPC, vol.13, p.397–9.

12. *Ibid.*

13. Bishop, J.G., *A Guide to Brighton Pavilion Brighton*, 1885, p.17

14. Surveyor's report, dated May 18th, 1896; PPC, vol.21, p.488.

15. *Ibid.*, p.489.

16. Letter from F. C. May to J. D. Crace, dated April 5th, 1898. Royal Pavilion Archives.

17. Letter from J. D. Crace, no date recorded; PPC, vol.22, p.423–4.

18. *The Brighton Herald*, August 13th, 1898, p.4.

19. Letter from J. D. Crace, dated March 11th, 1899; PPC, vol.23, p.189–93.

20. *The Brighton Herald*, August 13th, 1898, p.4.

Conclusion   pp.181 to 182

1. London, 1968. The book was first published under the title *Pioneers of the Modern Movement*, London: Faber & Faber, 1936.

2. 'John G. Crace & Son', (July 1881), p.83.

3. *Ibid.*, 1 (May 1884), p.136. (JGC–22)

4. 'The Royal Jubilee Exhibition, Manchester 1887', (July 1887), p.99.

5. 'Contemporary House Decoration', (May 1, 1891), p.69.

6. 'Architecture and Painting, A Tradition', July 1906, pp.201–7.

Photographic Acknowledgements

The authors and publishers would like to thank the following for granting permission to reproduce copyright photographs or for making photographs available.

Brighton Reference Library 4:21, 6:3, 8:3

British Architectural Library/R.I.B.A. 1:16, 4:5, 4:23, 4:24, 4:25, 4:26, 4:40, 4:41. *Colour:* 12, 18, 21, 22, 23

Christie's *colour:* 28

Lord and Lady Cobbold, Knebworth House *colour:* 13, 14, 15

Cooper-Hewitt, National Museum of Design, Smithsonian Institution 1:2, 1:4, 1:7, 1:8, 1:10, 1:11, 1:13, 1:14, 2:1, 4:1, 4:2. *Colour:* 3, 4

Country Life 1:16, 4:7, 4:8, 4:32, 4:33. *Colour:* 6, 24, 25

The Duke of Devonshire and the Chatsworth Settlement Trustees *colour:* 8, 9

Government House, Perth, W Australia 4:18

Leeds City Art Gallery *colour:* 1

Metropolitan Museum of Art, New York, Harris Brisbane Dick Fund, 1927 2:12

National Library of Australia 4:42

The National Trust 4:31

Private collection 1:1, 1:15, 2:2, 2:3, 2:4, 2:5, 2:6, 2:8. *Colour:* 26

Royal Commission on the Historical Monuments of England 4:35, 4:38

Royal Pavilion, Art Gallery and Museums, Brighton 3:1, 3:2, 3:4, 3:5, 4:16, 8:1, 8:2, 8:5, 8:6, 8:8. *Colour:* 5

Traditional Homes *colour:* 10

Trustees of Sir John Soane's Museum 1:3. *Colour:* 2

Sotheby's 3:3, 3:6

Stockport MBC Leisure Services Division, Museum and Art Gallery Service 4:14, 4:15. *Colour:* 16

Temple Williams Antiques 1:9

The Board of Trustees of the Victoria and Albert Museum, London 1:12, 2:7, 2:9, 2:10, 4:3, 4:4, 4:6, 4:9, 4:11, 4:12, 4:13, 4:17, 4:19, 4:20, 4:22, 4:27, 4:28, 4:30, 4:34, 4:36, 4:37, 4:39, 5:1, 5:2, 5:3, 5:4, 5:5, 6:1, 6:2, 8:4, 8:7. *Colour:* 7, 11, 17, 27, 30, 31

Windsor Castle, Royal Library © 1990. Her Majesty the Queen *colour:* 19, 20

Index